The politics of sustainable development

Theory, policy and practice within the European Union

Edited by Susan Baker, Maria Kousis, Dick Richardson and Stephen Young

ROUTLEDGE

London and New York

First published 1997
by Routledge
11 New Fetter Lane, London EC4P 4EE

Simultaneously published in the USA and Canada
by Routledge
29 West 35th Street, New York, NY 10001

Typeset in Times by Routledge
Printed and bound in Great Britain by
Creative Print and Design (Wales), Ebbw Vale

British Library Cataloguing in Publication Data
A catalogue record for this book is available from the British Library

Library of Congress Cataloguing in Publication Data
The politics of sustainable development: theory, policy and practice
within the European Union / edited by Susan Baker ... [*et al.*]
p. cm. – (Environmental politics)
Includes bibliographical references.
1. Sustainable development–European Union countries.
2. Sustainable development. 3. Environmental policy–European Union
countries. I. Baker, Susan, 1946– . II. Series.
HC240.Z9E573 1997
333.7′096–dc21   96–29598

ISBN 0–415–13873–6 (hbk)
ISBN 0–415–13874–4 (pbk)

The politics of sustainable development

The concept of sustainable development has achieved broad acceptance among politicians, academics and professionals as the path to an
environmentally better future. Uniting theory, policy and practice, *The
Politics of Sustainable Development* explores the possibilities of how
sustainable development theory might be applied within Europe at all
levels of government.

The study begins with an analysis of the ambiguities inherent in
sustainable development and the contestable nature of the concept.
The contributors explore how far it is possible to reconcile economic
growth with environmental needs, asking whether sustainable development can promote equity and development. Subsequent Chapters
examine how sustainable development has been interpreted at EU and
sub-national levels within the member states, drawing examples from
the Mediterranean and Northern European countries.

Introducing the 'Ladder of Sustainable Development', a concept
that enshrines the alternative frameworks for putting sustainable development into practice, this study offers many insights into the
possibilities of sustainable development and how it might be achieved
in practice.

Susan Baker is a Senior Research Fellow, the School of Social and
Administrative Studies, University of Cardiff; **Maria Kousis** is Asso-
ciate Professor of Sociology, University of Crete; **Dick Richardson** is
Reader in International Relations and Green Politics, University of
Teesside; and **Stephen Young** is Senior Lecturer in the Department of
Government, University of Manchester.

Contents

List of illustrations

Notes on contributors

Susan Baker is a Senior Research Fellow in the School of Social and Administrative Studies at University of Wales College of Cardiff, UK.

Henry Buller is a holder of an ESRC Global Environmental Change Fellowship at Kings College London, UK, and also a Lecturer in Geography, University of Paris VII, Paris, France.

Dimitrios Konstadakopulos is a Research Associate in the European Regional Studies Unit at the University of West of England, Bristol, UK.

Maria Kousis is an Associate Professor of Sociology in the University of Crete, Rethimno, Crete, Greece.

Angela Liberatore is a Scientific Officer in the Unit on Socio-Economic Environmental Research of the Directorate-General for Science, Research and Development of the European Commission.

Philip Lowe is Duke of Northumberland Professor of Rural Economy Director of the Centre for Rural Economy at the University of Newcastle upon Tyne, UK.

Tim Marshall is a Lecturer in Planning at Oxford Brookes University, UK.

Arne Naess is Professor Emeritus in the Centre for Development and the Environment, University of Oslo, Norway.

Geoffrey Pridham is Professor of European Politics and Director of the Centre for Mediterranean Studies at the University of Bristol, UK.

Michael Redclift is Professor of Rural Sociology in the Environment Section, Wye College, University of London, UK.

Dick Richardson is Reader in International Relations and Green Politics at the University of Teesside, UK.

Yvonne Rydin is a Senior Lecturer in the Department of Geography at the London School of Economics, UK.

Allan Schnaiberg is Professor of Sociology at Northwestern University, Evanston, Illinois, USA.

Neil Ward is a Lecturer in the Department of Geography at the University of Newcastle upon Tyne, UK.

Stephen Young is a Senior Lecturer in the Department of Government, University of Manchester, UK.

Preface

The Politics of Sustainable Development is the first full-scale academic study to analyse the political aspects of the concept of sustainable development within the European Union, covering theory, policy and practice. Many efforts were pooled together in the making of the book, which had its genesis in an international conference on sustainable development held at the University of Crete, Rethimno, under the auspices of the European Consortium for Political Research (ECPR) from 21 to 23 October 1994. The book is not, however, a collection of conference papers. The Chapters have been specially commissioned, in the light of the conference discussions, to address the central themes which emerged at Rethimno.

Part I of the book concerns the concept of sustainable development, and deals with the philosophical and theoretical dimensions of the subject. It focuses on the legacy of the Brundtland Commission's Report and explores its impact upon perceptions of, and approaches towards, economic development on the one hand and environmental protection on the other (Chapters 1–3). Part II explores the practice of sustainable development within the EU. It begins by looking at the policy of sustainable development formulated by the EU (Chapters 4–5), followed by an analysis of policy implementation in 'top-down' practice (Chapters 6–9). This is followed by a parallel but complementary view from a 'bottom-up' perspective. Integration of theory and practice is cemented through an Introduction which develops the concept of a Ladder of Sustainable Development for advanced industrial societies, while possibilities for the future are analysed in the Postscript (Chapter 12).

The editors gratefully acknowledge the financial and other support from various bodies which contributed to this publication. ECPR established a Research Group on the Politics of Sustainable Development and facilitated the initial communication between the editors at a meeting at the University of Trondheim, Norway, in November 1991. Financial support for the conference itself came from the Global Environmental Change (GEC) Programme of the Economic and Social Research Council (ESRC); the European Commission (DG XII for Science, Research and Development); the Greek Ministry for the Environment, Physical Planning and Public Works; and the Greek Bank for Industrial Development. Henry Buller's contribution was made possible through the support of an ESRC (GEC) Research Fellowship, while Maria Kousis's work was funded in part by the European Commission (DG XII) under the Environment and Climate Programme (SEER II).The Erasmus University of Rotterdam, University of Crete, University of Teesside and University of Manchester also provided resources in support of both the conference and the final publication. In particular, the editors would like to thank Jean Connell and Beryl Wilkinson of the University of Teesside for collating the final manuscript and generally easing the work of the editors.

Susan Baker, Maria Kousis, Dick Richardson and Stephen Young

Introduction

The theory and practice of sustainable development in EU perspective

Susan Baker, Maria Kousis, Dick Richardson and Stephen Young

This Introduction explains the importance of focusing on sustainable development in a Northern industrialized context. In considering sustainable development from this perspective, the authors are aware that many of the key, critical components of the concept are more sharply revealed from a perspective that takes account of the global dimension, and in particular the inequalities in global resource use and life chances that exist between the North and the South. However, the literature on the struggle over the environment in the South is already well developed, whilst that on the North is underdeveloped. The authors therefore seek to fill an appreciable gap in political science literature by focusing on the promotion of sustainable development in a Northern, industrialized context, and in particular the European Union (EU) context in terms of theory, policy and practice. Accordingly, the Introduction has been divided into five sections. The first examines the theoretical debates surrounding the concept of sustainable development and argues that the concept is contestable *by its very nature*. The second defends the position that sustainable development needs to be understood as a social and political construct and, as such, the study of the operationalization of sustainable development through the implementation of specific policies provides *the* critical focus for research. The third develops a Ladder of Sustainable Development as a heuristic device for situating and grouping the range of policy imperatives associated with the promotion and implementation of sustainable development policies. The fourth looks at the role of government, at both the national and sub-national levels, and of bottom-up participation in this process of implementation. The final section looks at the implementation of sustainable development policy within the EU – the main focus of this book.

The Introduction also provides, by way of background for the book, a brief overview of the EU's position with respect to the promotion of sustainable development. If sustainable development is to become an integral part of EU policy, as is suggested by the Fifth Action Programme, then there is an urgent need to begin a wider and deeper investigation not only of the EU's understanding of sustainable development but also of the manner in which this policy is being implemented at the member-state level. This understanding is aimed at revealing new insights into the EU policy-making process, particularly as it relates to environmental policy formulation (see Chapters 4 and 5). At the same time, it is hoped that the economic, social, administrative and cultural barriers to implementation that exist at both the EU and member-state level can be identified (see Chapter 6).

THE CONCEPT OF SUSTAINABLE DEVELOPMENT: THEORETICAL DEBATES

The Brundtland legacy

The 1960s and the 1970s were marked by an intensification of concern about pollution. They were also marked by an awareness that environmental problems arise within the context of a complex interrelationship between humankind, the global resource base and the social and physical environments (Turner 1988). As a consequence, questions about the acceptability of conventional growth objectives, strategies and policies were brought to the forefront of public debate. Initially, this was followed in some quarters by a call for zero-growth strategies (Daly 1977). An important inspiration for this argument was the publication of the Club of Rome report *The Limits to Growth* in 1972 (Meadows *et al.* 1972).

The limits to growth argument was widely criticized and was partially displaced by the argument that environmental protection and continuing economic growth could be seen as mutually compatible, and not necessarily conflicting, objectives. The term 'sustainable development' was used to refer to this new point of view. In 1980 it entered the public arena when the International Union for the Conservation of Nature and Natural Resources presented the *World Conservation Strategy* with the overall aim of achieving sustainable development through the conservation of living resources (IUCN 1980). However, the World Conservation Strategy was limited in the sense that its prime focus was *ecological* sustainability, as opposed to linking sustainability to social and economic issues.

A broader understanding of sustainable development was used by the United Nations Environment Programme, in particular in the report *Our Common Future*, published by the World Commission on Environment and Development (WCED 1987). This Report is also known as the Brundtland Report, after its president. The now widely quoted definition of sustainable development given in the Brundtland Report is 'development that meets the needs of the present without compromising the ability of future generations to meet their own needs' (WCED 1987: 5). The Report argued that the concept provides a framework for the *integration* of environmental policies and development strategies, thus breaking the perception that environmental protection can only be achieved *at the expense of* economic development. With the popularization of the Brundtland concept of sustainable development, environmental quality and economic development have come to be seen as interdependent and mutually reinforcing. Thus the mainstream debate has shifted from its earlier concern with whether environment and development are compatible objectives to a new preoccupation with how to achieve environmentally sustainable forms of development.

The Brundtland Report's understanding of sustainable development contains within it two key concepts. First, the concept of *needs*, in particular the essential needs of the world's poor, to which overriding priority must be given. Seeing needs as socially and culturally determined, Brundtland argued that sustainable development requires the promotion of values that encourage consumption patterns that are within the bounds of the ecologically possible and to which all can reasonably aspire. Changes in consumption are particularly important for Northern developed societies. Second, there is the concept of *limitations* on the environment's ability to meet present and future needs, limitations that are imposed by the state of technology and social organization.

However, while the fundamental objectives of sustainable development were brief, the Commission was much more elaborate about what Lélé has termed the 'operational objective' of sustainable development (Lélé 1991: 611). The Brundtland Report linked the achievement of sustainable development at the global level with a number of major political and social changes: elimination of poverty and exploitation, equal distribution of global resources, an end to the current pattern of military expenditure, new methods of ensuring just population control, lifestyle changes, appropriate technology, and institutional changes including democratization, achieved through effective citizen participation in decision-making (WCED 1987: 8–9). According to the Brundtland Report, sustainable development also implies a concern for both inter-generational and intra-generational equity in resource use. Inter-generation equity refers to including the needs of future generations in the design and implementation of current policy. Intra-generational equity highlights the importance of meeting the basic needs of present generations, where poverty is seen as both a cause and a consequence of unsustainable behaviour. In addition, intra-generational equity applies to those trapped in poverty in Northern countries, especially in inner-city areas in EU member-states (Young 1996a). In short, sustainable development was linked to questions of power and the removal of the disparities in economic and political relationships, especially between North and South (WCED 1987: 46).

The Brundtland Report also argued that there is no single blueprint of sustainable development, given that economic and social systems and ecological conditions differ widely among countries. Thus, despite seeing sustainable development as a global objective, *Our Common Future* pointed out that each nation would have to work out the concrete policy implications for itself. It thus left to policy-makers the task of translating into practice what are in effect highly generalized, declaratory political statements.

The Brundtland Report adopted an anthropocentric position with respect to sustainable development, arguing that 'Our message, is, above all, directed towards people, whose well-being is the ultimate goal of all environment and development polices' (WCED 1987: xiv). Furthermore, it argued that economic growth and development involve changes in the physical ecosystem and that every ecosystem everywhere cannot be preserved intact. This anthropocentricism is also seen in the argument that sustainable development requires the conservation of plant and animal species because their loss can greatly limit the options of future generations. However, a number of commentators, including Achterberg, have pointed out that the Report also strikes different, non-anthropocentric notes (Achterberg 1993: 86). For example, the Report argued that the case for the conservation of nature should not rest only with development goals. It is part of humankind's moral obligation to other living beings and future generations (WCED 1987). Thus, in the discussion of the various positions on sustainable development, including the anthropocentric position, care must be taken not to fit political actors into too tight a conceptual categorization. Political reality and its ideological underpinning are always more messy than this.

SUSTAINABLE DEVELOPMENT AS A POLITICAL AND SOCIAL PROCESS

Post-Brundtland diversification of meaning

By the late 1980s and early 1990s the Brundtland formulation had come to represent the mainstream of sustainable development thinking, with an increasing number of organizations and agencies subscribing to at least some, and often most or all, of these objectives. These include the EU, the United Nations Environment Programme (UNEP) and the World Bank. However, the broadening of the concept of sustainable development, coupled with its popularity, has given rise to ambiguity and lack of consistency in the use of the term. Even a quick glance at the large volume of writings on sustainable development reveals that there is no general agreement on exactly what sustainable development means. Pezzey has, for example, produced a ten-page listing of the most common definitions used in the decade of the 1980s (Pezzey 1989). A similar widening of the range of definitions was noted in an appendix to the Pearce Report in 1989 (Pearce *et al.* 1989).

This lack of clarity is not without its advantages. It has, for example, allowed groups with different and often conflicting interests to reach some common ground upon which concrete policies have been developed. However, some have argued that the concept's ambiguity severely diminishes its usefulness. There is concern among environmentalists and ecologists that the lack of clarity in the definition allows anything to be claimed as 'sustainable' (Jacobs 1991: 59–60; see also Chapter 1). To counteract this, it is argued, 'sustainable development' needs to be precisely defined so that a set of measurable criteria can be specified which will allow individuals and groups with widely differing values, political preferences or assumptions about human nature to agree whether the criteria are being met in a concrete development programme (Brooks 1992, quoted in Beckerman 1994: 192–193).

Denying the usefulness of 'sustainable development' as an analytic concept or the attractiveness of it as a normative concept, however, does nothing to impinge on either its popularity or importance as a political concept (Lafferty 1995: 223–224). More importantly, the search for a unitary and precise definition of sustainable development may well rest on a mistaken view of the nature and function of political concepts. From an alternative standpoint, however, the concept per se can be dismissed as a misguided attempt to pursue a policy of 'political correctness' at international level (see Chapter 1).

Sustainable development as a social and political construct

Viewing sustainable development as a social and political construct makes it possible to move beyond the search for a unitary and precise definition, and to focus instead on the objectives underlying the original formulation of each of the two concepts 'sustainable' and 'development'. The concept 'sustainable' – or, to be more precise, 'sustainability' – originated in the context of discussions about harvesting and managing renewable resources, such as forest and fisheries, in such a way as not to damage future supplies (Lélé 1991: 609). Most proponents of sustainability take it to mean the maintenance of the existence of ecological conditions necessary to support human life at a specific level of well-being through future generations. In short, sustainability had its roots in the notion of ecological sustainability. This emphasizes the constraints and opportunities that nature presents to human activity (Lélé 1991: 609). The task is to establish forms of development that do not lead to widespread and irreversible damage. Thus, for example, fish stocks need to be maintained, but renewable energy sources can be exploited.

The major development in the debate since then has been the realization that in addition to, or in conjunction with, the need to maintain ecological conditions, there are social conditions that influence the ecological sustainability of the interaction between humankind and nature (Lélé 1991: 609–610). Putting 'development' and 'sustainability' together, 'sustainable development' becomes a form of societal change that, in addition to traditional developmental objectives, has the objective or constraint of maintaining ecological sustainability (Lélé 1991: 610).

The promotion of sustainable development forms part of a conscious process of achieving social change. Thus it comes as no surprise that policy-makers are increasingly using the term to cover a broader set of concerns than those embedded in the original idea of ecological sustainability, including health, education and social welfare concerns. This reflects a growing understanding that the promotion of sustainable development involves a new focus on the impacts of policies that were previously conceived more narrowly. The provisional list of sustainability indicators produced by the UK Local Government Management Board in 1994 forms one example: here more than one-third of the themes into which sustainable development indicators were divided do not relate strictly to the narrow environmental field (Jacobs 1995a: 13; Lemb 1995).

Understanding sustainable development as a social and political construct also makes it possible to see the variety of positions on sustainable development that have developed since Brundtland as reflecting differing sets of beliefs that exist about the world. These differences lie deep in religion, philosophy and history. As many commentators have argued, especially Lafferty, Jacobs and O'Riordan, sustainable development is best seen as similar to concepts such as 'democracy', 'liberty' and 'social justice' (Lafferty 1995; Jacobs 1995b; O'Riordan 1985: 52). For concepts such as these there is both a readily understood 'first-level meaning' and general political acceptance, but around a given set of 'core ideas' there lies a deeper contestation. Similarly, sustainable development is an essentially contestable concept (Connolly 1983, quoted in Lafferty 1995: 223). According to Jacobs and Lafferty, in liberal democracies the debates around these contested concepts form an essential component of the political struggle over the direction of social and economic development (Jacobs 1995b: 5; Lafferty 1995). Substantive political arguments are part of the dynamics of democratic politics and the process of conscious steering of societal change. O'Riordan also agrees with this, arguing that rather than seeing sustainable development as an end in itself, which is a tendency among those who seek out an ever clearer definition of the term, it is best to see sustainable development as *a catalyst* to genuinely creative thinking and practice (O'Riordan 1985: 52).

If attention is focused on sustainable development as a social and political concept, attention can be turned away from sterile debates about the precise meaning of the term, and focused instead on the contemporary process of implementing sustainable development policies and the alternative conceptions that are developing concerning how sustainable development should be interpreted *in practice*. It is through this process of implementation that the nature of the interface between environmental protection and economic development is being constructed. It is the dynamic of the initial attempts of the EU to interpret sustainable development through implementation that forms the subject matter of this book.

Sustainable development is examined in this book as a political concept, understood in the wide sense as embracing the social, economic and political processes of change within society. The focus is on how the meaning of sustainable development is interpreted in a variety of ways, developed into policies and programmes, and then reinterpreted in the light of the experience of implementation (Barret and Fudge 1981). Sustainable development is thus mediated through the process of implementation. An essential task is to examine the new insights into the relationship between social, economic and environmental phenomena that arise from analysing the implementation of sustainable development policy in the context of the developed world, and in particular the European Union. Given this, the book examines the traditional objectives of development and identifies how they have been expanded or modified to include the objective of 'sustainable development' (see Chapters 1, 2, 3, 7, 8 and 10). This, in turn, leads to an examination of a number of related issues. These include the extent to which ecological sustainability has been successfully integrated into the traditional development objectives of the EU; the nature of the barriers to integration, including at the administrative and institutional levels (see Chapters 4 and 5); the development areas, or sectors, in which integration has – or has not – occurred (see Chapters 3, 6, 7, 8 and 9); whether a working consensus has been developed between different interests, especially those at the regional and local level, in order to effect a shift to a sustainable development (see Chapters 6, 7, 8, 9 and 10); and whether this process has facilitated genuine local participation in the construction and management of social change (see Chapters 10 and 11). However, it should be pointed out that no attempt is made to offer a comprehensive review of policy implementation in all EU member-states: instead the book examines key issues within a selection of member-states, chosen because of their capacity to cast light on deeper issues facing the EU as it seeks – at least in theory – to shift the Northern, developed, part of the globe towards a sustainable development path.

THE LADDER OF SUSTAINABLE DEVELOPMENT

The diversity of policy options associated with the different meanings attributed to sustainable development can best be seen in terms of a Ladder (see Table 0.1).[1] Each column focuses on a different aspect of sustainable development. Reading across the Ladder identifies the political scenarios and policy implications associated with each rung of the Ladder. This enshrines a number of alternative frameworks for putting sustainable development into practice: the treadmill approach; weak sustainable development; strong sustainable development; and the Ideal Model.

Philosophical underpinning

The variety of approaches to sustainable development are an indication of differing ideological beliefs about the natural world, which for simplicity can be divided into the 'anthropocentric' and 'ecocentric'

Table 0.1 The Ladder of Sustainable Development in advanced industrial societies

Approach to sustainable development	Role of economy and nature of growth	Geographical focus	Nature	Policies and sectoral integration	Technology	Institutions	Policy instruments and tools	Redistribution	Civil society	Philosophy
'Ideal Model' of sustainable development	Right livelihood; meeting needs not wants; changes in patterns and levels of production and consumption	Bioregionalism; extensive local self-sufficiency	Promoting and protecting biodiversity	Holistic inter-sectoral integration	Labour-intensive appropriate technology	Decentralization of political, legal, social and economic institutions	Full range of policy tools; sophisticated use of indicators extending to social dimensions	Inter- and intra-generational equity	Bottom-up community structures and control. New approach to valuing work	**Ecocentric/biocentric**
Strong sustainable development	Environmentally regulated market; changes in patterns of production and consumption	Heightened local economic self-sufficiency, promoted in the context of global markets	Environmental management and protection	Environmental policy integration across sectors	Clean technology; product life-cycle management; mixed labour- and capital-intensive technology	Some restructuring of institutions	Advanced use of sustainability indicators; wide range of policy tools	Strengthened redistribution policy	Open-ended dialogue and envisioning	
Weak sustainable development	Market-reliant environmental policy; changes in patterns of consumption	Initial moves to local economic self-sufficiency; minor initiatives to alleviate the power of global markets	Replacing finite resources with capital; exploitation of renewable resources	Sector-driven approach	End-of-pipe technical solutions; mixed labour- and capital-intensive technology	Minimal amendments to institutions	Token use of environmental indicators; limited range of market-led policy tools	Equity a marginal issue	Top-down initiatives; limited state-environmental movements dialogue	
Treadmill	Exponential growth	Global markets and global economy	Resource exploitation	No change	Capital-intensive production technologies; progressive automation	No change	Conventional accounting	Equity not an issue	Very limited dialogue between the state and environmental movements	**Anthropo-centric**

positions.[2] According to the literature, the ecocentric perspective is based on a view about nature in which nature is used as a metaphor for unity, interdependence and a new moral order (O'Riordan 1985: 54; Eckersley 1992; Pepperman Taylor 1996). Those who hold this view locate the causes of environmental problems in the anthropocentric worldview. Sustainable development therefore requires the construction of a new moral and ethical view of nature which takes account of the interests and values of all living things (Pepperman Taylor 1996). As such, ecocentrics have visualized sustainable development as part of 'nature's way', a way designed to assist society by allowing nature to set the parameters of economic behaviour. This interpretation of nature 'serves to put mankind in its place in the cosmic order' (O'Riordan 1985: 54). Here humankind is situated *in* nature, not above it, and in the final analysis nature is seen as conditioning economic, social and political activity. As John Seymour asserts:

> We are a part of nature. That is the primary condition of our existence. And only when we recognise this will we awake from the evil dream that has led us down the path of self-destruction for the last two or three hundred years. That is the dream that we, mankind, can 'conquer nature'. For only when we abandon this dream will we realise again that you cannot conquer something of which you are a part.
>
> (Seymour 1989: 1)

In this context, sustainable development is an 'externally guided' policy option aimed at the creation of partnership based on reciprocity between human beings and nature.

In contrast, the anthropocentric view is based on a more interventionist approach to nature, because the wealth of nature is seen only in relation to what it can provide in the service of humankind (O'Riordan 1981). This was epitomized by the Industrial Revolution of the eighteenth and nineteenth centuries and the development of a technocentric approach towards nature – the subjects of Seymour's strictures in the extract above (Seymour 1989). Certainly, the extreme form of the anthropocentric position sees sustainable development as a challenge to enhance humankind's superiority on earth, though nowadays through a superiority of creative effort rather than brute force. From this perspective, sustainable development is seen as an 'inner-directed' notion, which structures a much more human-conditioned approach to planning and management.

These two perspectives have important implications for the design and implementation of policies aimed at the promotion of sustainable development. The ecocentric approach espouses 'appropriate' technology; that is, technology that is in keeping with natural laws, small in scale, understandable to lay people and workable and maintainable by local resources and labour. This is also closely connected with a belief in community empowerment achieved though the generations of community or 'grassroots' consciousness, and improvement in environmental quality through co-operative endeavours and local initiatives (see Chapter 11). It is symbolized by the Danish community-owned wind farms. In this view, the objective of sustainable development policy is the maintenance of social and communal well-being rather than being limited merely to considerations of the harmonious use of natural resources. Here there is greater emphasis on social purposes and values.

In contrast, in the anthropocentric approach, at least in its extreme form, economic behaviour is viewed in terms of the brute forces of industrial, economic and technological improvement. This approach is, according to O'Riordan, identified by a number of elements, including rationality, a so-called 'objective' appraisal of means to achieve given goals; by managerial efficiency, the application of organizational and productive techniques that produce the most for the least; and by a sense of optimism and faith in the ability of man to understand and control physical, biological and social processes for the benefit of present and future generations (O'Riordan 1981: 12). O'Riordan goes on to argue that these elements form the ideology of technocentrism that downplays the sense of wonder, reverence and moral obligation that are the hallmarks of the ecocentric approach. The policy implications that are associated with this approach are clearly elaborated by O'Riordan:

> The technocentric mode has left its legacy in environmental policy-making in a number of ways. First, its *optimism* over the successful manipulation of techniques to extract and allocate resources. . . . Second, its determination to be '*value free*' in advice and analysis, leaving the 'tough' judgements to a political arena that is already shaped by their advice. Third, its *disavowal of widespread public participation*, especially the input of lay opinion, a philosophy much admired by politicians equally intent on preserving their rightful role in acting authoritatively on behalf of the public. . . . Finally, its disquieting *fallibility*, the constant evidence of error and mis-interpretation and of hunches that do not quite pay off.
>
> (O'Riordan 1981: 19)

The treadmill approach

At the bottom of the Ladder is the 'treadmill' approach, as epitomized by transnational industrial corporations and the world of high finance. Adherents to this approach, for example, Simon and Kahn (1984), who represent the most extreme expression of this belief, view development in terms of an extension of Western capitalism into areas which have not as yet felt the benefits of development in material terms. An underlying assumption of this approach is that, given the freedom to innovate, human ingenuity, especially expressed through technology, can solve any environmental or technical problems. According to Simon and Kahn, there is no limit to the capacity for human understanding and hence humankind's ability to manipulate environmental systems.

In the treadmill approach the natural environment is seen in terms of its utility to the economic system. Within this approach sustainable development becomes merely a synonym for sustainable growth where, in its crudest form, development is measured solely in terms of the expansion of gross national product (GNP). Conventional approaches to accounting remain intact. In this conventional approach the focus is on a narrow range of variables, in particular income, investment, profit and exports. In the treadmill approach policy tools continue to aim at maximizing production and growth. The limitation of this approach in the context of sustainable development is that it focuses on the monetary dimension of economic activity and ignores the environmental impact of this activity (Pearce *et al.* 1989: ch. 4; Department of the Environment (DoE), UK 1994: ch. 34). Conventional growth has knock-on effects on road traffic, energy consumption and land use, to take just a few examples, whereas the promotion of sustainable development requires the elaboration of accounting systems that monitor whether or not different approaches to economic development are reducing the negative environmental impacts of economic activity.

Essentially, the treadmill approach is geared to the production imperative with little or no concern for environmental consequences (see Chapters 1 and 3). This was the dominant position adopted by European industry up until the early 1980s and is still to a large measure reflected in the behaviour of small and medium enterprises within the EU (EEA 1995). It was encapsulated in a 1985 statement by the Managing Director of BP (Britain); when discussing growing environmental awareness and the increase in regulatory environmental regimes, he argued: 'as far as industry is concerned, the primary aim must be to ensure that the environmental regulations do not place them at a disadvantage with their international competitors and . . . that their costs do not render the project concerned uneconomic' (Cazalet 1985: 88).

Weak sustainable development

Immediately above the treadmill approach on the Ladder is the concept of 'weak' sustainable development, whose aim is to integrate capitalist growth with environmental concerns. This position is closely associated with David Pearce and the highly influential Pearce Report, which argued that the principles of neo-classical economics can be applied to the solution of environmental problems (Pearce *et al.* 1989; see also Grayson and Hobson 1994: 32). The objective of policies to promote weak sustainable development remains economic growth, but environmental costs are taken into consideration through, for example, accounting procedures. This is possible because the environment is considered to be a measurable resource (Pearce *et al.* 1989). In this respect the treadmill approach is subject to a series of constraints: humans will identify the environmental cost of growth and decide whether there should be a trade-off; the finite nature of the earth's resources is recognized in the setting of 'resource harvest rates' at levels no higher than natural or managed regeneration rates; the use of the environment as a 'waste sink' is based on the principle that waste disposal rates do not exceed the rate of natural or managed assimilation by the counterpart ecosystem. According to this approach, sustainable development is economic growth achieved by economic efficiency within a system, subject to constancy of the natural capital stock – that is, the stock of environmental assets is held constant while the economy is allowed whatever social goals are deemed appropriate.

Pearce argues that there are two fundamental dimensions of sustainability: the first is sustainable development, which he takes as meaning the sustainable growth of per capita real incomes over time – the traditional economic growth objective. The second feature is the sustainable use of resources and environment. For him the issues are reduced to the belief that:

> Just as sustainable economic development . . . implies some reasonably constant rate of growth in per capita real incomes, without depleting the nation's capital stock, so the sustainable use of resources and the environment . . . implies some rate of use of the environment which does not deplete its capital value.
>
> (Pearce 1985: 9)

This is a position he later reaffirms (Pearce *et al.* 1994).

Weak sustainable development has had a growing influence on international agencies, including the World Bank, the United Nations, and, according to Redclift and Goodman, has become almost synonymous with environmental management (Redclift and Goodman 1991: 5). It is closely associated with an anthropocentric and technocentric view of nature, wherein nature is seen as providing both material and environmental wealth but both forms of wealth have only a social purpose: nature is seen as full of potential in the service of humankind. Material and environmental wealth creation are viewed as a partnership, but one which is capable of technical manipulation by enlightened managers, albeit with the aid of new managerial and administrative tools. These tools include environmental impact assessment; cost benefit analysis that takes account of the non-market aspect of environmental goods and services (through, for example, the creation of environmental shadow prices); and marginal adjustment to market forces to take account of market failure, through such policy tools as fees, taxes and tradable permits.

Many are critical of this approach. Redclift and Goodman (1991), for example, argue that the resource accounting method that it endorses is highly ethnocentric and biased in favour of the Northern view of the development process. Another limitation is that weak sustainable development values the environment only in monetary terms, and not for what it is worth, for example, in cultural or spiritual terms. It thus leaves the neo-classical paradigm, with all its limitations, intact (Redclift 1993: 13). It also reduces environmental problems to managerial problems, solvable within the context of the dominant political and economic system. Environmental conservation thus becomes a key target of policy, understood as the achievement of efficiency through the removal of waste. Rather than stimulating radical reform, sustainable development here becomes a cachet of ever-expanding improvement. However, the beneficiaries of development are primarily the present generation. Furthermore, the environmental management approach often ignores or devalues the experience of local people and, as a consequence, governments and policy-makers can run the risk of importing inappropriate solutions to environmental problems from elsewhere, typically from the core to the periphery (Baker *et al.* 1994; see also Chapter 9).

Strong sustainable development

The third rung on the Ladder is the 'strong' sustainable development represented by thinkers such as O'Riordan (1981) and Weale (1992). Whereas Pearce (1985, 1995) asserts that economic development is a precondition of environmental protection, advocates of strong sustainable development assert that environmental protection is a precondition of economic development. This, as Brundtland argues, involves a different kind of economic development, which is more focused on the environmental dimension than has been the case in the past. The strong sustainable development position requires that political and economic policies be geared to maintaining the productive capacity of environmental assets (whether renewable or depletable); and protecting, keeping or creating environmental assets which are either worthy of preservation as they are (for example the tropical forests) or capable of being improved (for example degraded soils). This will require market regulation and state intervention using a wide range of tools and mechanisms, but, in particular, it will require the involvement of local communities when discussing changes to the local economy and the sustainable utilization of the local environment. There is less emphasis on quantitative growth with this approach; however, although the accent is on a switch to qualitative growth, the overall objective of economic growth remains. This approach is epitomized by 'ecological modernization' among some of the larger EU firms (EEA 1995; Weale 1992).

While playing a role in both the weak and strong approaches to sustainable development, the use of policy instruments is particularly important for the strong approach. For example, legal, economic and fiscal instruments are advocated in order to influence or force changes in behaviour. In the environmental field, these include legal regulations and land-use planning, financial incentives and economic instruments such as green taxes and pollution charges, tradable resources and pollution permits, subsidies and deposit-refund schemes, various kinds of public expenditure, and encouraging changes in behaviour through information, publicity and persuasion. Under its Fifth Environmental Action Programme, the EU is committed to expanding the range of policy instruments that it uses to bring about changes in the patterns of consumption, and in particular making increased use of market-based policy instruments. In this respect, it is promoting a form of sustainable development that is closer to the weak end of the spectrum. In contrast, in the strong model of sustainable development, legal, economic and planning tools focus on the management of resources, taking account of a wider range of social issues than is found in the weaker model, a focus that is also reflected in the development of a broader range of sustainable development indicators.

The Ideal Model

The top rung on the Ladder represents the Ideal approach to sustainable development, associated with thinkers such as Arne Naess (1989), Edward Echlin (1993, 1996) and Edward Goldsmith (1992). The Ideal Model offers a profounder vision aimed at structural change in society, the economy and the political systems, which is premised upon a radical change in the attitude of humankind towards nature. This position has been termed the 'ecologist' approach, as represented, for example, by the deep ecology movement (Achterberg 1993: 84). It envisages a form of 'pure' sustainable development whereby humankind puts as much into the ecosystem as it takes out. There is no overall growth in quantitative terms, as traditionally measured, since humankind is envisaged as living within the finite ecological constraints of the planet. Growth is measured in qualitative terms – through quality of life rather than standard of living. There might, for example, be quantitative growth in some areas, notably in the Third World or (perhaps) poorer areas of Europe, but only through negative growth in already highly developed areas. Echlin (1993) has described the position as one of 'sustainable sufficiency', while Naess makes it clear that the ecological position is biocentric, concerning the totality of life on earth rather than simply human life (see Chapter 2). Not only is non-human life seen as valuable in its own right, but its intrinsic value is independent of its usefulness to humans. This ecocentric worldview seeks to be morally egalitarian in its understanding of the value of different forms of life, adopting a holistic approach that recognizes the interrelatedness of all life. Value is located in natural processes and groups rather than in individual living entities (Pepperman Taylor 1996).

The Ideal Model stresses the social dimensions of development, and sees existing approaches as offering only a limited means of measuring these (Ekins 1992: 62–71; LGMB 1995). It thus requires the elaboration of a more detailed set of development indicators that focus on the quality of life. It also means that greater account is taken of work and production activities that lie outside the formal, economic system in the social economy, for example through the not-for-private-profit contributions of community-based organizations (see Chapter 10). Such activities are seen as improving the quality of life and creating non-monetary wealth. The promotion of policies aimed at the Ideal Model would encourage these forms of activity and incorporate them into more sophisticated eco-accounting systems.

Individual thinkers hold different opinions as to the exact policy implications of the Ideal Model, but they are all agreed that environmental protection not only is necessary but will require severe restraints on the consumption of the Earth's resources and humankind's related economic activities. Deep ecologists, for example, argue that environmental protection requires radical constraints on economic activity (see Chapter 2). Because of this they are critical of the popularization of the concept of sustainable development, arguing that by failing to specify exactly what degree of environmental protection is required it offers governments and industry a means of embracing environmentalism without commitment (see Chapter 1). At the extreme, the current international and national commitments to sustainable development give rise to cynicism. This is a position adopted by the *Ecologist* (Ecologist 1992: 122). Albrecht, to take another example, has argued that in the hands of many Western governments, the concept of sustainable development 'has been welcomed as the means by which the existing mode of economic production and its associated values can continue with only minor modifications' (Albrecht 1994: 97). Thus, not all environmentalists have endorsed the concept of sustainable development and many are deeply suspicious of its underlying assumption, namely that human beings can and ought to manage the environment. The promotion of the sustainable development project is here seen as part of the wider modernist project of societal self-determination (Jacobs 1995b: 1478), a project which ecologists reject. Ecologists, in fact, argue that the Ideal Model represents not so much the top rung of a Ladder of Sustainable Development but a new development paradigm in its own right (Echlin 1996; see also Chapter 1).

The previous point notwithstanding, the four approaches on the Ladder offer a useful heuristic device for understanding the policy imperatives associated with the different approaches towards the promotion of sustainable development. However, the reader should be aware that the four approaches to sustainable development given in the Ladder are not entirely discrete. Rather they are a representation of broad schools of thought which can, and often do, overlap. For example, at the level of strong sustainable development there have been tentative moves to develop the role of the not-for-private-profit organizations operating in the social economy (see Chapter 10). But this approach would be much more highly developed in the Ideal Model.

Thus, the Ladder is best seen as representing positions that spread along a series of rungs. Both ends should be considered the extremes which represent all the possible visions, from superficial to radical, on the nature of, and solution to, the contemporary environmental crisis and on the relationship between humankind and nature. It is this flexibility which is the key to understanding sustainable development as a political construct and, in particular, the approach that has evolved under the influence of Brundtland.

The Brundtland approach may be ambiguous, as has already been argued, but it can also be asserted that within the ambiguity lies a neutrality which allows it to incorporate elements of each of the four approaches identified on the Ladder. Theoretically, it is possible for governments to adopt any position on the Ladder, and it might be viewed as normal for them to opt for progressively higher positions on the Ladder given the continuing overall diminution of the Earth's resources and increases in pollution. In practice, however, governments can move down the Ladder as well as up, and indeed might move in different directions in different policy areas. This is the case at the European Union level. Brundtland symbolizes this enigma in both theory and practice.

SUSTAINABLE DEVELOPMENT, THE ROLE OF GOVERNMENT AND BOTTOM-UP PARTICIPATION

The role of national, regional and local governments

The state has a key role to play in the shift to sustainable development. This role arises, in part, because the market mechanism generates environmental problems, including the negative externalities of pollution, the subordination of weak interests that cannot be expressed in terms of money, and the failure to supply collective goods, such as a healthy and safe environment (Achterberg 1993: 90). The existence of market failure, particularly in relation to the failure of markets adequately to protect the environmental resource base, provides governments with a key strategic and managerial role. Governments need to use a range of instruments to correct for market failure, which include the imposition of regulations, levies and subsidies, the setting of environmental ambient standards and the use of economic and fiscal instruments to bring about changes in consumption and production behaviour. Governments within member-states of the EU are expected to use these instruments in order to steer demand and supply towards more sustainable patterns (CEC 1993). However, opinions on the degree of government intervention needed to effect a shift to sustainable development vary across the spectrum of viewpoints on sustainable development outlined in the Ladder above. Many of these differences of opinion are centred around views about the role of the market (Turner *et al.* 1995).

Some claim that sustainable development requires centralized planning, which in turn demands a high degree of state intervention, particularly with respect to industrial policy (Meadowcroft 1995). Redclift, for example, has argued that sustainable development becomes a model for planning, a strategy involving purposeful management of the environment (Redclift 1993: 7). This is because containing economic activity within the limits of the environment's carrying capacities requires economic planning that centres around controlling the market and gearing the economy towards achieving a set of environmental targets (Eckersley 1995).

Others argue that centralized planning is inappropriate. Pearce (1985, 1995), for example, believes that it is possible to promote sustainable development through the use of economic instruments that decentralize decisions to the marketplace. Also, centralized planning may give rise to tensions within the EU as it runs counter to the trends of deregulation and marketization that are characteristic of economic policy within the emerging Single European Market. It also runs counter to the ideological position of radical political ecologists, who wish to see a reduction, rather than an increase, in the role of the centralized state. Furthermore, planning demands an approach that places the requirements of the economic system above those of the individual. This in turn will involve ethical judgements about the role and rights of present individuals versus the system's survival and the welfare of future generations (Turner *et al.* 1995). These are all contentious political issues.

While it is recognized that the role of central government is an important one, it is also now widely recognized that much of the implementation of policies aimed at shifting economies to a sustainable development path will have to take place not at the level of national government, but above and below that, at the international and local levels, respectively. This was stressed at the 1992 Rio Earth Summit. At the national level, governments have limited responsibilities in relation to the implementation of policies that are directly relevant to tackling the promotion of sustainable development. Thus a shift to sustainable development requires not only an increased role for central government, but also an enhancement of the involvement of sub-national levels of government in environmental management. The sub-national level of government includes the regional, city and commune levels.

Local authorities have a particularly important role in the shift to sustainable development, given their areas of legal competence. They manage ambient environmental quality, apply tools for modifying behaviour, shape land-use planning, stimulate economic development, deal with waste disposal, transport, urban renewal, and the provision of education, health, housing and welfare services. This wide range of functions makes local government key players in the design, and more especially the implementation, of strategies to promote sustainable development (Haughton and Hunter 1994). This role has been recognized by the EU in both the Fifth Environmental Action Programme and the Green Paper on the Urban Environment (CEC 1990, 1993) and in the Local Agenda 21 strategies that followed the Rio Earth Summit. Thus it is clear that the successful implementation of sustainable development policies is now seen as requiring the involvement of local actors. As a consequence, this book pays particular attention to sustainable development practices taking place at the local level within EU member-states (see Chapters 7, 8, 10 and 11).

Using the Ladder of Sustainable Development: local government and the imperatives of sustainable development

A more detailed examination of the competences of local governments and their relationship to the promotion of sustainable development can help elaborate the Ladder of Sustainable Development more fully, and illustrate its usefulness in understanding the different policy imperatives associated with the promotion of sustainable development. For example, in the economic sphere, local governments can be situated either on the weak or the strong rung of the Ladder of Sustainable Development. More particularly, through their involvement in economic development and planning, local governments can move beyond reactive responses (weak sustainable development) to proactive environmental management (strong sustainable development). A good example is to be found in site-protection policy, where proactive involvement acts to steer development away from sites that are more environmentally important: sites with abandoned industrial works, for example, can be used for development, thus avoiding greenfield encroachment. Similarly, local governments can adopt an approach to wildlife in keeping with strong sustainable development by, for example, promoting biodiversity through site protection and the creation of wildlife corridors. However, there is also scope for local government to encourage new forms of economic activity that move policy closer to the Ideal Model. Green technology parks are an example, where firms which can exploit each others' waste products can be located together.

The range of local government competences also means that there is scope for the development of local policies aimed at equity in environmental resource use and distribution. The intra-generational equity aspects of this are linked to redistribution in the Ladder of Sustainable Development. For example, inner urban areas in European cities experience widespread poverty, deprivation and bad housing, and local governments have the opportunity to steer resources into tackling the social aspects of regeneration that form a necessary part of the shift to sustainable development (Haughton 1995; see Chapters 7, 8 and 10).

Sub-national governments also play an important role in relation to the integration of environmental considerations into sectoral programmes (the fifth column in the Ladder). Integration is in keeping with the imperatives associated with the strong interpretation of sustainable development. Transport and land-use planning provide clear examples of sectors where the integration of environmental considerations is more easily achieved at the local, rather than at the national, level (Haughton and Hunter 1994). Here there is also scope for local government to move towards the holistic approaches characteristic of the Ideal Model of sustainable development. However, in practice progress is slow. This depends on how far local governments can develop an improved understanding of the policy dynamics associated with a shift to sustainable development, particularly the need to set targets and appraise policy success through the use of broad-based indicators.

Local governments have a crucial role in relation to the use of existing environmental policy instruments and tools, and in the development of new tools appropriate to the promotion of sustainable development. The capacity to implement policies is related to the effectiveness of available instruments, but currently the instruments are limited and narrow in their focus. Sustainable development indicators can provide new techniques for assessing policy and appraising the appropriateness of existing instruments and resources. They also have a communicative function as they help to inform the wider community about trends in the environment and provide a conduit for public participation (Jacobs 1995a: 19). Furthermore, given that sub-national governments are charged with the monitoring and evaluation of policies, the elaboration of sustainable development indicators provides a good example of the proactive role that local government can adopt. Such improved understanding and participation is fundamental, given the ambiguities embedded in the notion of sustainable development.

Successful implementation of policies aimed at shifting to a sustainable development path also requires institutional innovation and reform. This poses a challenge to local government, which includes the introduction of reform aimed at the elimination of administrative barriers to policy integration as well as a reduction in institutional fragmentation. Resource mobilization and co-ordination, for example, are particularly difficult to achieve in the context of small municipalities and where institutional fragmentation is high. Furthermore, stronger forms of sustainable development require a more holistic approach based on inter-sectoral integration, which in turn requires a reduction in the autonomy of different units within a local authority. This holistic approach is politically sensitive and is more common in Denmark and The Netherlands than it is in Britain (Batley and Stoker 1991).

Sub-national governments are closer to their electorates and to civil society than national governments. Strengthening the links between local governments and their electorates is thus an important ingredient in the promotion of sustainable development (see the tenth column of the Ladder). The strength of local governments' commitment to sustainable development can, in part, be evaluated by the extent to which they have moved from overreliance on 'top-down' strategies (inherent in the weak interpretation of sustainable development) towards the encouragement of 'bottom-up' initiatives (more characteristic of strong sustainable development and the Ideal Model). Promoting a bottom-up approach requires a much more enabling and empowering proactive strategy on the part of local government. This provides a key concern of this book, namely identifying the extent to which local groups have been incorporated into open policy-making fora, or conscripted into more closed neo-corporatist arrangements by government organizations operating at the local, regional, national and EU levels (Young 1996b; see Chapters 8, 10 and 11).

The importance of 'bottom-up' involvement

The failure of the state adequately to address the problem of environmentally damaging activities affecting public welfare, and thereby securing social harmony, often generates opposition at the grassroots level (Cable and Benson 1992). In such case, legitimation concerns of the polity can act as political opportunity structures for grassroots activists to pressure the state and gain concessions (Modavi 1993). Certainly, during the last three decades securing bottom-up participation in the policy process has been a target of citizens and grassroots groups. In the postwar period there has been a steady and increasing growth in grassroots environmental activism across class, gender and race. In the developed world, many contentious grassroots actions have aimed at stopping forms of land use that are not approved locally, often without support from larger environmental organizations (Gould *et al.* 1993; Freudenberg and Steinsapir 1991). These movements share the belief that they should participate in the decisions that affect their daily lives. Citizen groups may also demand that producers and the state implement or create environmental protection measures and policies. These largely defensive grassroots environmental actions stem from the generalized environmental degradation that threatens livelihoods and welfare. They are legitimately labelled 'new social movements' because they respond to social needs which have been recently generated by world developments (Fuentes and Gunder Frank 1989).

The promotion of sustainable development needs to take into consideration such reactions from the grassroots. Certainly bottom-up involvement could help in attaining more successful sustainable development agendas. Furthermore, the promotion of sustainable development must be participatory if it is to succeed. There are a number of reasons for this. In particular, sustainable development polices, at least in their Ideal form, will mean sacrifices for the Northern populations that include accepting a reduction in levels of consumption. This may also – though less certainly – be true of strong sustainable development. If implemented, such policies will require changes in the structure of the economy, industry, transport, agriculture and food production – in short the entire Northern way of life. These changes will threaten acquired rights and established interests, which means that widespread public support from citizens is a necessary condition for a permanent, structural solution to the environmental crisis (Achterberg 1993: 82). Local participation in, and contribution to, the development of policies based on sustainable development is therefore crucial, as the co-operation of actors at the local level is vital if the project of sustainable development is to be realized, not least in terms of ensuring the management of specific, locally based resources. Furthermore, argues Achterberg, participation in the decisions which affect one's own life is a central political value of democracy and, for strategic reasons, the required changes of lifestyle connected with a shift to sustainable development can never be lasting if they are imposed in an authoritarian way. Voluntariness is an imperative of successful sustainable development policies. However, achieving bottom-up participation is an extremely difficult political process (see Macnaghten *et al.* 1995: 7; Young 1996b).

Planning for a sustainable future also involves an increased role for government, an increase which may not necessarily be accepted at grassroots level. It therefore requires the construction of 'a shared public basis on which to ground the legitimacy of restrictions and corrections' if sustainable development policies are to be successfully implemented (Achterberg 1993: 91). But participation is not just a means whereby pre-existing sustainable development policies can be legitimized. Increasingly, participation is seen as a necessary part of the formulation and implementation of policy. Cohen and Uphoff distinguish four types of participation, namely in decision-making, implementation, benefit distribution and evaluation (Lélé 1991: 615). This distinction can be useful for widening understanding of the role of participation in sustainable development. Here participation becomes a process of respecting and drawing upon an indigenous community's own understanding of, and interactions with, the natural environment. This form of participation will give rise to new indicators of progress, which, as Jacobs has pointed out, embrace cultural traditions, local distinctiveness and local knowledge (Jacobs 1995a:14). Participation can allow policy-makers to draw upon the rich understanding of local resources held by local people. This is particularly important for resource management, as the practices of resource management, which characterize long-established local cultures, have usually evolved over extended time periods in an attempt to maintain local social and ecological systems (Murdoch and Clark 1994: 19). Participation ensures that sustainable development is aimed not just at environmental management but at societal continuation. In order to realize its full potential, that is to move from its weak to strong and ultimately Ideal form, sustainable development must grow from within and rely on local control over resources, local participation in decision-making and the empowerment of local people, especially the underprivileged and marginalized (Thrupp 1989; de la Court 1990; Brechin and West 1990).

Finally, participation is significant because in the strong and Ideal models of sustainable development the 'community' dimension is as important as the ecological dimension. As O'Riordan has argued, the nucleus of the notion of strong sustainable development involves the interweaving of the citizenship and educational aspects of development with the fusion of material and environmental wealth creation.

Doing this, he argues, has important political and policy consequences: it leads to a shift in the balance of priorities towards the longer term, towards global survival, towards the happiness and creative potential of our descendants, and towards a much more 'earth conscious' approach towards policy formulation and investment planning (O'Riordan 1985: 53). To return to a point made earlier, sustainable development is here seen not as a blueprint, but as a catalyst for change. In contrast to a top-down policy approach, bottom-up participation has the potential to facilitate and catalyse radical social change.

These arguments about the importance of participation were recognized at the Rio Earth Summit and are implicit in Agenda 21. Participation is central to Local Agenda 21 for three reasons. First, the need to construct broad-based consensus approaches was acknowledged and agreed. Second, Chapter 28 of Agenda 21 specifically mentioned the need to involve different interests and minorities in the process, including young people, indigenous peoples and those with their own cultural traditions, women, non-governmental organizations (NGOs), local authorities, trade unions, business, the scientific and technical communities and farmers. In agreeing to Agenda 21, governments have accepted the need to involve all groups in society and not just the more articulate, self-presenting groups. Third, almost all interpretations of sustainable development focus on the notion of equity. Although related to North/South issues and Third World poverty, equity has also been linked to making opportunities available to marginalized groups in inner-city and remote rural areas in industrialized countries. Certainly, if equity issues are to be addressed it is necessary to establish effective participation processes at the policy-making stage. It is also important to stress the consequences of what was agreed at Rio for the participation process. Producing consensus and involving minorities has meant that participation is now seen as an integral part of the promotion of sustainable development. Participation is no longer an optional extra and the Rio Summit has given participation a new status (Young 1996a: 2).

In view of the importance of bottom-up participation, it is important to analyse the extent to which sustainable development strategies, when applied to local projects, take account of what O'Riordan refers to as the 'cultural, administrative and aspirational differences among communities' (O'Riordan 1985), and to evaluate the various ways in which local people experience and perceive sustainable development. This entails a discussion of power and the involvement of local interests in non-local socio-economic and political structures. In this respect a key concern is the extent to which sustainable development policies, originating from the EU, including those under the Fifth Environmental Action Programme, make use of people's knowledge and expertise concerning their environment. The book explores these issues by focusing on rural agricultural peripheral economies where sustainability entails delicate balances (see Chapter 11); on urban economies where new forms of urban sustainability need to be developed (see Chapters 7 and 8); and on the involvement of local communities in forming their own projects to promote sustainable development (see Chapter 10).

It can be seen, therefore, that there is a tension at the heart of the sustainable development process. On the one hand, it requires top-down input and gives a key role to government and international agencies. On the other, it recognizes that the various stakeholders in society have their own role to play – and local, bottom-up perceptions of sustainable development policies may differ from those held by central policy-makers. Perhaps inevitably, therefore, at least in the liberal democracies characteristic of EU member-states, the outcome of participation is usually a policy or set of policies representing a compromise between competing interests. In this respect, EU environmental policy is an excellent example of the process of compromise. In practice, local people may mobilize against projects in order to protect their environment and sustain their resource base and this can include local mobilization against centrally inspired sustainable development projects (see Chapter 11).

Overall, promoting successful sustainable development polices depends upon maintaining a satisfactory balance between the imperatives of top-down strategic planning and bottom-up participation in the policy-making process. However, whilst current sustainable development models reject a simple top-down structure, they leave us unclear as to how the imperatives of top-down management and bottom-up participation can be reconciled into new policy paradigms. Even in mid-1996, when this Introduction was written, it was still too early to assess this issue as, across the world, very few Local Agenda 21s had been formulated, let alone implemented. Thus, whilst recognizing the importance of participation, it should not be assumed that the involvement of local and environmental interests in policy formulation and implementation will necessarily ensure project success. Lélé, in particular, is very critical of this assumption. She sees participation as a necessary, but not a sufficient, condition for achieving the equity and social justice imperatives embedded in the strong form of sustainable development. Rather, participation, seen as an institutional process, is a framework for bargaining and negotiation in which cer-

tain groups of people can become involved and, as such, may not necessarily reinforce ecological sustainability. She argues that equity in
resource access may not lead to sustainable resource use without the
construction of new institutions for resource management (Lélé 1991:
616).

SUSTAINABLE DEVELOPMENT POLICY WITHIN THE EU

The promotion of sustainable development

The growth of multinationals, the transnationalization of capital and
the intensification of the search for markets across the world are some
of the factors implicated in the emergence of the global economy. This,
in turn, has fuelled pressures for states to promote trade liberalization
and economic growth with minimal inflation. In the EU case, these
factors, combined with the need to respond to the competitive threat
posed by Asian economies, lie behind the decision to complete the
Single European Market and to amend the original Treaty establishing
the EU through the Maastricht Treaty.

The EU's attempts to promote sustainable development in the 1980s
and 1990s have to be seen in the context of these global economic
pressures. These pressures also impose constraints on member-states'
attempts to promote sustainable development. This is because, first,
treaties such as the Maastricht Treaty impinge on the rights of states
to protect their domestic economies. Such agreements can have significant effects on some economic sectors, which in turn can have an
impact on local economies. Yet within the Single European Market the
right of governments to counteract or alleviate such impacts can be
quite seriously circumscribed. The contraction of Europe's coal, steel
and shipbuilding industries in the 1980s gives clear examples, as, more
recently, does the case of the fishing industry (Stenson and Gray
1995). Second, global economic pressures make it hard for projects
based on the promotion of sustainable development to survive in the
competitive European marketplace. It is easy to point to isolated
examples, as in specialized niche markets in the food sector or in sustainable tourism. However, in general, economic pressures mean that
major firms can undercut local companies. Third, capital investment
programmes routinely aim to replace jobs through automation, thus
moving away from the sustainable development goal of a more labour-
intensive economy.

Collectively, these pressures all fuel the demand for economic
growth to provide jobs, create wealth, promote exports and thus pay

for the cost of public spending programmes that cover everything from infrastructure development to welfare and training provision. The conventional economic growth model underlines the need to reorient economies, as growth threatens the supply of finite resources and the carrying capacities of ecosystems (see Chapter 3). The global economic pressures do not just create the need to move towards sustainable development: they undermine the initial attempts to change course to more sustainable forms of economic activity. This then strengthens the need to break out of the circular pattern that increasingly endangers the planet's capacity to sustain species within their broader interlocking ecosystems.

Although the forces associated with the process of globalization are very powerful, there are some counter-trends that need to be noted. First, there are the decisions reached at the Rio Earth Summit, including the launching of the Agenda 21 process. Second, there are moves to address environmental issues through the development of clean technologies and ecological modernization (Mol 1995; Young and van der Straaten 1997). There are now new markets for pollution control equipment and new jobs in the service sector connected with enhanced environmental management. While these are still focused on economic growth, they are moving towards promoting a different kind of growth. Third, there are the attempts by sub-national governments to stimulate local economies through, for example, the promotion of local purchasing agreements. Finally, although spending under the EU Structural Funds and various urban programmes is relatively small, the existence of targeted programmes is establishing an important precedent. They can potentially be reoriented and refocused on sustainable development objectives. Globalization pressures and the creation of international agreements do indeed act as constraints on individual states. But the extent to which they do is often exaggerated.

A Northern focus

As has been argued, the flexibility of the term sustainable development is theoretically problematic but of immense policy significance: it can help forge a consensus or commitment to promote sustainable development, while at the same time allowing individual policy-makers a great deal of flexibility in their interpretations of the policy imperatives associated with that commitment. Sustainable development is thus a powerful tool for political consensus (Repetto in Lélé 1991: 612). This is evidently the case in the EU context, as it has allowed the EU as a whole to commit itself to the reconciliation of economic and environmental interests, while at the same time allowing member-states as well as individual Directorate-Generals within the Commission a great deal of latitude with respect to their choice of policy options to put this commitment into practice.

Given the EU commitment to sustainable development and the flexible policy responses at the Commission and member-state levels, the empirical focus of this book is on the implementation of sustainable development policy in the North – that is, on developed economies and predominantly industrialized societies. There are good theoretical justifications for this. First, as Redclift has argued, from the early 1980s the ecocentric and strong approaches to sustainable development have become very concerned with the structural relationship between developed and less-developed countries. In particular, within the radical green perspective the implications of sustainable development action must ultimately bear on the North as well as the South: on 'us' as well as 'them'. In this context it becomes legitimate to begin to ask 'what does sustainability mean for us?' (Redclift 1987: 10–11; see also Chapter 12). Most research to date has framed discussion within the global context of North–South relations. This arises directly from the Brundtland Commission's exposure of the links between poverty, uneven development, population growth and environmental degradation. However, while this framework raises legitimate issues of a global nature, it is not necessarily the most suitable for understanding the dynamics of environmental policy-making within the fifteen member-states of the European Union. Following the publicity surrounding the Rio Earth Summit both policy-makers and the general public have become increasingly familiar with environmental and development issues as problems of international relations. What is less familiar is how the concept of sustainable development relates to the European context as such, as opposed to the European context in its relation to the underdeveloped or developing world. It is important that this dimension is addressed.

Second, as a major trading bloc and increasingly important international political actor, the European Union plays a leadership role and sets precedents regarding the manner in which the principle of sustainable development is operationalized in policy terms. The Dublin Declaration on the environment stated that the Community must use its position of moral, economic and political authority to advance international efforts to promote sustainable development, and that the Union's credibility as an international environmental leader rested on this (CEC 1988). As a major regional economic power, the EU will also play a role in shaping future patterns of production and consumption, and thereby also the success of policy aimed at achieving sustainable development at the global level. The Union is still committed to this role and, as the Commission stated in 1992:

> The Community, as the largest economic/trading partner in a world where it is increasingly seen that growth has to be environmentally sustainable, must exercise its responsibility to both present and future generations. To this end it must put its own house in order and provide an example to developed and developing countries alike in relation to the protection of public health and the environment and the sustainable use of natural resources.
>
> (CEC 1993)

The EU's approach

In the Fifth Environmental Action Programme (1992–1997), the EU committed itself to a policy of sustainable development in an attempt to reconcile its historical commitment to economic development with its new concern to protect the environment (Baker 1993). Furthermore, under the 1986 Single European Act it is legally obliged to integrate environmental considerations into all other policy sectors. A key concern is whether this commitment can in practice help to reconcile economic and environmental interests within the Union. It is reasonable to suggest that the most relevant changes necessary to make a successful transition to sustainable development on a global scale are not necessarily the same as those most pertinent to ensuring the transition to sustainable development within a European context. Furthermore, the internal policy and institutional changes that need to be achieved within the EU relate less to resolving food security and extreme hunger than to the nature of the links between the Western economic development model and the environment. The significance of the decision-making process of the Union and its institutional capacity for shaping the response of the Union to the challenge of sustainable development is also of importance for this book (see Chapter 5).

Across the EU, there is only limited understanding of the changes required in present production and consumption patterns if a Northern path to sustainable development is to evolve. There is also uncertainty as to the limitations that current economic trends within the EU, more especially the liberalization of markets and increase in competition under the Single European Market, pose for developing sustainable development policy initiatives (see Chapter 4). Similarly, there is a lack of clarity in relation to how strong a role the EU needs to play in effecting a transition to sustainable development, and how this role can be reconciled with the interests of member-states and their sub-national actors, and with the new EU commitment to the principle of subsidiarity (see Chapter 5). This book looks at the ways in which the EU and its member-states have tried to link economic development to environmental sustainability. At the EU level, the commitment to sustainable development has occurred across a number of different planes, which for convenience can be grouped into two categories: formal, legal and declaratory statements; and policy programmes.

The formal commitment

Environmental policy within the EU is framed in terms of action programmes. The Fifth Action Programme for the Environment and Sustainable Development (1992–1997) is formed around the explicit aim of breaking the perception that there is a trade-off between environmental protection on the one hand and economic development on the other. The crucial starting-point for the Programme' is the linking of environmental protection with sustainable economic development (Europe an Environment 1992).

The incorporation of the concept of sustainable development as a central theme of the Fifth Programme is important. First, it is of symbolic importance: the Union has now set an environmental target towards which all its policies must aim – at least in theory. Second, even if policies fall far short of this aim – and they most certainly will – the setting of sustainable development as a target of policy has provided an important environmental criterion against which EU policy can in future be appraised. However, the question remains as to whether or not the concept will allow the Union to move beyond a policy approach that was dominated by the evolution of an ever-tighter regulatory framework to a new more positive approach, where environmental protection is seen as an integral part of economic activity. This requires an examination of the tension between the EU's historical commitment to economic growth, on the one hand, and its recent acceptance, in the Fifth Action Programme, of the concept of sustainable development, on the other. Attitudes towards this new policy change from time to time among both elites within Europe (see Chapter 4) and key environmental groups (see Chapter10).

A good deal of uncertainty remains concerning the meaning the EU attributes to the very term 'sustainable development' (see Chapters

1 and 4). One of the legacies of the Brundtland formulation – on which the EU commitment is based – is that the concept is analytically 'contentless'. Thus the operationalization of the concept has been left up to individual institutions and/or governments. The EU, for example, sees the implementation of sustainable development as involving policies aimed at promoting sustainable consumption and sustainable production. Sustainable consumption can be understood as 'the use of goods and services that respond to basic needs and bring a better quality of life, while minimising the use of natural resources, toxic materials and emissions of waste and pollutants over life-cycles, so as not to jeopardise the needs of future generations' (Minister of the Environment, Norway 1995: 9). In this sense, the promotion of sustainable consumption can be seen as bringing together a number of key issues: meeting needs, enhancing quality of life, improving resource efficiency, increasing the use of renewable energy sources, minimizing waste, taking a life-cycle perspective and taking into account the equity dimension. This focus also means that a central question for the EU becomes how to provide the same or better services to meet the basic requirements of life and the aspirations for improvement for current and future generations, while continually reducing environmental damage and risk to human health. However, a danger associated with this focus is that the improvements in environmental quality may be sought through the substitution of more efficient and less polluting goods and services, rather than through the reduction in the volumes of goods and services consumed. In other words, this focus may encourage a tendency to limit policy goals to the achievement of changes in the patterns of consumption as opposed to levels of consumption, a tendency which confines policy to the weak rung of the sustainable development Ladder (Baker 1996).

Similarly, sustainable production is based around the idea of cleaner production, which is seen as a preventive strategy that aims at promoting the use and development of cleaner processes, products and services, thus protecting the environmental resource base upon which production is dependent. The EU argues that there is increasing evidence that sustainable production can bring both economic and environmental benefits. This is closely linked with the EU policy of encouraging ecological modernization among firms (see Chapter 4). Again, however, this focus is limited to achieving changes in the *patterns* of production as opposed to the *levels* of production.

The integration of environmental considerations into sectoral policy

In order to be truly successful, the policy of sustainable development has not only to be applied in the area of environmental policy but also to be integrated into all other policy areas within the Union. This integration now forms a major objective of EU environmental policy. In particular, under the Fifth Environmental Action Programme, the Commission is committed to achieving integration in five sectors, namely tourism, industry, energy, transport and agriculture. This poses particular difficulties for the EU as the Union has historically been committed to ensuring economic growth through the implementation of traditional economic goals and objectives. To take an example, transport is an area that poses major problems for the environment. In response to the environmental problems posed by the transport sector the Commission has adopted a policy of 'sustainable mobility'. This involves initiatives of three kinds: technical measures, transport policy measures and measures which can influence human behaviour (Baker and Young 1996). However, how sustainable mobility can be achieved given the other policy priorities of the Commission in the transport sector, in particular the commitment to developing the Trans European Network, remains uncertain (Baker and Young 1996). Similar problems exist within the agricultural sector, especially given the fact that environmental management received only marginal consideration in the reform of the Common Agricultural Policy (CAP) (Baker and Young 1996). Tourism also poses its own difficulties, not least of which is the lack of EU legal competence in this sector, combined with heavy anticipated growth in tourist activity, particularly in the Mediterranean regions (see Chapter 6). Overall, therefore, there are formidable institutional as well as economic barriers to the incorporation of environmental considerations into other policy areas (see Chapters 4 and 5).

The promotion of sustainable development policies is also difficult given the current EU priority of completing the internal market. In peripheral regions, for example, the belief persists that there is a sharp trade-off between environmental protection on the one hand and economic development on the other. Furthermore, implementation of sustainable development policies in the periphery can be hampered by the fact that underdeveloped regions may lack the basic physical infrastructure and administrative capacity necessary to implement this policy (Baker *et al.* 1994).

Because of their importance in the context of Northern industrialized economies, it is necessary to analyse the policy imperatives associated with the promotion of sustainable development in urban areas. In this book this analysis takes place within the context of a wider discussion of the policy process, especially as it relates to economic interests (see Chapters 7, 8 and 10). To date in western Europe land-use planning controls aimed at environmental management have tended to influence the location of development, not its occurrence. This method of intervention is primarily aimed at facilitation rather than at serious curtailment of the production activities that are central to industrial economies (Redclift 1987: 135). In the area of land-use planning, for example, most environmental responses to the existence of conflict over development have been what Holling calls 'protective and reactive response' (Holling 1978). This has resulted in two tendencies: first, policy-makers treat each case of controversy over land use as if it were unique; second, they try to separate the environmental consequences of development from the social and economic ones. Thus existing environmental management methods in the area of land-use planning will need substantial reform if land-use planning is to become an instrument in the promotion of anything beyond weak sustainable development (see Chapter 7). This reform will have to take account of the fact that merely undertaking land-use assessment does not mean that effective policy measures are implemented to ensure that land is used in the most appropriate and sustainable way (Redclift 1987: 134–137).

Furthermore, as Redclift has argued, environmental management, imbued with the contradictions that afflict all management science, represents an attempt to mediate the contradictions of industrial society by minimizing the social costs of conflict (Redclift 1987). As such, its role in the promotion of strong sustainable development may well be a limited one. As numerous Chapters in this book implicitly argue, the environmental management approach is closely associated with the weaker end of the sustainable development Ladder. It has had limited success in promoting the more ambitious approaches higher up the Ladder. A key concern of this book, then, is to explore the new approaches to planning that are needed if policy-makers are to promote stronger forms of sustainable development (see Chapter 8).

The imperatives for successful implementation of sustainable development

The concept of sustainable development offers the hope that some common ground does exist where a fruitful and politically practicable partnership of ideas, values and policies can develop between policy-

makers and environmental groups (O'Riordan 1985). The incorporation of environmental groups into the EU policy-making process is a
necessary prerequisite for such a partnership to develop successfully
within the EU. However, further research is needed on the attitude of
environmental groups to the EU's new concern about sustainable
development and how they see their role in relation to participating in
the promotion of sustainable development across Europe (see
Chapters 10 and 11).

This participation is closely associated with the democratization of
the EU. Involvement in all stages in the policy-making process is a key
element in the sustainable development process. However, it is important to point out that there is no simple or uniform relationship
between environmentalism and democracy. As Pepperman Taylor has
argued: 'Environmentalist movements have generated a wide diversity
of attitudes and approaches towards democracy, and environmental
theorists have reflected this tremendous range of views, from radically
democratic to radically authoritarian' (Pepperman Taylor 1996;
O'Riordan 1994). Because of the integration and co-ordination
demands that sustainable development places on the policy-making
process as a whole, it is sometimes argued that a strong and centralized
state is needed as a necessary condition for ecologically sound development. Alternatively, it has been argued that in certain circumstances
democracy can be sacrificed in the interest of wider ecological goals.
This raises an interesting issue for analysis, namely how different state
traditions across the Union influence the promotion and implementation of sustainable development policies (see Chapter 6).

The democratization of the EU environmental policy process is but
one step. For sustainable development to be accepted politically within
member-states it is of crucial importance that it be seen to be an
achievable aim of policy. Successful implementation of sustainable
development strategies hinges on whether the policy recommendations
are seen as affordable, achievable, accessible and (socially, culturally
and politically) attractive (Minister of the Environment, Norway
1995).

The range of policy tools

The Fifth Environmental Action Programme stressed the need to
expand the range of policy tools used to implement sustainable development policy within the EU. The range of new policy tools that the
Commission is keen to put to use include legislative instruments,
market-based instruments, horizontal supporting instruments and

financial support mechanisms. The Commission believes that economic analysis can play a key role in the identification of policy instruments that can facilitate the implementation of the policy of sustainable development and, as such, is close to the weak rung of the Ladder of Sustainable Development. Following the publication of the *White Paper on Growth, Competitiveness and Employment*, the Commission has said it aims to rely as much as possible on market mechanisms (Baker and Young 1996). Here, however, there may be an unwarranted assumption that policy tools are 'neutral' – that is, that they are applicable in all countries, across all sectors, for all policy objectives. In these circumstances, it will be necessary to ascertain in more detail which tools are of most use in different socio-political-cultural settings and which are most useful in the five sectors targeted by the Fifth Environmental Action Programme for integration. This is a task for future research.

CONCLUSION

Sustainable development will remain a contestable concept and, like many political and social concepts embedded in liberal democratic societies, it will continue to give rise to a variety of different interpretations as to how it is to be operationalized and achieved. Nevertheless, the flexibility of its meaning is at the root of the widescale acceptance of sustainable development as a goal of policy; and in particular it has allowed the concept to provide a means whereby policy-makers can reject the notions that environmental conservation constrains development and that development necessarily means environmental pollution. Others disagree with this assertion, however, and conflicts remain. But whatever the individual perspective on such matters, environmental protection in practice *does* mean the imposition of constraints on economic activity; and economic growth and environmental protection will remain uneasy partners (Jacobs 1991: 61).

NOTES

1   In developing this Ladder, the authors have made use of O'Riordan's 'A possible map of the sustainable transition', 'Democracy and the sustainability transition', paper presented to the Environment and Democracy Project, Mansfield College, Oxford, September 1994.
2   The term 'biocentric' is also used, both in some of the succeeding Chapters and in the relevant literature. The two terms 'ecocentric' and 'biocentric' are often used interchangeably; but it should be noted that 'ecocentric' is some-

times used to refer specifically to ecosystems, whereas 'biocentric' is given a wider meaning which may encompass the social dimension.

REFERENCES

Achterberg, W. (1993) 'Can liberal democracy survive the environmental crisis? Sustainability, liberal neutrality and overlapping consensus', in A. Dobson and P. Lucardie (eds) *The Politics of Nature: Explorations in Green Political Theory*, London: Routledge, pp. 62–81.

Albrecht, G. (1994) 'Ethics, anarchy and sustainable development', *Anarchist Studies* 2: 95–117.

Baker, S. (1993) 'The environmental policies of the European Community: a critical review', *Kent Journal of International Relations* 7(1).

—— (1996) 'Sustainable development and consumption: the ambiguities – the Oslo Ministerial Roundtable Conference on Sustainable Production and Sustainable Consumption', *Environmental Politics*, 3: 93–9.

Baker, S. and Young, S. C. (1996) 'The implementation of sustainable development policy in member-states: an appraisal of EU policy to date', paper presented at the ECPR Joint Sessions of Workshops, Oslo, April 1996.

Baker, S., Milton, K. and Yearley, S. (eds) (1994) *Protecting the Periphery: Environmental Policy in Peripheral Regions of the European Union*, London: Frank Cass.

Barret, S. and Fudge, C. (eds) (1981) *Policy and Action*, London: Methuen.

Batley, R. and Stoker, G. (eds) (1991) *Local Government in Europe*, Basingstoke: Macmillan.

Beckerman, W. (1994) 'Sustainable development: is it a useful concept?', *Environmental Values* 3: 191–209.

Brechin, S. R. and West, P. C. (1990) 'Protected areas, resident peoples and sustainable conservation: the need to link top-down with bottom-up', *Society and Natural Resources* 3: 77–79.

Brooks, H. (1992) 'Sustainability and technology', *Science and Sustainability*, Vienna: International Institute for Applied Systems Analysis.

Cable, S. and Benson, M. (1992) 'Acting locally: environmental justice and the emergence of grassroots environmental organizations', paper presented at the American Sociological Association Conference, Pittsburgh, revised version.

Cazalet, P. G. (1985) 'But we do also have to run a business: the implications for industry of environmental regulation – conflict or partnership?', in The UK Centre for Economic and Environmental Development (CEED) *Sustainable Development in an Industrial Economy*, Proceeding of a Conference held at Queen's College, Cambridge, 23–25 June, Cambridge: UK Centre for Economic and Environmental Development.

CEC (1988) Commission of the European Communities, *Dublin Declaration on the Environment*, Brussels: CEC.

—— (1990) Commission of the European Communities, *Green Paper on the Urban Environment*, Luxembourg: CEC.

—— (1993) Commission of the European Communities, 'Towards sustainability: a European Community programme of policy and action in relation to the environment and sustainable development', *Official Journal*, NOC 138/5.

Connolly, W. E. (1983) *The Terms of Political Discourse*, Princeton: Princeton University Press.

Daly, H. E. (1977) *Steady-State Economics*, San Francisco: W. H. Freeman.

de la Court, T. (1990) *Beyond Brundtland: Green Development in the 1990s*, London: Zed Books.

Department of the Environment (DoE), UK (1994) *Sustainable Development: The UK Strategy*, London: HMSO.

Echlin, E. P. (1993) 'Theology and "sustainable development" after Rio', *The Newman* 30: 2–7.

—— (1996) 'From development to sufficiency', *The Aisling* 18: 32–34.

Eckersley, R. (1992) *Environmentalism and Political Theory: Towards an Ecocentric Approach*, New York: UCL Press.

—— (ed.) (1995) *Markets, the State and the Environment: Towards Integration*, Basingstoke: Macmillan.

The Ecologist (1992) *Whose Common Future?*, London: Ecosystems Ltd.

EEA (1995) European Environmental Agency, *Environment in the European Union, 1995: Report for the Review of the Fifth Environmental Action Programme*, K. Wieringa (ed.), Copenhagen: EEA.

Ekins, P. (1992) *Wealth Beyond Measure*, London: Gaia Books.

European Environment (1992) 'EEC: Fifth Action Programme for the Environment and Sustainable Development', *European Environment*, Supplement, no. 386 (5 May).

Freudenberg, N. and Steinsapir, C. (1991) 'Not in our backyards: the grassroots environmental movement', *Society and Natural Resources* 4(3).

Fuentes, M. and Gunder Frank, A. (1989) 'Ten theses on social movements', *World Development* 17(2): 179–191.

Goldsmith, E. (1992) *The Way*, London: Rider.

Gould, K. A., Weinberg, A. S. and Schnaiberg, A. (1993) 'Legitimating impotence: pyrrhic victories of the modern environmental movement', *Qualitative Sociology* 16(3): 207–246.

Grayson, L. and Hobson, M. (1994) 'Sustainability', *Inlogov Informs* 4 (Birmingham: University of Birmingham Institute of Local Government Studies).

Haughton, G. (1995) 'Regional resource management, sustainable development and geographical equity', paper presented at the ESRC Sustainable Cities Seminar, September 1995.

Haughton, G. and Hunter, C. (1994) *Sustainable Cities*, London: Jessica Kingsley.

Holling, C. (ed.) (1978) *Adaptive Evaluation Assessment and Management*, Chichester: John Wiley.

IUCN (1980) *World Conservation Strategy: Living Resource Conservation for Sustainable Development*, Gland, Switzerland: International Union for Conservation of Nature and Natural Resources, UNEP, WWF.

Jacobs, M. (1991) *The Green Economy: Environment, Sustainable Development and the Politics of the Future*, London: Pluto Press.

—— (1995a) 'Reflections on the discourse and politics of sustainable development: part 1: faultlines or contestation and the radical model', paper presented at the Planning Sustainability Conference, Political Economy Research Centre, University of Sheffield, 8–10 September 1995.

—— (1995b) 'Justice and sustainability', in J. Lovenduski and J. Stanyer (eds) *Contemporary Political Studies*, Proceedings of the Political Studies Association, Belfast: Political Studies Association, 3: 1470–1485.

Lafferty, W. M. (1995) 'The implementation of sustainable development in the European Union', in J. Lovenduski and J. Stanyer (eds) *Contemporary Political Studies*, Proceedings of the Political Studies Association, Belfast: Political Studies Association, 1: 223–232.

Lélé, S. (1991) 'Sustainable development: a critical review', *World Development* 19(6): 607–621.

LGMB (1995) Local Government Management Board, *Sustainability Indicators: Research Project Consultants Report on the Pilot Phase*, Luton: LGMB.

Macnaghten, P., Grove-White, R., Jacobs, M. and Wynne, B. (1995) *Public Perceptions and Sustainability in Lancashire: Indicators, Institutions, Participation*, Report by the Centre for the Study of Environmental Change Commissioned by Lancashire County Council, University of Lancaster: Centre for the Study of Environmental Change.

Meadowcroft, J. (1995) 'Planning for sustainability', paper presented at the Planning Sustainability Conference, Political Economy Research Centre, University of Sheffield, 8–10 September 1995.

Meadows, D. H., Randers, J. and Behrens, W. W. (1972) *The Limits to Growth*, London: Earth Island.

Minister of the Environment, Norway (1995) *Report: Oslo Ministerial Roundtable Conference on Sustainable Production and Consumption*, Oslo: Miljøverndepartmentet.

Modavi, N. (1993) 'State response to land use initiative in Hawaii: demobilizing and depoliticizing environmental opposition', *Journal of Political and Military Sociology* 21: 11–36.

Mol, A. P. J. (1995) *The Refinement of Production: Ecological Modernisation Theory and the Chemical Industry*, The Hague: Koninklijke Biblioteek.

Murdoch, J. and Clark, J. (1994) *Sustainable Knowledge*, Newcastle upon Tyne: Centre for Rural Economy, Working Paper no. 9.

Naess, A. (1989) *Ecology, Community and Lifestyle*, Cambridge: Cambridge University Press.

O'Riordan, T. (1981) *Environmentalism*, 2nd edn, London: Pion Press.

—— (1985) 'What does sustainability really mean? Theory and development of concepts of sustainability', *Sustainable Development in an Industrial Economy*, Proceeding of a Conference held at Queen's College, Cambridge, 23–25 June, Cambridge: UK Centre for Economic and Environmental Development.

—— (1994) 'Democracy and the sustainability transition', paper for the Oxford Environment and Democracy Project, Mansfield College, Oxford, 9–11 September 1994.

Pearce, D. (1985) 'Sustainable futures: the economic issues: the compatibility of industrial development and care of the environment', *Sustainable Development in an Industrial Economy*, Proceeding of a Conference held at Queen's College, Cambridge, 23–25 June, Cambridge: UK Centre for Economic and Environmental Development.

—— (1995) *Blueprint 4: Capturing Global Environmental Value*, London: Earthscan/CSERGE.

Pearce, D., Atkinson, G. D. and Dubourg, W. R. (1994) 'The economics of sustainable development', *Annual Review of Energy Environment* 19: 457–474.

Pearce, D. W., Markandya, A. and Barber, E. B. (1989) *Blueprint for a Green Economy: A Report for the UK Department for the Environment*, London: Earthscan.

Pepperman Taylor, B. (1996) 'Democracy and environmental ethics or environmental ethics and the perils of ideological politics', in W. Lafferty and J. Meadowcroft (eds) *Environment and Democracy*, London: Edward Elgar, pp. 86–107.

Pezzey, J. (1989) *Definitions of Sustainability*, UK Centre for Economic and Environmental Development, Working Paper no. 9.

Redclift, M. (1987) *Sustainable Development: Exploring the Contradictions*, London: Routledge.

—— (1993) 'Sustainable development: needs, values, rights', *Environmental Values* 2: 3–20.

Redclift, M. and Goodman, D. (1991) 'Introduction', in D. Goodman and M. Redclift *Environment and Development in Latin America: The Politics of Sustainability*, Manchester: Manchester University Press.

Seymour, J. (1989) *The Ultimate Heresy*, Bideford: Green Books.

Simon, J. L. and Kahn, H. (1984) *The Resourceful Earth: A Response to Global 2000*, Oxford: Blackwell.

Stenson G. and Gray, T. S. (1995) 'The tragedy of the Common Fisheries Policy', in T. S. Gray (ed.) *UK Environmental Policy in the 1990s*, Basingstoke: Macmillan, pp. 263–282.

Thrupp, L. A. (1989) 'Politics of the sustainable development crusade: from elite protectionism to social justice in third world resources issues', *Environment, Technology and Society* 58: 1–7.

Turner, R. K. (1988) *Sustainable Environmental Management: Principles and Practice*, London: Belhaven.

Turner, R. K., Doktor, P. and Adger, N. (1995) 'Assessing the economic costs of sea-level rise', *Environment and Planning A*, 27: 1777-96.

WCED (1987) World Commission on Environment and Development, *Our Common Future: Report of the World Commission on Environment and Development*, Oxford: Oxford University Press (this is popularly referred to as the Brundtland Report).

Weale, A. (1992) *The New Politics of Pollution*, Manchester: Manchester University Press.

Young, S. C. (1996a) 'Participation strategies in the context of Local Agenda 21: towards a new watershed?', in I. Hampsher-Monk and J. Stanyer (eds) *Contemporary Political Studies*, Proceedings of the Political Studies Association, Belfast: Political Studies Association, 2: 858–870.

—— (1996b) *Promising Participation and Community-based Partnerships in the Context of Local Agenda 21: A Report for Practitioners*, Manchester: Government Department, Manchester University, European Policy Research Unit Paper.

Young, S. C. and van der Straaten, J. (1997) *Ecological Modernisation*, London: Routledge.

Part I

The concept of sustainable development

1 The politics of sustainable development

Dick Richardson

Sustainable development is a political fudge: a convenient form of words, promoted, though not invented, by the Brundtland Commission, which is sufficiently vague to allow conflicting parties, factions and interests to adhere to it without losing credibility. It is an expression of political correctness which seeks to bridge the unbridgeable divide between the anthropocentric and biocentric approaches to politics.

Beneath the rhetoric of the political platform, the reality is that the concept of sustainable development as presently used is inherently contradictory and begs a number of important questions. There are two basic approaches: the anthropocentric, sometimes referred to as the environmental, and the biocentric, sometimes referred to as the ecological or Gaian. The former approach, adopted by the traditional political parties, by business and trade union interests, and by governments and bureaucracies generally – the European Union among them – presupposes no great changes in the political and economic process or the relationship between humankind and nature. In contrast, the biocentric approach, adopted by ecological interest groups and the majority of Green parties, is predicated upon a fundamental change in the relationship between humankind and nature, with consequential social, political and economic implications.

This Chapter will address the political implications of the differing approaches to sustainable development. It will consider the challenges faced by governments at all levels – international, national and local – within a planetary system of finite resources. It will argue that for the concept to have any real meaning, other than as a consensual phrase of political agreement, it needs to be radically redefined along purely ecological lines. If that is not possible it should be totally abandoned.

ANTHROPOCENTRICITY, BIOCENTRICITY AND SUSTAINABLE DEVELOPMENT

The rise of industrial society in the late eighteenth and nineteenth centuries stimulated the emergence of anthropocentric rather than biocentric ways of thinking (Richardson 1994: 4). By the mid-twentieth century the industrial worldview, based on the conquest of nature, materialism and consumption, had achieved almost universal acceptance. In the industrialized world, consumers and politicians look to ever-increasing material standards of living; in the less-developed countries (LDCs) politicians seek to emulate the achievements of the established industrialized states. The achievement of economic growth, measured quantitatively through gross national product (GNP) or through GNP per capita, has become the touchstone of success.

The essence of the anthropocentric approach to the natural world is that humankind is above nature and has the right – divine or otherwise – to subjugate it. Often called domination theory (Richardson 1994: 4), this approach has two main aspects – religious and secular. Of the major religious traditions, the Christian is by far the most anthropocentric (White 1967: 1205), calling on humankind to impose its will on the natural world, to subdue it (Genesis: 26, 28). This tradition, through industrialism, has become allied and entwined with the secular: the scientific-rationalist concept, grounded in the ideas of Bacon, Newton and Descartes, that planet Earth exists for the benefit of, and exploitation by, the human race. Humankind is seen as something separate from the rest of life on earth – and superior to it.

It was not until the 1960s that the industrial worldview was seriously challenged, by newly emergent biocentric thinkers and practitioners in what has been termed 'The Green Challenge' (Richardson 1994: 4–11).[1] Central to the biocentric analysis is that humankind is part of nature, not above it; that all life forms, of which humankind is only one, are interconnected in a self-sustaining biosphere (planet Earth). It follows that the part (humankind) cannot dominate the whole (the natural world). Thus, by seeking to subjugate the planet, by imposing human domination, humankind is threatening its own existence. This self-destruction, it is suggested, can be seen in the language of terrorism, genocide, breakdown, pollution and exhaustion (Schumacher 1974: 10–11, 246–247).

In practical day-to-day terms, the anthropocentric approach to the human condition within the natural world is based on materialism and the pursuit of wealth, expressed primarily through industrial expansion and economic growth. Following the teachings of Bacon, Newton and Descartes, explanations of life are reduced to the material. Anything that cannot be proved scientifically is deemed not to exist; anything that cannot be measured does not matter. It is this impersonal, rationalizing outlook, with its emphasis on purely economic and scientific values in measuring human progress, which is integral to the concepts of capitalism, communism, liberalism, socialism and conservatism – and to the political parties which stem from them. The pursuit of wealth and exploitation of the planet may take place on an individualist basis (conservatism), on a collectivist basis (socialism and communism) or on a mixed basis (liberalism and social democracy); but in practice the only differences between the anthropocentric political parties are their methods of *organizing* the pursuit of wealth and material expansion, dependent as they are on the exploitation of the Earth's resources.

The biocentric approach to the human condition is radically different. It is anti-materialist in that it eschews the pursuit of wealth as a goal in itself and seeks to enhance the non-material (some would say spiritual) dimension of the human experience. There is emphasis on the quality of life as distinct from the quantity of material possessions, on feelings and values, on the inner rather than the outer self. Partly this is a question of recognizing the wholeness of the self (material and non-material) as well as the wholeness of the planet. But more fundamentally, from the point of view of the present Chapter, it is a question of recognizing that the pursuit of wealth through industrial expansion and economic growth is ultimately incompatible with the Earth's finite resource base. Central to this approach is the view that the Earth's resources should be used as capital rather than as income, otherwise humankind is merely consuming what rightly belongs to future generations (Schumacher 1974: 12–14, 16). The concept is that of Right Livelihood. Consumption should be based on human need rather than human greed.

The late 1960s and early 1970s saw the climax of what came to be known as the Great Doom debate, between the anthropocentric establishment and its emergent biocentric critics. Major attacks on the industrial worldview came from E. J. Mishan with *The Costs of Economic Growth* (1967), the Club of Rome's *The Limits to Growth* (Meadows *et al.* 1972), the Ecologist's *Blueprint for Survival* (1972) and E. F. Schumacher's *Small is Beautiful* (1974). The first national Green party in Europe, with a specifically biocentric basis, was founded in 1973 – the UK Green Party – then known simply as 'People'. By the early 1980s Green parties had been established in most western European states, and in West Germany Die Grünen entered the

Bundestag in March 1983. In subsequent years, Greens have entered national and local assemblies throughout Europe and pose not only an intellectual threat to the prevailing anthropocentrism of the traditional political parties, but a political threat as well.[2]

Anthropocentrism in its various guises remains the dominant force within national and international society. But in recent years, with the development of the ecological critique of the industrial worldview and the appearance of Green parties in national assemblies, there has been an attempt on the part of anthropocentric thinkers and practitioners to dilute the impact of their biocentric critics. For example, a watered-down version of domination theory has gained currency. As regards the religious aspect, this has found expression in the concept of stewardship, whereby the human race is extolled to 'take all possible action to ensure man's responsible stewardship over nature' (Echlin 1988: 5). This is seen by some as a middle way between the environmental destruction associated with the industrial worldview, and ecological determinism (O'Riordan 1976: 204), but in reality the concept of stewardship is as human-centred as the cruder forms of anthropocentric theory. Humankind is still in charge of the natural world. Similarly, as regards the scientific-rationalist aspect of domination theory, watered-down anthropocentrism can be seen in the concept of sustainable development, which in practical terms has come to mean that a modicum of attention is paid to environmental – as distinct from ecological – concerns, within the overall context of the continued plundering of the Earth's resources (Orton 1994: 13).

The term 'sustainable development' is hardly a new one. The Canadian government began to use the term, intermittently and anthropocentrically, in the early 1980s. However, it was the publication of the Brundtland Report, *Our Common Future*, in 1987 which popularized and politicized the term. The report itself, the product of three years' work by the United Nations' World Commission on Environment and Development, was a series of compromises between the opposing views of twenty-three commissioners from twenty-one different states from around the globe. Typical of the compromises was that on the definition of sustainable development: 'development that meets the needs of the present without compromising the ability of future generations to meet their own needs' (WCED 1987: 8). It was a 'catch-all' definition which left all the commissioners happy: a good political fudge – and an excellent political slogan – but on deeper analysis a vague, contradictory, even meaningless concept.

The key to understanding the Brundtland approach to the natural world is that it frames anthropocentric programmes and the industrial worldview in the language of biocentricity. At the level of rhetoric, Brundtland unites the supporters of treadmill production such as Simon and Kahn (1984) with those who would mitigate its effects on the environment, through either a market-reliant environmental policy (Pearce *et al.* 1989) or an environmentally regulated market (Jacobs 1991). Similarly, in terms of a Ladder of Sustainable Development (see the Introduction) the Brundtland phraseology unites the advocates of exponential growth with the exponents of 'weak sustainable development' and 'strong sustainable development'. In essence, the supporters of Brundtland do not seek to question the concept of quantitative growth measured in traditional terms, although adherents of strong sustainable development may wish to see it redirected in part along qualitative lines. In contrast, the advocates of a biocentric approach question the very concept of quantitative growth.

Given their inherent anthropocentricity and support of the industrial worldview, it is hardly surprising that the Brundtland principles have been endorsed, indeed welcomed, by governments at all levels. They are the basis of the European Union's Fifth Environmental Action Programme. They are written into the Maastricht Treaty, which aspires to 'sustainable and non-inflationary growth respecting the environment'. They are reflected in the agreements reached at the Earth Summit in Rio in June 1992: the Rio Declaration; the Convention on Biodiversity; the Statement of Forest Principles; the Framework Convention on Climate Change; and Agenda 21. Principle 12 of the Rio Declaration, for example, lays down that 'States should co-operate to promote a supportive and open international system that would lead to economic growth and sustainable development in all countries'. This approach is further reflected in the United Nations Commission on Sustainable Development, established after Rio as a promotional vehicle to offset the threat of the political ecology movement to national governments and global multinational business (Orton 1994: 14). The UK Government's report to the UN Commission on Local Agenda 21 stated specifically that 'Sustainable development is not incompatible with economic growth' (UKLGMB 1993: 2).

The problem with the Brundtland Commission was that it tried to unite the ununitable – the anthropocentric and biocentric approaches to the natural world – by means of an agreed form of words. It was an act of political consensus which sought to bring together not only governments (both Left and Right), but the business community, the scientific establishment, non-governmental organizations (NGOs) and even environmentalists. In this it has achieved considerable success. It is almost universally subscribed to. It gives hope to developed states, in particular their scientific and business communities, that economic expansion can be achieved without adversely affecting the environment. It gives hope to LDCs and underdeveloped regions that their development needs will be met. It has given environmentalists credibility. In reality, however, by the very fact that it based its findings on the need for political consensus, the Brundtland Commission begged the very questions that it was established to analyse. What, in fact, constitutes development? What is the relationship, if any, between development and growth? How can needs be identified? How should future needs be compared with present needs? What are needs as distinct from desires? *Which* future generations should be taken into account in formulating policy? The next generation? The next but one? Or, given the problem of nuclear waste, the next but twenty-one?

THE TERMINOLOGICAL IMPLICATIONS OF POLITICS

For the concept of sustainable development to have any utility – except as a political slogan – it needs to be radically redefined. Given its inherent contradictions, there is a good case for abandoning it altogether. However, its assimilation into the political vocabulary as an icon of political correctness makes redefinition, at this stage, a justifiable and potentially productive exercise. Essentially, this means coming to terms with three main issues: development, needs and sustainability.

The anthropocentric view of development is that it is synonymous with growth, growth which follows the Western development paradigm based on international free trade, the maximization of output and the expansion of individual economies, local and national, measured in terms of GNP. In practice, it is this development paradigm which has been adopted by ruling elites on a worldwide basis. Terminologically, it has much to be said for it. Indeed, it is backed by the *Shorter Oxford English Dictionary*. Development, according to dictionary definition, has four main meanings: a gradual unfolding, in the sense of a fuller working out of details; evolution, in the sense of the production of a new form or matter; growth of what is in the germ; and growth from within. In other words, all four definitions entail some kind of expansion or growth, and in the first three definitions this is primarily physical. Only the fourth definition – inner growth – allows for purely non-physical growth.

The biocentric approach to development is opposed to the anthropocentric in that it concentrates on the fourth definition of growth – inner growth – measuring well-being in terms other than that of annual consumption. The biocentric premise is that since consumption is merely a means to human well-being, whether individual or collective, the aim should be to obtain the maximum of well-being with the minimum of consumption (Schumacher 1974: 47–48). This, of course, poses the question of what should be indicators of human well-being. The problem here is that it is difficult to formulate indicators which relate to feelings and values and the non-material world. Birth and death rates, adult literacy levels and life expectation have all been put forward, but they are deficient in that objective factors cannot adequately measure subjective values.

What, then, constitutes development? In theory, there is no one answer, or the answer is ambiguous. But in practice, in the parlance and actions of the political world, the answer is that development is equated with growth, in its material sense. Indeed, the interconnection between development and growth has been enshrined in documentary form, as for example in the Maastricht Treaty and Rio Declaration. Further, it has taken root in the acceptance of the growth-oriented Western development paradigm across the globe. Nevertheless, in the final analysis the equation of growth with development is unrealistic, since exponential economic growth is a physical impossibility given the finite limits of the planet. The consequence, therefore, is that those who wish to define development in terms of non-material, non-physical growth, or in terms of social and cultural growth as well as economic and technological growth, are left with a conundrum. Should they continue to use a term – development – which has effectively been hijacked by the anthropocentric proponents of the industrial worldview, or should they seek a new or refined term which encapsulates their own ideas and feelings?

The question of needs is in many ways similar to that of development, given that there is a material and a non-material element to both. The anthropocentric approach is concerned solely with the material side. Needs are identified and quantified in economic terms, on the grounds that the accretion of wealth, assessed through GNP or GNP per capita, makes it possible to meet the material needs of all. This is the basis of the 'Brundtland consensus', which identifies the problem as 'meeting the basic needs of all and extending to all the opportunity for a better life' (WCED 1987: 44). Yet there is no distinction between the perceived needs of people in the industrialized North, with their often extremely high standards of living, and those of the industrializing South, where standards of living are in most cases extremely low.

It is a basis of the Western development paradigm that needs are *unmet and unfulfilled*, as this gives rise to aspirations for greater material growth. Unhappiness and discontentment are deliberately fostered, in the sense of people and governments wanting more than is obtainable at any one moment (Sadie 1960: 302). At the individual level, the 'have-nots' of the industrialized world aspire to the standards of living and material possessions of those that 'have'. Similarly, at governmental level the 'have-not' states of the industrializing world aspire to the standards of living and material possessions of the 'have' states. The suffering and dislocation that may be caused to the ecosystem or its human subsystems in the process of attempting to meet these aspirations may be objectionable, but is the price to be paid for economic 'progress'.

Thus the problem with the anthropocentric approach to needs, enshrined as it is in the Brundtland consensus, is not only that it fails to give due weight to non-material needs, but also that it fails to distinguish between needs and wants, indeed deliberately encourages wants. This is especially important when comparing the putative needs of the industrialized North with those of the 'industrializing' South. A 'need' in the former is likely to be considered a luxury in the latter. This is equally true within the EU context when comparing, for example, a hyper-developed region of the Netherlands with an economically underdeveloped region in Greece or Portugal or a decaying inner-city urban area such as Moss Side in Manchester. In all cases, however, the fundamental criterion from the anthropocentric standpoint is not the existence of need but the aspiration for 'more'.

The biocentric approach to need is fundamentally different, since it is predicated upon a baseline of physical and material needs common to both the industrialized and industrializing world. The exact nature of these basic physical needs might be debatable, but certainly they would cover the right to sufficient food, clean water and adequate clothing and shelter. Anything above the agreed baseline would be termed a want or luxury, as, for example, the word processor on which this manuscript is written. But the biocentric approach is not limited to purely physical or material needs; it also encapsulates the fulfilment by human beings of non-material or spiritual needs, together with respect for the needs of non-human life on the planet and, indeed, the Earth itself, because of their intrinsic value independent of human life (Naess 1984: 266).

Thus, as with development, there is a basic incompatibility between the anthropocentric and biocentric approaches to needs. Again, dictionary definitions do not help much. The *Shorter Oxford English Dictionary* gives five main definitions: violence, constraint or compulsion, exercised by or upon persons; necessity arising from the facts; an imperative demand for the presence or possession of something; a condition placing one in difficulty or distress; and a condition marked by the lack or want of some necessary thing. The first three might be taken to support the anthropocentric approach, the fourth the biocentric, while the fifth could be taken as supporting either, given its obfuscation of needs and wants. In practice, however, what is important in relation to sustainable development is the way that needs are assessed in terms of economic and social policy; and in this respect it is clear that the anthropocentric definition, the Brundtland consensus, is paramount. The measurement of need by governments across the globe is based not on the biocentric concept of sufficiency, with an agreed common baseline, but on the aspiration for 'more', whatever the existing base. As a consequence, therefore, those who wish to define need in biocentric terms are left with a similar conundrum to those who wish to redefine development along biocentric lines. Should they continue to use a term – in this case 'need' – which has effectively been hijacked by the anthropocentric proponents of the industrial worldview? Or should they seek a new or refined term which encapsulates their own ideas and feelings?

If a basic contradiction exists between the anthropocentric and biocentric approaches to development and needs, there is an even greater contradiction in their approach to sustainability. The implicit assumption of the traditional anthropocentric approach – and the explicit assumption of the business community and the greater part of the scientific establishment – is that, in practice, the Earth's resources are infinite and that the question of sustainability does not therefore arise. New reserves of resources, or alternative materials, will be found to replace any that are exhausted. Equally, the traditional anthropocentric approach evades the question of future generations, since new or replacement resources will always be found if any individual resources are exhausted.

The biocentric approach to sustainability is based on the fact that the Earth has finite limits, and that consumption, based on economic growth, cannot go on for ever. Otherwise, sooner or later, the Earth will reach the limits of its carrying capacity in relation to its human subsystem. It is not a question of 'if'; it is a question of 'when'. In this respect, three limits in particular must be borne in mind: those imposed by non-renewable resources; those imposed by renewable resources; and those imposed by environmental decay through pollution. Industrial civilization will break down once the relevant limit has been reached. This might occur because key non-renewable resources have become exhausted or it has become uneconomical to exploit them further. It might occur because the renewable resource system has been overexploited – for example the soil will be unable to feed the growing world population. Or it might occur because the planet's ecological system is unable to filter out the pollutants that humankind has loaded on to it. In this respect, it is irrelevant which limit is reached first. The end result will be the same: ecological (including human) disaster. The planet will not be inhabitable for future generations.

The biocentric critique of industrial society in the late 1960s and early 1970s had a profound effect on political leaders, more especially since it was difficult to refute that on a finite planet with finite resources there must be a point at which those resources will become exhausted, with the inevitable impact on future generations. The debate on this point could be seen in the workings of the Brundtland Commission, which was obliged to accept, as a philosophical principle, the concept of ecological limits. What it did not accept, however, was the conclusion that industrial society, based on economic growth, would necessarily reach these limits and inevitably decline. For, to accept this conclusion would mean adopting policies which would seriously disrupt the existing social, political and economic status quo, indeed require revolutionary change. Instead, it produced a modicum of ideas which could be accommodated within the existing anthropocentric paradigm, such as environmental costing, resource conservation and the quality (as distinct from quantity) of growth.

In the event the Brundtland Commission produced a formula – sustainable development – which by the manipulation of terminology endeavoured to obscure the contradiction between the anthropocentric and biocentric approaches to sustainability. Beneath the rhetoric, however, as with development and needs, the Brundtland concept of sustainability can be seen to be totally anthropocentric in character. *Our Common Future* not only emphasized that economic growth was still an objective of human society, but also advocated a five- or even tenfold increase in world manufacturing output. It accepted the Western development paradigm and the profligate Western lifestyle as a model for the industrializing world. Ecological sustainability was not seen as primary in the policy-making process, but rather as only one of a number of factors. In essence, the industrial worldview was accepted, albeit in the language – or at least some of the language – of biocentricity.

In practice, therefore, as with development and needs, those who wish to define sustainability along ecological lines are left with a conundrum. Should they continue to use the term sustainability when, to all intents and purposes it has been hijacked by the anthropocentric proponents of the industrial worldview? Or should they seek a new or refined term which encapsulates their own interpretation? Before giving a final answer, it is necessary to consider the *political* implications of the anthropocentric and biocentric interpretations.

THE POLITICAL IMPLICATIONS OF TERMINOLOGY

The importance of the current 'Brundtland consensus' on terminology lies not in what it has accomplished – which is very little – but in what it symbolizes. It connotes a grudging acceptance by anthropocentric politicians and bureaucrats that the biocentric critique is real, powerful, difficult to answer in terms of morality and ethics, and, at least as regards sustainability, impossible to answer in terms of science and logic. But putative acceptance from a philosophical standpoint is different from practical acceptance from a policy standpoint.[3] It is easy for politicians to accept the general principle that the Earth's natural resources should be conserved and, where possible, replenished. It is not too difficult for them to accept – as a philosophical principle – that on a finite planet with finite resources there must be a point at which those resources will become exhausted. But a rhetorical commitment will not produce the changes required to ensure survival in the longer term. Only political action and commitment will do so.

Here lies the problem. Political action will be taken only if it is clear that inaction will prove more costly (Blowers 1992: 3). States will only take action to prevent or rectify environmental damage if it is in their interests to do so (Grove 1990: 13). Besides, there is the question at both state and individual level of reconciling concern for the environment and ecological damage with aspirations for a better standard of living. In this latter respect, it is pertinent – in the words of the Brundtland Commission – to ask *whose* environment and *whose* development is to be sustained. That of Gaia? Of a peasant in the Sahel? An Amazonian Indian? The executives of multinational corporations? Or even international academics?

The potential for conflict over sustainable development at political level is clear (Grayson and Hobson 1994: 2). Not only are there traditional differences to reconcile on the Left–Right spectrum, from an anthropocentric standpoint there are new and emerging differences between the advocates of treadmill production and the supporters of weak and strong sustainable development (see the Introduction). It was these differences which caused the issue to be fudged by Brundtland and which explain why it has continued to be fudged by governments at all levels in subsequent years. To illustrate reality, I will take examples of the anthropocentric paradigm of sustainable development at three levels – global, European and local. I will then compare them with the biocentric paradigm.

At global level, the anthropocentric paradigm is best illustrated by the Earth Summit held at Rio in 1992 under the auspices of the United Nations Commission on Environment and Development (UNCED). On the surface Rio was a considerable success, uniting North and South through the concepts of free-market environmentalism and growth based on the position and policies advocated by the major multinational corporations (MNCs) and the Business Council for Sustainable Development. But in ecological or biocentric terms Rio was a failure, doing nothing to reverse the historic process whereby trade-led growth has led to ecological degradation through the overexploitation of natural resources. Thus there was a convention on biodiversity, but none on free trade; a convention on forests, but none on logging; a convention on climate, but none on cars; an Action Plan (Agenda 21) which had clauses on enabling the poor to achieve sustainable livelihoods, but none on enabling the rich to do so (Ecologist 1992: 122). In other words, the reality of UNCED was that it was concerned with defending the power, interests and living standards of the 'haves' of the industrialized North at the expense not only of the 'have-nots' of the industrializing South but also of Gaia.

At the European level, the situation is somewhat similar. On the surface, the European Union has accomplished a great deal in the area of environmental protection. By 1990 it had introduced 160 directives for environmental protection and improvement, covering questions and problems such as water quality (drinking and bathing), food, air quality, noise pollution, toxic waste and vehicle emissions. And subsequently, the Community has become even more proactive in relation to environmental questions, notably in its Fifth Environmental Action Programme of March 1992. This programme not only accepts the concept of sustainable development, albeit from an anthropocentric standpoint, but identifies five main areas where action is specifically to be promoted – agriculture, energy, industry, tourism and transport. Further, since 1993 the European Commission has sought to incorporate environmental considerations into policy-making in general, for example through the process of environmental impact assessment, and to create a co-ordination unit within Directorate-General XI (Environment).

Beneath the surface, however, the measures implemented – or about to be implemented – by the EU are little more than cosmetic. There are no effective means of policing the EU's directives, and by 1994 not a single one of the 160 environmental directives already referred to had been implemented by all member-states (Green Party 1994: 3). Moreover, environmental questions are low on the EU agenda. For example, environment and climate change constitute only one of fifteen priority areas in the Commission's Research and Development Programme, with only 9 per cent of the Fourth Framework budget devoted to environmental projects (Grayson and Hobson 1994: 7). In ecological terms, as with the Rio Summit, the EU programmes have been a failure. A telling indictment is the EU transport programme, one of the Fifth Environmental Action Programme's priority areas. The chief feature of the EU transport programme is not the commitment to public transport, but the expenditure of 120 billion ECU (£93 billion) on the construction of over 50,000 km of new roads, including 12,000 km of new motorways: the so-called Trans-European Road Network (TERN). In comparison, the amount allocated for railways is miniscule.

In reality, at the European level as well as at the global level, environmental policy is made and implemented in terms of the vested interests in government and industry who wish to consolidate their power and follow the path of economic growth. For example, the TERN plan was based on proposals made by the Motorways Working Group – on which there were representatives from the International Roads Federation, the European Round Table of Industrialists, the oil industry and the Association of European Car Manufacturers, but none from environmental pressure groups (Whitelegg 1994: 1). The fact that the consequences of TERN, in terms of the production of greenhouse gases such as carbon dioxide, can be considered to be in direct contravention of the EU's commitments in the Framework Convention on Climate Change at Rio did not even enter the equation.

At local level, the anthropocentric paradigm is best illustrated through the evolution of Local Agenda 21. In the UK this resulted in the framing of a major report by the UK Local Government Management Board in May 1993. This report went some way towards defining the practical implications of accepting that the world has finite limits. For example, it urged that policy decisions be taken on the precautionary principle, by which there is an assumption *against* actions whose environmental impact is uncertain, and drew up a list of actions and policies that could be undertaken by both local and central government (UKLGMB 1993: 7, 20–31). At the same time, the thrust of the report, like that of Brundtland, was that sustainability and growth are not incompatible and that continuous environmental improvement is possible provided that natural resources are used more efficiently. Moreover, there was an inherent contradiction in the report, in that it envisaged the poor and disadvantaged having greater access to resources – in other words increasing their consumption of resources – which ran counter to the report's stated principle of reducing overall consumption levels. Unless, that is, the rich are required to reduce their consumption, a question which is politically difficult and which the report deliberately avoided – just as Brundtland did.

It is to avoid the question of making difficult political choices that governments at all levels have taken the anthropocentric approach to the environment. If consumerism, the pursuit of ever-increasing wealth levels and the profligate use of natural resources engender ecological damage on a worldwide basis, they also constitute the basis of the quality of life of Western civilization. It is difficult to envisage the metaphorical man and woman in the street voluntarily accepting reduced standards of living; and it is even more difficult to envisage traditional politicians advocating such a course; thus the current preoccupation with assimilating the anthropocentric approach into the ecological imperative by adopting Brundtland rhetoric and incorporating environmental costs into neo-classical economics.

For biocentrists, attempts to mitigate the environmental consequences of treadmill production through so-called weak or strong sustainable development are foredoomed to failure, since the anthropocentric approach to the natural world, despite the terminology of sustainability, is still based on the progressive liquidation of the natural capital that we call planet Earth. Ultimately, industrial economics, founded on expanding consumption and the maximization of production, will deplete the very resource base on which industrial society depends. It will be the author of its own destruction. As Bertolt Brecht put it:

> And they were sawing off the branches on which they were sitting, and eventually they dropped off and those who watched them shook their heads and kept on sawing.
>
> (Brecht, quoted in Echlin 1993: 4)

The problem is that human economic activity is already exhausting non-renewable resources and expending renewable resources far more quickly than the planet can regenerate them, while producing wastes and pollution beyond the carrying capacity of the Earth. With the continuing population explosion, the economic aspirations of LDCs and underdeveloped regions – in particular the People's Republic of China – and the even greater aspirations of the industrialized world, the situation can only get worse, not better, unless there is a radical redirection of human effort and understanding.

For biocentrists, the central problem is not the incorporation of the environment into economic policy, but the incorporation of economic policy into sustaining the biosphere. This, however, would require a very different approach to the human condition and lead to a very different kind of society to the current Western model. Essentially, it would entail a steady-state economy which could afford a tolerable standard of living for all humankind while respecting the intrinsic value and life of the non-human world and the natural environment. It would require a change in the nature of production and consumption and the adoption of no-growth or even negative-growth policies; it would require resource conservation rather than resource exploitation; a reduction in population; redistribution of resources between North and South and interregionally; it would require the cessation of activities which would penalize future generations (Blowers 1992: 3). In the final analysis, it might require de-industrialization.

CONCLUSION

So what, then, is the future of sustainable development? The concept as defined by Brundtland is not only a political fudge; it is a sham. It attempts – unsuccessfully – to obscure the basic contradiction between the finiteness of the Earth, with natural self-regulating systems operating within limits, and the expansionary nature of industrial society (Orton 1994: 19). The divide between the anthropocentric and biocentric approaches is unbridgeable, and the attempt by Brundtland to obfuscate the incongruity by promoting a new terminology is, ultimately, foredoomed to failure.

At the same time, it is possible that in future years we may come to see Brundtland in a better light, by considering the concept of sustainable development not as an end in itself but as a tentative first step which took politicians along the road from anthropocentricity to biocentricity. To some extent, for the industrialized North this can be viewed in terms of a Ladder of Sustainable Development (see the Introduction). But the ladder analogy can be taken too far. There is no natural progression from treadmill production to weak sustainable development to strong sustainable development, let alone to the Ideal (biocentric) Model. Indeed, governments can move down the Ladder as well as up. Moreover, despite their differences in policy terms, there is a basic link between the treadmill approach to the natural world and that of both weak and strong sustainable development, in that they all have anthropocentric underpinnings and are all based – to a greater or lesser extent – on the pursuit of quantitative growth. There is no such link between the anthropocentric and biocentric paradigms.

In practice, therefore, there can be no direct progression from even strong sustainable development to the biocentric ideal. Not only are the philosophical underpinnings entirely different, so too are the policies and objectives they give rise to. In contrast to the capital-intensive 'high-tech' future offered by the anthropocentric development paradigm, the biocentric paradigm is associated with Right Livelihood, appropriate technology, labour-intensive, small-scale production, the active promotion of biodiversity, inter- and intra-generational equity and 'bottom-up' community control. Overall, indeed, the biocentric approach would involve the wholesale restructuring and reorientation of political, social, legal and institutional structures.

Given the intrinsic differences between the anthropocentric and biocentric development paradigms, there is a need for new terminology to evaluate and understand the biocentric approach. Sustainable development, with its anthropocentric underpinning and inherent contradictions, must go. It has no place within the biocentric paradigm since it has been effectively hijacked by the proponents of anthropocentrism. The question is what to replace it with. One possibility is that put forward by Edward Echlin in the annual Newman Lecture in 1993. It is that of 'sustainable sufficiency'. As Echlin puts it, it is a question of 'living lightly within the soil as if the future mattered' (Echlin 1993: 7); or, to put it another way, of satisfying our vital physical and material needs – together with our non-material or spiritual needs – within the ecosystem; putting in as much as we take out. But to do this, as John Seymour (1989: 1) suggests, we must first accept that we are a part of nature and not above it.

Political scientists are familiar with the now discredited Marxist progression from feudalism through capitalism to socialism. It is possible, however, in the none-too-distant future, that they will be analysing the transition from capitalism to ecologism and from anthropocentrism to biocentrism. As regards development paradigms, they may be analysing the transition from sustainable development to sustainable sufficiency.

NOTES

1 That is not to say that biocentric thinkers and activists, whether religious or secular, did not exist in the late nineteenth and early twentieth centuries; rather they represented a minority point of view.

2 It should be noted, however, that many Green parties have anthropocentric elements within them.
3 In this respect, the Brundtland Report and the Rio Summit can be said to be analogous to the Muraviev Circular and the first Hague Peace Conference of 1899, which encapsulated the philosophical acceptance of the concept of disarmament by governments, who meantime strove officiously to avoid its practical implications (Richardson 1989: 29–32).

REFERENCES

Blowers, A. (1992) 'Sustainable urban development – the political prospects', in M. Breheny (ed.) *Sustainable Development and Urban Form*, London: Pion.
Echlin, E. (1988) 'The rainbow covenant: conservation as if Christians matter', *The New Road* (January–March): 4–5.
—— (1993) 'Theology and "sustainable development" after Rio', *The Newman* 30: 2–7.
The Ecologist (1972) *A Blueprint for Survival*, London: Ecosystems Ltd.
—— (1992) *Whose Common Future?*, London: Ecosystems Ltd.
Grayson, L. and Hobson, M. (1994) 'Sustainability', *Inlogov Informs* 4 (Birmingham: University of Birmingham Institute of Local Government Studies).
Green Party (1994) *European Election Manifesto 1994*, London: UK Green Party.
Grove, R. (1990) 'The origins of environmentalism', *Nature* 345: 11–14.
Jacobs, M. (1991) *Sustainability and Socialism*, London: Socialist Environment and Resources Association.
Meadows, D. H., Meadows, D. L., Randers, J. and Behrens, W. W. (1972) *The Limits to Growth*, London: Earth Island.
Mishan, E. J. (1967) *The Costs of Economic Growth*, Harmondsworth: Penguin.
Naess, A. (1984) 'A defence of the deep ecology movement', *Environmental Ethics* 6: 265–270.
O'Riordan, T. (1976) *Environmentalism*, London: Pion.
Orton, D. (1994) 'Struggling against sustainable development', *Z Papers* 3: 13–19.
Pearce, D., Markandya, A. and Barbier, E. (1989) *Blueprint for a Green Economy*, London: Earthscan.
—— (1989) 'Process and progress in disarmament: some lessons of history', in V. Harle and P. Sivonen (eds) *Europe in Transition*, London: Pinter.
Richardson, D. (1994) 'The Green challenge: philosophical, programmatic and electoral considerations', in D. Richardson and C. Rootes (eds) *The Green Challenge*, London: Routledge, pp. 4–22.
Richardson, D. and Rootes, C. (eds) (1994) *The Green Challenge*, London: Routledge.
Sadie, J. L. (1960) 'The social anthropology of economic underdevelopment', *Economic Journal* 70: 294–303.
Schumacher, E. F. (1974) *Small is Beautiful*, London: Abacus.
Seymour, J. (1989) *The Ultimate Heresy*, Bideford: Green Books.

Simon, J. L. and Kahn, H. (1984) *The Resourceful Earth: A Response to Global 2000*, Oxford: Blackwell.

UKLGMB (1993) *The UK's Report to the UN Commission on Sustainable Development: An Initial Submission by Local Government*, Luton: UK Local Government Management Board.

WCED (1987) *Our Common Future*, Oxford: Oxford University Press.

White, L. Jr (1967) 'The historical roots of our ecological crisis', *Science* 155: 1203–1207.

Whitelegg, J. (1994) *Driven to Destruction*, London: Greenpeace.

2 Sustainable development and the deep ecology movement

Arne Naess

What I have to say falls into two parts: first, I describe the false direction of present developments; second, I explore the role of the deep ecology movement.

In common usage, the terms 'sustainable' and 'development' are seen as bywords for progress when we talk about communities, societies or states. Groups with different policies try to make them their own. Consequently, the terms are open to a confusing diversity of interpretations. In particular, sustainable development as a goal is often explicitly or implicitly limited to the fairly shortsighted interests of one species, the human species. This is in contrast to the deep ecology movement, which focuses on the long-term defence of life conditions on Earth – 'full ecological sustainability'. In practice, in the many conflicts between animals and humans concerning territory, the limiting of concern *only* to humans would go against the long-term interests of both humans and animals.

There is a tendency today, even among politicians – who have no animal voters – to call for respect for *all* other living beings. But they often complain that only a minority of people feel that way. The question of how far one should go in concern for the richness and diversity of life will always give rise to different views. Supporters of the deep ecology movement go far, but no extreme views are implied. The movement is broad and is realistic when it comes to practical applications.

ECOLOGICAL SUSTAINABILITY

General sustainable development I take by definition to imply continuity over generations without very severe negative consequences. This implies ecological sustainability as one aspect of general sustainable development. Opinions about what would constitute a very severe consequence, however, will naturally differ. Some would reckon only catastrophes which hit humans hard as very severe consequences; that is, if what is obviously useful for humans is saved, but the richness and diversity of life on Earth very severely damaged, there might still be ecological sustainability. In contrast, supporters of the deep ecology movement ask for a high degree of protection of life conditions in general: no more interference than is necessary in order to satisfy *vital* human needs; the term 'vital' being interpreted as wider than 'basic'.

It is not enough that there is a demand in the market for some kind of product. We should ask: how much can safely be produced by the human population when we have several thousand million more people to offer a decent material standard of living? And how should such products be produced? ('Energy efficiency?') An ethical axiom says: don't live a life you cannot seriously wish that others might also live, if they wish to live that way. At the global level, can we seriously wish people in India and China to live our wasteful Western life? No, obviously not, since the demographic/resource pressures would make this course ecologically unsustainable, and we could not leave it to our children to face the ensuing problems realistically. We must change our lives, and let the poor improve their material standard of living. The necessary investment in such a process must increase year by year. We in the rich countries must start now to change policies, downscaling material production for ourselves. For example, we should only support economic growth – that is, *production* – if *consumption* of what is produced happens outside the rich countries.

There is no sure gain in development without a gain in the direction of ecological sustainability. Since the 1960s there has been enough information to make it clear that the First World is moving in the direction of *increasing*, not decreasing ecological *un*sustainability. The per capita negative influence on life conditions has so far been small in the Third World, though especially in Southeast Asia a *false* kind of change in a Western direction is rapidly taking place. The book *Limits to Growth* (Meadows *et al.* 1972), published by the Club of Rome, was important. *Beyond the Limits* (Meadows *et al.* 1992), published by the same authors twenty years later, is no less important, but much less read. It is especially important in that it highlights the backlash against the Green movement which started in the 1980s: a swarm of organizations, mostly far right politically, which have tried to stop, weaken or repeal environmental legislation and environmental efforts in general. *Beyond the Limits* also shows that the curves illustrating present global development, which should rise, point downwards, whilst conversely those which ought to point downwards, rise. Not only has there been an increase in CO_2 emissions and ozone defects in the atmosphere, but an indisputable *increase* in erosion and *decrease* in arable land and forests.

All over the world we see the scramble to pass from a low material standard of living to the *false* kind of high standard that exists in the richest countries. Why false? What I refer to is the wasteful use of energy, increasing production of goods not used to satisfy vital needs, and a population at or above replacement level. The developing nations of eastern Europe even neglect the few *good* aspects of life among the rich. In the Scandinavian countries, cycling to work is common. In Danish cities there are big parking lots for bicycles. In Sweden it is possible to ride a bike on special lanes through all cities. New kinds of bicycles make cycling in Norwegian hilly regions very comfortable. In contrast, in eastern European countries cycling is rare. People make the transition straight from walking to private driving. In Warsaw and many other cities, cycling is now too dangerous for most people and there are rarely any special lanes. This is only an example. Rich countries' trade and tourism encourage the false direction of development.

Nevertheless, we can change our policies, showing clearly that we are aiming for a decreased level of material standard of living, while keeping or improving our quality of life. In 1988 the World Watch Institute estimated that it would require the investment of an annual sum of US$149 billion to start a worldwide decrease in unsustain-ability. Factors included decreasing erosion, decreasing deforestation and increasing reforestation, stopping the trend towards diminishing the area of good soil, decreasing energy waste, and a couple of other items. Conclusion: ecological sustainability is still obtainable through an investment of only a fraction of the investment in advertising. But every year the cost of – or, more accurately, the necessary *investment* in – future life conditions, increases exponentially.

THE DEEP ECOLOGY PLATFORM

Now, what is the deep ecology movement? Something quite new started in the 1960s – an international concern about the threats to life conditions on Earth through chemicals. The hostile reactions of the chemical industry, in close co-operation with the US Department of Agriculture, started even before Rachel Carson published her famous book *Silent Spring* in 1962. The book made evident the dangers of the heavy use of pesticides. Within a few years environmental legislation started. Grassroots participation in the struggle was able to move the politicians to an astonishing degree. Later in the 1960s Europe woke up and we got a truly international environmental – or, better, ecological – movement. But with President Reagan and British Prime Minister Margaret Thatcher a counter-movement sprang up which still is very strong, the so-called 'Green backlash' (Rowell 1996).

It seems that without the enthusiastic participation of a sizeable minority of people environmental policies leading to global sustainable development will be unobtainable. Politicians must be sure that courageous environmental initiatives are met with goodwill at the polls. They are *not* sure today.

It was already clear in the 1960s that those who participated in the international environmental movement looked upon their work in different ways. There are two terms which often are used to define the difference, in spite of their being slightly misleading: the 'anthropocentric' view and the 'ecocentric' or 'biocentric' view. The former is more or less completely motivated by the threats to humans, their health and their need to enjoy unspoiled nature. Many people find that this priority of fellow humans makes it natural to say they are anthropo- or human-centric rather than centring on ecosystems or on life conditions for living beings in general. My conclusion is that it is better to avoid talk about a centre, because many of those who talk about threats to humans nevertheless support radical protection of other life forms on Earth, whatever their 'usefulness' for humans. And so-called ecocentrics may insist that we have very special responsibilities and obligations towards fellow humans. Supporters of the deep ecology movement are mostly conceived as being firmly ecocentric, but they still affirm the very special obligations we have towards fellow humans. They press for the elimination of extreme hunger and oppression just as much as the so-called anthropocentrics.

As I see it, supporters of the deep ecology movement essentially ask for extended and deepened care for humans as well as non-humans. But what is fairly *new* is the vivid expression of deep concern for non-humans. At the same time, the deep ecology movement does not subscribe to the view that if one cares for other beings than fellow humans there is less left for the humans – as if care were handed out from a small container. The term 'deep' in the name 'deep ecology' refers to depth of premises motivating its supporters – and the depth of the social changes necessary to overcome the environmental crisis.

What follows is a characterization of the deep ecology platform based on the 'deep ecology eight points'. They express fairly general and abstract views which all or nearly all supporters accept. In detail the views may be formulated somewhat differently. Here is a recent version:

1 Every living being has intrinsic or inherent value.
2 Richness and diversity of kinds of living beings have intrinsic or inherent value.
3 Humans have no right to reduce this richness and diversity except to satisfy vital human needs.
4 The flourishing of human life and cultures is compatible with a decrease of the human population. The flourishing of non-human life requires such a decrease.
5 Present human interference with the non-human world is excessive, and the situation is worsening.
6 Policies must be changed in view of points 1 to 5. These policies affect basic economic, technological and ideological structures.
7 The appreciation of a high quality of life will supersede that of a high standard of living.
8 Those who accept the foregoing points have an obligation to try to contribute directly or indirectly to the implementation of the necessary changes.

The firm acceptance of the two first points of the platform is of considerable social and political importance. As long as major efforts to protect and, as far as it is still possible, to *restore* richness and diversity of life on Earth are argued solely on the basis of narrow utilitarianism, they will be piecemeal. Cost benefit analysis here is difficult. It can scarcely be carried out with maximal perspective in space and time. Without respect for the biosphere as a whole, efforts will continue to be focused on special spectacular items, such as pandas, wolves, acid rain, the ozone layer, CO_2. In contrast, respect for the planet as a whole facilitates acceptance of long-range efforts including appropriate changes in human societies. Ecologically sustainable development will automatically refer to the whole planet and not to the ecologically arbitrary boundaries of nations.

The terms 'life' and 'living' as used in this movement need comment. When a campaign was launched in Lapland to protect a river against so-called development, the slogan 'Let the river live!' did not concern the H_2O of the river, but a somewhat vaguely conceived ecosystem as a whole – a 'living' whole including people who did not interfere, the Sami (Lapland) people. It included people who lived along the river and used the river in an ecologically responsible, sustainable way. This broad ecologically inspired way of interpreting the term 'life' of a river is important when forming strategies for the conservation of resources. It is clear that most campaigners for the protection of a river against major interference do not have only narrow usefulness in mind, but feel that the interference touches or reduces *the meaning of their own lives*. People try to protect a vital need for meaning and what is necessary to maintain that meaning; a development which is expected to reduce that meaning is not sustainable. We are led to a concept of sustainable development for this satisfaction of human needs which protects the planet also for its own sake.

Philosophers who are dubious about the notion of 'rights' propose its elimination, for instance using the phrase 'humans should not . . . ' instead of 'humans do not have the right to . . . '. Nevertheless, the postulation of certain 'human rights' has a positive influence today, and as long as the term is used in this connection it *might* also be used to refer to non-humans. Some, undoubtedly, would say that humans can have rights because they have obligations, and that as animals do not have obligations they therefore have no rights. Such a limitation on the meaning of 'rights', however, is not found in everyday usage of the term. Examples are the rights of lunatics and of small children.

The acceptance of point 3 does not, strictly speaking, depend on the acceptance of the existence of rights for humans and non-humans. If a mother says to her son, 'You have no right to prevent your little sister from eating all her birthday cake', this does not imply any doctrine of rights of sisters to eat. There is an important everyday usage of the expression 'no right to' which has to do with injustice and related phenomena. The same applies to 'no right to' in the formulation of point 3. If one dislikes the expression 'does not have the right to', the somewhat weaker 'should not, ethically speaking', is at our disposal.

Not included in the eight points, but quite expressive of opinions among supporters of the deep ecology movement, is the following formulation: 'Every living being has the right to live and flourish.' Logically perhaps more satisfying is: 'There is a right that every living being has: the right to live and flourish.'

The question of standards of living versus quality of life is of especial concern to the deep ecology platform. In this respect, the gigantic gross national product of the rich industrialized states is unfortunately a measure of gigantic pollution and waste with doubtful gain for the quality of human life. In fact, in Green circles GNP was being referred to as 'gross national pollution' (rather than gross national product) as early as the 1960s. Certainly, an increase in GNP does not guarantee an increase in the satisfaction of vital needs. This fact is painfully obvious in poor countries, where increases so far have had little influence among the desperately poor.

Where to draw the limit between vital and non-vital needs is a question that must be related to local, regional and national particularities – though in practice a certain area of disagreement must be taken to be normal.

Two points of the deep ecology platform have occasioned particularly lively discussion, points 4 and 6. Point 4 was originally worded like this: 'A decrease of world population would be good for humans, and very good for non-humans.' The phrase 'decrease of . . . humans' caused strong negative feelings: the memories of Hitler and of people publishing hostile utterances about humanity seem to have caused a shudder. People in poor countries might mistakenly imagine that point 4 is aimed primarily at them. As early as the 1970s it was usual to say something like: 'There are not too many now, but it would be good to stabilize the number at the present level.' People who in the 1970s said this tend to say the same today, thereby avoiding the word 'decrease'.

Objections to point 4 are often made on the basis of the view that a *quick* decrease is ethically objectionable, and that if many centuries are needed, the point is without interest. As I see it, many centuries are needed, but it is nevertheless important to have it in mind in city planning and many other long-range enterprises. Some believe that a decrease will hurt the economy. Not many economists discuss how to maintain good economic conditions under very slow decrease, for instance 0.25 per cent annually. Assuming conditions are otherwise stable, however, economists make us aware of the following excellent consequences: per capita real capital increases, per capita natural resources increase, interference in the ecosystems and crowding decrease. These consequences hold good in abstract generality, but in practical life will depend on local and regional peculiarities. When discussing per capita interference with the ecosystems it is of prime importance to stress that in the last couple of centuries the industrial countries have caused very much more destruction than non-industrial countries. A hundred babies born in Bangladesh may cause less interference than one single baby born in a rich country.

Point 6 has caused lively discussions because it has been widely held that new technologies will make it possible for all people to reach the material affluence of the present rich countries without catastrophic consequences: 'Business as usual! But new technologies are needed.' Since 1960, however, many promising inventions have been made – solar energy technology is an instance. But whether inventions will be used on a sufficiently large scale depends upon social and political factors.

How do supporters of the deep ecology movement react to concrete

ecological problems such as that of global warning? They tend to agree
with the International Panel on Climate Change (IPCC) that without
great changes in policies the warming is unavoidable. And they
support any drastic change in policy necessary, insisting that changes
need not reduce quality of life. The warming is due to the excesses of
the rich nations, and the worst consequences of continuing present
policies will hit the Third World. It is therefore the clear duty of the
richest countries to co-operate much more intensively with the poor to
counteract those consequences. In general the realization of ecological
sustainability in the Third World is dependent on the co-operation of
rich and poor. Present efforts are symbolic rather than realistic.

THE DEEP ECOLOGY PLATFORM AND SUSTAINABLE
DEVELOPMENT

In pressing for *ecologically* sustainable development, supporters of the
deep ecology movement are in favour of investments of considerable
scope because their philosophy of life is such that the devastation they
see now reduces their own life quality. The role of supporters is important because they actively work for change and because politicians can
always count on their enthusiastic endorsement of plans which are
radical enough to reduce the increasing unsustainability of the
contemporary Western world.

In contrast to the ideas of the deep ecology platform, extensive free
markets and a development towards an 'enterprise culture' create
conditions favourable to a deepening of ecological unsustainability.
The average distances travelled by humans and the volume of trade
and prevalent conceptions of 'economic growth' are negative factors.
Negative, not in the sense that such factors *necessitate* increasing
ecological unsustainability, but rather in the sense that they make it
harder to avoid. There is within the deep ecological movement a clear
tendency to be open to considerably different views about the
economics and politics of how to overcome the ecological crisis. But
there is an agreement that the way to go is democratic and non-violent.
Important publications are written in the spirit of the deep ecology
movement – without using its terminology.

One of the great obstacles facing rich countries, including some in
the European Union, is the mobility explosion and the availability of
fossil fuels at absurdly low prices. The average number of kilometres
travelled per capita shows an exponential increase. The same applies to
the transport of goods. Technical advances which decrease the pollution per kilometre cannot keep up. The vaster the markets in square

kilometres, the greater mobility must be expected unless strong, unpopular measures are introduced. The violent increase in trade over long distances creates problems which are well known to environmental experts in the European Union.

In short, it seems impossible to mobilize efforts to gain ecologically sustainable development within, let us say, the next thirty years. Unfortunately, there has been a tendency to view any increase in trade as a plus, whereas a more moderate view is to warn against what may be called 'excess' trading. Recently there was an international conference in New York considering negative consequences of the globalization of the economic system. Supporters of the deep ecology movement take these consequences seriously.

It is not the view of Green political theory that *the* main political problem of the next century is that of decreasing ecological unsustainability. Rather there are two other *equally* important problem areas: those of peace and the elimination of extreme poverty and oppression, including the use of torture. It is a massive goal to make everybody in the rich countries active in support of a movement in favour of solving the three main largely political problems! Each country, and power constellations like the European Union, must contribute in relation to their resources.

A distinction must be made between Green (with a capital 'G' – ecological) political theory and green (with a small 'g' – environmental) political theory. Green ('G') theorists foresee the need for greater policy changes. I would mention here three influential books relating to political parties: the well-established economist Hazel Henderson published her *The Politics of the Solar Age* in 1981; Jonathan Porritt published his *Seeing Green: The Politics of Ecology Explained* in 1984; and Charlene Spretnak and Fritjof Capra also published their *Green Politics* in 1984. The main difficulty which Green (ecological) politicians meet is that of integrating green (environmental) political proposals into a general political framework. A Green politician must have general political credibility – credible opinions about every small political subject of the day – whilst still remaining true to her (or his) principles. Equally, Green political theorists must relate their general political framework to proposals emanating from Green politicians, including those supporting the deep ecology platform.

Outstanding among Green political theorists, I am glad to say, is a woman, Robyn Eckersley. Her *Environmentalism and Political Theory* (1992) is level-headed but insists that policies must change significantly. Three other authors should be mentioned because of their contribution to understanding the Green movement: Andrew Dobson, *Green Political Thought* (1990); John Dryzek, *Rational Ecology* (1987); and Robert C. Paehlke, *Environmentalism and the Future of Progressive Politics* (1989). The hint of the word 'progress' in the latter title may evoke memories of the red–blue political axis of the time of the Soviet Union, but rather faintly. The term 'radical environmentalism' is generally avoided by supporters of the deep ecology platform because of the misleading association with that axis; they very rarely (or don't at all) have opinions characteristic of the far Left or far Right. Perhaps the most expressive title, however, is that of Dryzek, who focuses on the irrationality of politics which ignores the complete dependence of humanity upon natural conditions and the rationality of taking the future seriously.

As might be expected, every Green theorist favours democratic regimes. The necessary changes are much too complex for any dictatorial management. They need active co-operation in wide circles of the population. In addition, the theorists reject authoritarianism for reasons of ethics. However, nobody knows what will happen politically if countries are faced with ecological catastrophes on a grand scale. Some people reason that 'fascism' of some kind will appear, or authoritarian measures by the powerful, rich countries trying to impose ecologically strong policies in poor areas of the world. It is often said that pollution 'knows no borders', and it is clear that winds and other forces lead to the wide distribution of pollution. As to climatic changes, each country tends to calculate what changes will largely benefit its people and what changes may have largely negative influences.

Most of the thousands of people engaged in studies on climatic changes are interested in specialized research, not in philosophical enquiry about life. It may sound absurd, but some people who talk critically about the deep ecology movement believe that its supporters find it to be a serious drawback that researchers on climate and in other ecological, scientific occupations do not take up questions of philosophical and political foundations. On the contrary, supporters of the deep ecology platform are grateful that work of great importance is carried out. The general ecological movement needs competent people in a myriad areas. It is all very well *espousing* ecologically sustainable development, but the rhetoric needs to be fortified with practical proposals for implementation.

It has been said that the eight points of the deep ecology movement open up the possibility of 'fascist' interpretations. Some versions of point 1 may be interpreted in such a way that *individual* living beings, including individual humans, do not have inherent value. To counteract this possibility I have proposed that point 1 be reformulated, for instance this way: 'Every living being has inherent value', that is, it makes sense to do something purely for its own sake. Point 2 will then attribute inherent value to the manifold manifestations of life on Earth. Finally, point 8 may end with the adverbs 'democratically' and 'non-violently'. There are no Green theorists who envisage the use of violent means, though critics may point to the theoretical possibility. In short, there is no place for 'fascist' interpretations. Imputations in this direction must be expected, however, as long as there is a Green backlash – as epitomized by the efforts of organizations whose aim is to get rid of environmental legislation and non-governmental implementation of policies in the direction of ecological responsibility.

CONCLUSION

The deep ecology platform has outlined a set of principles that is broad and undogmatic enough to function as a rallying point for groups of widely different views on the causes of the ecological crisis. There is room for people who wish to emphasize masculinity as the major cause of the crisis, and there is room for those who insist on the relevance of human domination of humans as a cause of human 'domination' also over nature. But above all, the basic function of the terminology of the deep ecology movement is to facilitate the formulation of policies which will reach deep enough to ensure a global change from increasing to decreasing ecological unsustainability.

REFERENCES

Brown, L. *et al.* (1988) *State of the World*, New York: Norton.
Carson, R. (1962) *Silent Spring*, Boston: Houghton Mifflin.
Dobson, A. (1990) *Green Political Thought*, London: Unwin Hyman.
Dryzek, J. (1987) *Rational Ecology*, Oxford: Blackwell.
Eckersley, R. (1992) *Environmentalism and Political Theory: Toward an Ecocentric Approach*, New York: University of New York Press.
Henderson, H. (1981) *The Politics of the Solar Age: Alternatives to Economics*, Garden City, NY: Anchor Press.
Meadows, D. H., Meadows, D. L., Randers, J. and Behrens, W. W. (1972) *The Limits to Growth*, London: Earth Island.
Meadows, D. H. *et al.* (1992) *Beyond the Limits*, London: Earthscan.
Paehlke, R. C. (1989) *Environmentalism and the Future of Progressive Politics*, New Haven, CT: Yale University Press.
Rowell, A. (1996) *Green Backlash*, London: Routledge.
Porritt, J. (1984) *Seeing Green: The Politics of Ecology*, Oxford: Blackwell.
Spretnak, C. and Capra, F. (1984) *Green Politics*, London: Hutchinson.

3 Sustainable development and the treadmill of production

Allan Schnaiberg

A major input into the Brundtland Report was a growing sense that our current economic systems are ecologically unsustainable. More controversial is the question of whether these systems are *socially* unsustainable. This Chapter explores whether and how sustainable development can be, first, attainable within a reasonable period and, second, durable once it has been attained (Davis 1991), using local recycling as a case study and model. The conclusion reached is that the contemporary world economic system, based on the 'treadmill of production' (Schnaiberg 1980; Schnaiberg and Gould 1994) is incompatible with the logic of sustainable development as currently understood, since inherently it has institutionalized economic growth as the central national and transitional goal.

The treadmill's *economic* component has the publicly stated goal of expanding industrial production and economic development, as well as concomitantly increasing consumption. Its *political* component has a public confluence of interests among private capital, labour and governments in promoting this expansion. In *social* terms, there is a corresponding belief that advances in public welfare are achieved primarily through economic growth. From the standpoint of the world capitalist system and its apologists, therefore, the treadmill is politically, economically and socially sustainable. And certainly, in the absence of major political changes it will be difficult to dismantle in the foreseeable future.

Treadmill interests are manifest in private investments in fixed capital, in public institutions developed by the state to facilitate economic growth, and in the orientation of organized (and non-organized) labour toward these investments and institutions (Barnet and Cavanagh 1994; Schnaiberg and Gould 1994). Treadmill production uses fiscal capital to substitute more controllable physical technologies for more refractory human labour. In turn, such technologies have required the increased use of ecosystems as reliable feedstocks for production and as available sinks for industrial wastes. One way of understanding the treadmill, therefore, is to look on it as socially sustainable in that it meets the economic needs of only *some* of the present generation. Moreover, it will, through the political power of this *part* of the present generation, also meet the future economic needs of only *part* of the future generation. The future path of sustainable development thus rests on ongoing *intra*-generational conflicts between treadmill proponents and opponents.

Environmentalists and ecologists see the treadmill as an *unsustainable* political-economic system (Schnaiberg and Gould 1994). Ecologically, it threatens rural biodiversity, as well as other ecosystems within urban and suburban environments of industrial and industrializing societies. Socially, it has increasingly come to rely upon the 'low road' of development in the modern era of transnational competition. Thus, the treadmill has displaced and impoverished many stable working classes and subsistence agricultural groups. Harrison makes this case most clearly:

> managers try to beat out the competition by cheapening labour costs. They move whatever operations they can to low-wage rural areas or to Third World countries. They scrimp on training. They routinely outsource work to independent contractors who will not . . . pay decent wages, let alone provide basic benefits. . . . [They] try to squeeze the last ounce out of older capital equipment. . . . At the last extreme, a company that once made its own products, using domestic workers and paying them a living wage, now hollows itself out . . . to become . . . an importer of things made by foreign companies – or by their overseas subsidiaries.
>
> (Harrison 1994: 213)

Most treadmill actors are likely to offer substantial resistance to social policies that will actually promote genuinely sustainable development, since sustainable development must perforce restrict some forms of contemporary technological and labour organization (Redclift 1984, 1986, 1987) to preserve natural resources for future generations. This can be seen through an evaluation of the history of two earlier proposals for changes in the treadmill: that of Schumacher (1973) and his concept of 'appropriate' technology; and that of Graedel and Allenby (1995), Socolow *et al.* (1994) and Tibbs (1993a, 1993b), with their concepts of ecological modernization and industrial ecology. In both cases, the effect on the treadmill, its goals and its means was minimal.

In undertaking these evaluations, I will follow the outline of Hugh Stretton (1976), who outlined some socially and politically realistic scenarios about how a material 'levelling down' might take place under different political and social conditions. It should be noted, however, that his mixture of social coercions and seductions traced difficult policy *choices* between national growth, environmental protection and social equity in industrial societies of the European Union (EU), whereas, in contrast, many contemporary EU proponents of sustainable development envisage attaining *all three goals*. Subsequently, I will offer a brief historical analysis of post-consumer waste recycling programmes, since they appear to represent an integrated effort of the state, industry and labour (CEC 1993: ch. 8) towards some kind of sustainable development. Certainly recycling appears to capture many of the elements of ecological sustainability and political subsidiary in the EU – working at the lowest level of government operation possible. It will be seen, however, that even recycling has been strongly influenced by treadmill institutions.

INTERMEDIATE TECHNOLOGY: A HISTORICAL PRECURSOR OF SUSTAINABLE DEVELOPMENT?

Schumacher was a unique role model: a Northern manager of the European Coal Community, he had also worked in the South, on development projects. His concept of 'appropriate' technology (AT) (Schumacher 1973) was built on Buddhist economic or 'Right Livelihood' principles ('achieve the most social gain with the least material input'). What makes AT or its institutionalized form of intermediate technology (IT) so valuable as a comparison to sustainable development is that it drew favourable attention in both North and South among citizens, politicians and even some private-sector agents of the treadmill. Interestingly, like sustainable development, appropriate technology also generated little overt political resistance (Dickson 1975; Gould 1987; Schnaiberg 1982, 1983a, 1983b).

When we look at the achievements of AT some twenty years later, we see that there are some AT *projects*; but there are few sustained AT programmes of change in either the North or the South (Reddy 1979). 'Appropriateness' of technology, as projects were created in the South through Institutes for Intermediate Technology, gradually became disconnected from Buddhist economics. In practice, AT became translated into something intermediate between existing traditional labour-intensive production and highly capital-intensive treadmill-type production (UNIDO 1979). The term 'intermediate' provided useful ambiguity for operationalizing Schumacher's goals: the continuum between traditional labour-intensiveness and the pinnacle of capital- and energy-intensiveness is a large and elastic one, with few clear criteria to measure success. Likewise, IT moved away from Schumacher's social emphasis on relations of production and ecological emphasis on 'peace and permanence'. As applied, it became transformed into a much narrower technical concept of the 'right' technology for the *local* mix of labour, natural resources, and the local or extra-local sources of capital (Gould 1987; Leonard *et al.* 1989).

Why did AT not develop into broader programmes? Mostly the projects had one of the following trajectories (Schnaiberg and Gould 1994: ch.8):

- If they were successful in expanding their markets beyond marginal clientele they were incorporated into treadmill firms.
- If they were dealing only with marginal workers they had uncertain funding, local ambivalence and mistrust, and erratic performances.
- Political support, necessary to ensure local mobilization and protection from treadmill interventions (including sabotage and rapacious competition), was erratic, because of the lack of an established party and sustained political constituency for it (see Higgins and Lutzenhiser 1993).
- Where projects were sustained, they fitted one of two conditions: either they were incorporated as a technology in a larger treadmill entity; or they met some local basic needs that other treadmill firms found it too costly or inefficient to meet.

In practice, the proliferation of small-scale AT/IT 'deeds' never seriously challenged the treadmill for any length of time. The projects were either incorporated (and thereby transformed into treadmill principles, using other technologies), crushed through competition or allowed to operate as a supplement to the treadmill, serving low-income and low-skill citizen-workers. In none of these circumstances were they expanded to be a competitor system challenging the treadmill. Mostly, in Redclift's (1984) terms, they were often neither very 'red' (having progressive relations of production) nor very 'green' (having technologies with low ecological withdrawals and/or additions). Equally important, during the periods of expanding, stagnating and declining AT/IT, there was rarely overt political opposition by treadmill agents (corporate and state). Most of their actions were 'backstage' political ones, including scientific and technological arguments (Schnaiberg 1977), or quiet market transactions, incorporating or crushing (Schnaiberg 1975). So AT/IT had a historical trajectory of 'noisily positive words' and 'quietly negative deeds' (Gould *et al.* 1993; Schnaiberg and Gould 1994: chs 8–9).

INDUSTRIAL ECOLOGY AND ECOLOGICAL MODERNIZATION: CURRENT PRACTICES AND FUTURE PROJECTIONS

Tibbs (1993a), following some of the earlier work of Ayres (1989), outlined a model of *industrial ecology* (Graedel and Allenby 1995; Socolow *et al.* 1994), also called *ecological modernization*. Industrial ecology is a form of re-engineering to reduce the environmental disruption generated by treadmill production. Before a sociological audience, Tibbs articulated a broader 'hierarchy' of social needs, including 'social functioning' and 'personal actualization'. He also suggested that 'Designs that meet, say, only basic technical criteria may well be effective over the short run. It is only when such partial solutions are deployed extensively for long periods that their environmental and other shortcomings threaten "unsustainability"' (Tibbs 1993b:13).

This poses two immediate problems: first, treadmill organizations have increasingly been operating in the *short* run, even while becoming more spatially dispersed (Barnet and Cavanagh 1994); second, treadmill agents have exerted considerable effort to diminish public sensitivity to the negative environmental and social externalities of treadmill production (Murphy 1994; Schnaiberg 1994). Tibbs (1993a), however, offered a number of examples of the recent 'greening' of particular corporations, as testimony to the *potential* for a future widespread industrial ecology and the immanence of a socio-environmental decision hierarchy (Tibbs 1993b: 13ff). His premise is that these examples were one or the other of the following:

- evidence of a widespread historical turnabout, representing a new corporate interest in longer-term ecological protection;
- evidence that, under certain favourable conditions, corporations can and will adopt a 'green' perspective.

In practice, the 'greening' of corporations such as those cited by Tibbs appears to be more a social construction put upon disparate corporate activities and motives. Most of the effects of environmentalism were *mediated* through standard treadmill parameters, which always influence decision-making about 'technical operations' for managers (Schnaiberg and Gould 1994: ch. 3). Exceptions exist in some European Union societies with stronger communal values, and in smaller, privately held businesses. Private owners may be resident in their communities of operation rather than absentee; they may thus value their local environments, and they may have enduring relationships with their community of operations (Schnaiberg and Gould 1994: chs 3–4). Overall, however, there is little evidence of universal internalization of negative externalities through 'getting the prices right' (European Commission 1993). Managers have increasingly had to confront the realities of increasing transnational competitiveness, which has in turn pressured them to externalize as many waste processes as possible (Murphy 1994).

Ironically, one widely used case study offered by Tibbs, of Asnaes in Denmark, is precisely a deviant corporate case, since it worked through '*geographically close participants*' and it is built around issues of *local* water conservation (Tibbs 1993a: 11). The complex Tibbs describes was an impressive illustration of what is possible under such conditions (and in a particular kind of society). Another case in Tibbs was that of General Motors, whose 'industrial ecosystem' recycled platinum. This too fits the more dominant treadmill and technical-operation decisional model, since 'the high value of platinum was obviously an important factor' (Tibbs 1993a: 12).

In contrast, Tibbs's report (1993a: 18) of 'dematerialization' by electrical utilities through conservation programmes obscures the fact that these programmes were primarily reactions to pressure from environmental movements. Political movements prevented the expansion of nuclear generating facilities in the 1970s and 1980s, through raising their political and economic costs. Citizen and scientific coalitions arose because of health fears (exacerbated by the Three Mile Island shutdown in 1979, and the Chernobyl disaster in 1986). The actual history of the 1965–1993 period was one of intense political conflict between the Edison Electric Institute and its members, on the one hand, and environmental movements, on the other.

One final illustration in Tibbs was Minnesota Mining and Manufacturing (3M) (Tibbs 1993b: 20). Alone among the examples Tibbs offered, this is a rather hopeful scenario for moving from the treadmill into industrial ecology and, eventually, into sustainable development. 3M has been an industry leader in energy consumption control, introducing van pools well before the small number of other corporate adopters. Perhaps the concentration of a highly skilled labour force, a relatively 'clean' and homogeneous community (Minneapolis) and a long tradition of local (as well as national) social investment helped drive their anti-pollution drive. But even here, their corporate slogan was that 'Pollution Prevention *Pays*', another treadmill bottom line. Moreover, during the period in which the 3M programme was introduced, both the Toxic Substances Control Act (TSCA) and the Resource Conservation and Recovery Act (RCRA) were created, to control many of the kinds of effluents that 3M generated (Landy *et al.* 1990; Szasz 1994). Therefore, 3M can be seen as at least as *reactive* to government regulations as *proactive* with regard to citizen inputs. Optimists see such examples as a new 'greening' of corporations, but other corporate analysts remain more cautious:

> Questioning today's win-win rhetoric is akin to arguing against motherhood and apple pie. After all, the idea that environmental initiatives will systematically increase profitability has tremendous appeal. Unfortunately, this popular idea is also unrealistic. Responding to environmental challenges has always been a costly and complicated proposition for managers. . . .
>
> For all environmental issues, shareholder value, rather than compliance, emissions, or costs, is the critical unifying metric. That approach is environmentally sound, but it's also hardheaded, informed by business experience, and as a result, is much more likely to be *truly* sustainable over the long run.
>
> (Walley and Whitehead 1994: 46, 52; emphasis in the original)

To offer a more dynamic view of sustainable development paths, I outline next the arena of waste recycling. My colleagues and I have studied this in the United States over nearly a decade (Gould *et al.* 1996; Pellow *et al.* 1995; Schnaiberg 1992a, 1992b, 1993; Weinberg *et al.* 1995, 1996), tracing both the *social* and *environmental* outcomes of recycling.

RECYCLING REFORMS AND RESISTANCES: HARBINGER OF SUSTAINABLE DEVELOPMENT?

Recycling is a recent local 'environmental' response to national problems of solid waste treatment. Post-consumer waste recycling has become widely diffused in US cities and suburbs and increasingly in the European Union, especially in Germany (*The Economist* 1991; Swanson 1991; McCarthy 1991; Fishbein 1992). For some US analysts, it represents a socio-political ideal for solving 'environmental problems', through 'thinking globally and acting locally'. They see local government agencies, environmental movement organizations and large-scale capital owners as negotiating a mutually acceptable alternative to solid waste disposal through burial in landfills or through incineration (cf. Moberg 1991). In the context of this volume, it seems valuable to examine such recycling approaches as potentially exemplifying some early stages of sustainable development. Among other values of the recycling example, I would note its unusually neo-corporatist character within the United States. While the USA is generally viewed as a non-corporatist society, with little co-ordination between the state, major capital actors and other social institutions, recycling offers an apparent counter-example.

One set of US opinions envisages recycling as an environmental policy, preserving resources for future generations, as reforms *of* the treadmill. These arguments suggest that use-value concerns, supported by citizen-activists and the state through recycling policy, are coming to have relatively more influence than current exchange-value interests over the forces of production. We could thus argue that these can be seen as empirical instances of Stretton's (1976) social scenario of 'second chances', whereby the health of communities is maintained despite ecological contractions.

A second set of statements suggests more tensions within recycling programmes. These ideologies and interests represent the interaction between environmental movements. We might see these as reforms *within* the treadmill, which Stretton's (1976) social scenarios labelled 'business as usual', or 'the rich rob the poor', under stringent regulation over ecosystem access. These statements offer us a *dynamic* view of recycling processes during a ten-year period when kerbside recycling expanded to over 4,000 communities in the US, as well as to institutional recycling programmes, yet exchange-value interests reasserted more influence over recycling programmes. Recycling thus affords us an opportunity to test the validity of the several social models for the attainment of sustainable development. This is because it has been around long enough in some industrial societies for us to trace its trajectory. Most of the literature on American and European recycling has largely dealt with the forces of production – recycling technologies for converting wastes into remanufactured products. In addition, it has emphasized the economic dimensions of such technologies and the political role that the state can play in regulating some of these processes. For me, these ongoing technical and political debates are especially noteworthy. We can examine the underlying social relationships and market transactions in this example that may lead us to understand more about possible social trajectories towards sustainable development. I illustrate this by noting the changes from the initiation of recycling in the mid-1980s to the sustaining relationships and transactions since 1985.

A key policy instrument of the European Commission document on sustainable development was 'getting the price right', also noted in the report of the parallel US National Commission on the Environment (1993). However, such a process of internalization of negative environmental and social externalities has almost never been evident in the deeds or practices around recycling policies in the USA (Murphy 1994). Indeed, as I note below, the majority of US discussions around recycling tend to keep this approach off the policy agenda (Bachrach and Baratz 1973). Instead, they reinforce the view that recycling programmes need to focus on 'getting the right materials'. This is best characterized by Stretton's (1976) scenario of 'business as usual'. My assessment is based on analyses of US post-consumer waste recycling programmes (Schnaiberg 1992a, 1992b, 1993; Pellow *et al.* 1995; Weinberg *et al.* 1995, 1996), which demonstrated that the actual deeds of recycling–remanufacturing offer very little internalization of negative environmental and social externalities.

Since the inception of local kerbside recycling programmes in the mid- and late 1980s, public and private agencies have been gathering more and more post-consumer wastes. These have been separated in a variety of ways – ranging from systems in which consumers separate them to local and regional materials recovery facilities (MRFs). MRFs use a combination of newer physical technologies, as well as hand sorting, to separate components of the gathered waste stocks. The latter are sorted into two primary categories: the recyclables and the non-recyclables. Recent estimates suggest that, overall, some 20 per cent at least of the waste gathered by public agencies is non-recyclable. Such rejected materials are either incinerated or placed in landfills, rather than 'closing the loop' between consumption of and production from waste materials (Morris and Dickey 1991). For many community-based programmes, an even larger proportion of the materials gathered is never transformed into remanufactured products. This is because there are no organizations that can recycle these wastes 'economically'.

> Recycling is manufacturing, and manufacturing is business, not disposal. . . . Some practitioners think of market development simply as local business promotion. Others see it as the progressive restructuring of the world economy to fully accommodate recycling. It is, of course, both. . . . The ultimate goal in market development is to increase investment in industry's capacity to recycle. Goals such as getting municipal suppliers together with reliable consumers end up becoming secondary to questions like 'did companies financially commit to building new plants?'
>
> (Kacandes 1991: 53)

Finally, when there was insufficient demand for products remanufactured from waste materials, markets became glutted and materials
were not sellable by municipalities or were sold for a small fraction of
the costs of gathering and separating them. When markets have
improved recently (Bishop 1991; Morris and Dickey 1991; Holusha
1994), they have done so because of new corporate remanufacturing
investments and anticipated returns rather than because of new corporate environmental goals.

Paradoxically, much 'green marketing' has encouraged consumers
to recycle their packaging quite independently of the MRF selection
processes. This has created a collection glut, because of rising citizen
'recycling participation levels', on the one hand, and higher MRF
selectivity due to declining market prices for many recyclable materials on the other (Bishop 1991). In either case, municipalities and
other private-sector actors have increasingly focused on getting the
right materials, in contrast with the European Commission principle
of getting the prices right.

LEARNING ABOUT SUSTAINABLE DEVELOPMENT
TRAJECTORIES FROM APPROPRIATE TECHNOLOGY,
INDUSTRIAL ECOLOGY AND RECYCLING

If the recent history of limited implementation of both appropriate
technology and industrial ecology leads us to be cautious about the
availability of a well-paved road to sustainable development, the case
studies of recycling policies which have been implemented in the USA
and the EU make one even more reticent. State agencies in the USA
and Europe, increasingly committed to operating costly recycling programmes, have come under growing political criticism from
environmental movements and local officials operating under principles of subsidiarity. Critics have pointed to the rather limited
remanufacturing from waste materials (cf. Holusha 1994), the ecological costs of bypassing other recyclable materials and the ecological
impacts of remanufacturing. New attempts have thus been made to
'get the right regulations', in order to control at least the quantities
and some prices of recyclable materials which have been utilized in
remanufacturing operations (Morris and Dickey 1991; Beck and
Grogan 1991; McCarthy 1991). In the United States, these regulations
have been limited to specifying several criteria of minimal incorporation of both producer and post-consumer wastes in production (Beck
and Grogan 1991). Conversely, in the European Union, especially in
Germany, these mandates have been more extensive and intensive –

requiring both the maintenance of reusable containers *and* a timetable for absorbing all containers into some form of remanufacturing (Fishbein 1992; McCarthy 1991).

Interestingly, I note the relative absence of shadow pricing in recycling, which the European Commission (CEC 1993) notes is part of 'getting the price right'. Instead, the USA has relied on market pricing as a criterion for recycling–remanufacturing. Such reliance on market prices is rather unusual historically in arenas of both social expenses and public works. Shadow prices have been used historically to embed citizen concerns (such as health, safety or pollution) into a form of legitimizing public-sector intervention into private-sector markets. They 'tilt' private transactions into greater conformity to the *relations* of citizens to these market agents and actions. Without such shadow price enforcement, the 'sustainable development' policy of recycling is more influenced by treadmill institutions (Murphy 1994). In this regard, we can see a re-emergence of many of the factors that have limited past implementation of appropriate technology and/or industrial ecology.

Within the US, the state role has often focused on subsidies for remanufacturing. Local kerbside programmes, especially when they operate at a loss and are underwritten by citizen taxation, are one such subsidy (Rabasca 1993). Others include tax credits or tax write-offs for MRFs and remanufacturing plants, which have become more popular in less affluent US communities, as one way of attracting high-tech remanufacturing facilities to supply jobs and taxes. Another way for communities to act is to commit local publics to gather a sufficient supply of wastes through community-subsidized programmes. A final way is to subsidize some local consumption of the remanufactured goods as well (Beck and Grogan 1991). Interestingly, within the USA such 'minimum recycled content' laws have been increasing at the regional (but not the national) level. In contrast, there have been bolder EU interventions in the form of prohibitions, such as exclusions of materials and taxes on virgin products (Fishbein 1992; McCarthy 1991).

The primary agents supporting 'getting the laws right' currently appear to be moral and economic entrepreneurial organizations. They seek to modify standard market operations, using the European Commission concept of subsidiarity, to minimize substitution of extra-local regulation to replace local forces. The sharp limits of local enforcement of water pollution and toxic wastes, under similar principles of subsidiarity in North America, have been explored (Gould *et al.* 1995, 1996; cf. Hawkins 1984). Attempts to change the current synthesis between citizen use-values and treadmill exchange-values at an organizational level within local communities need far more careful support than both the EU and US policies of localism have offered to date.

In the absence of such relational forces, the critical role in modern US recycling concerns the physical technologies in remanufacturing and waste sorting. There is little attention to the social relations of citizen-workers (and citizen-taxpayers) to both waste sorting and remanufacturing. Thus, little attention is currently paid to the quality of labour inputs to waste sorting and remanufacturing (including occupational hazards), other than to reduce transaction costs and increase profits by minimizing labour costs. Community development (an aspect of sustainable development) is rarely addressed in most government recycling programmes in either the USA or the EU. This limits the *social* sustainability of recycling programmes – the degree to which these programmes meet the needs of all members of the current generation.

There is much more complexity in the ecological impacts of recycling and remanufacturing. Remanufacturing involves physical, chemical and/or biological manipulation of recyclable materials. This produces both ecological additions or pollution *and* energy and water inputs or withdrawals from ecosystems (Schnaiberg 1980, 1994). On the other hand, much of the existing remanufacturing processes and plants cannot operate with only recycled materials (Forman 1991). Physical, chemical and/or biological criteria for remanufacturing require some balancing of feedstock attributes. In all such instances, therefore, virgin materials must be added to the remanufacturing process. Such production requirements necessitate the extraction of virgin materials to mix with recyclable material in remanufacturing. But such extraction of virgin materials has historically been associated with the destruction of habitat and/or species in the ecosystem (see Rudel and Horowitz 1993).

Taken together, these two blind spots in current recycling programmes make this contemporary innovation a rather limited exemplar for a socially and ecologically sustainable form of economic development (Weinberg *et al.* 1995, 1996). At one extreme, the strict recycling model of closing the loop would also require each producer and citizen-consumer both to gather their wastes and to purchase back the remanufactured products generated from their *own* wastes. At the opposite extreme, which is close to the current US model of recycling, sets of actors are motivated primarily by exchange-value interests which dominate the entire process, including the socio-political citizen inputs into legislation and gathering wastes.

This tension is well articulated in Walley and Whitehead's cautions about the 'greening' of US corporations:

> Companies should seek to minimize the destruction of shareholder value that is likely to be caused by environmental costs rather than attempt to create value through environmental enhancements. . . . In an area like the environment, which requires long-term commitment and cooperation, untempered idealism is a luxury. By focusing on the laudable but illusory goal of win-win solutions, corporations and policymakers are setting themselves up for a fall with shareholders and the public at large. Both constituencies will become cynical, disappointed, and uncooperative when the true costs of being green come to light. Companies are already beginning to question their public commitment to the environment, especially since such costly obligations often come at a time when many companies are undergoing dramatic expense, restructuring and layoffs.
>
> (Walley and Whitehead 1994: 47)

Between the two extremes, there are possibilities of creating a variety of new social and political situations:

> the inquiry into the functioning of the market continued to be made in a manner which largely ignored the *social nature of the problem*. . . . New institutional economics looks at not only market coordination but also non-market coordination within and between enterprises, and also at the determinants of the scope of individual enterprises. . . . Our theory of state intervention also suggests that there are *many possible types of state intervention* . . . neither the market, nor the state, nor any other economic institution is perfect as a coordination mechanism. . . . [T]his means that each country has to decide on the exact mix between the market, the state and other institutions . . . through a process of institutional learning and innovation.
>
> (Chang 1994: 131–136; emphasis mine)

David's cautions about attaining and sustaining sustainable development, first expressed around the time of the Brundtland Report, still hold:

> The concept of sustainability can be interpreted in either a limited or a broad sense. From a narrow economic perspective, it is synonymous with wealth creation or economic growth. . . . However, in a more holistic sense, sustainability is essentially linked to broader societal goals: . . . the requirements of sustainability and justice

tend to coincide. This is related to the necessity of building durable social and economic structures, and of eliminating various forms of inequality.

(David 1988: 153)

REFERENCES

Ayres, R. U. (1989) 'Industrial metabolism and global change: reconciling the sociosphere and the biosphere – global change, industrial metabolism, sustainable development, vulnerability', *International Social Science Journal* 41(3): 363–374.

Bachrach, P. and Baratz, M. (1973) *Power and Poverty: Theory and Practice*, New York: Oxford University Press.

Barnet, R. J. and Cavanagh, J. (1994) *Global Dreams: Imperial Corporations and the New World Order*, New York: Simon & Schuster.

Beck, P. and Grogan, P. (1991) 'Minimum content legislation: an effective market development tool', *Resource Recycling* (September): 90–99.

Bishop, R. S. (1991) 'Defining the MRF . . . ', *Resource Recycling* (October): 36–43.

CEC (1993) *Toward Sustainability: A European Community Programme of Policy and Action in Relation to the Environment and Sustainable Development*, Luxembourg: Commission of the European Communities, DG XI.

Chang, H.-J. (1994) *The Political Economy of Industrial Policy*, New York: St Martin's Press.

David, W. L. (1988) *Political Economy of Economic Policy: The Quest for Human Betterment*, New York, Westport, CT, and London: Praeger Press.

Davis, D. E. (1991) 'Uncommon futures: the rhetoric and reality of sustainable development', *Environment, Technology and Society* 63: 2–4.

Dickson, D. (1975) *The Politics of Appropriate Technology*, New York: Universe Books.

The Economist (1991) 'Recycling: how to throw things away', *The Economist* (April 13): 17ff.

Fishbein, B. K. (1992) 'European packaging initiatives leading the way on source reduction', *Resource Recycling* (March): 86–94.

Forman, M. (1991) 'In my opinion . . . plastics recycling: let's cut the bull', *Resource Recycling* (May): 102–104.

Gould, K. A. (1987) 'The devolution of a concept: "appropriate" technology in a third world context', paper presented at the annual meetings of the Midwest Sociological Society, Chicago, March 1987.

Gould, K. A., Schnaiberg, A, and Weinberg, A. S. (1995) 'Natural resource use in a transnational treadmill: international agreements, national citizenship practices, and sustainable development', *Humboldt Journal of Social Relations* 21(1): 61–93.

—— (1996) *Local Environmental Struggles: Citizen Activism in the Treadmill of Production*, New York and Cambridge: Cambridge University Press.

Gould, K. A. Weinberg, A. S, and Schnaiberg, A. (1993) 'Legitimating impotence: pyrrhic victories of the modern environmental movement', *Qualitative Sociology* 16: 207–246.

Graedel, T. E. and Allenby, B. R. (1995) *Industrial Ecology*, Englewood Cliffs, NJ: Prentice Hall.

Harrison, B. (1994) *Lean and Mean: The Changing Landscape of Corporate Power in the Age of Flexibility*, New York: Basic Books.

Hawkins, K. (1984) *Environment and Enforcement: Regulation and the Social Definition of Pollution*, Oxford: Clarendon Press.

Higgins, L. and Lutzenhiser, L. (1993) 'Ceremonial equity: low-income energy assistance and the failure of socio-environmental policy', *Social Problems* 42: 601–625.

Holusha, J. (1994) 'Rich market for business of recycling', *New York Times* (8 October): 1.

Kacandes, T. (1991) 'Market development in New York: a report from the field', *Resource Recycling* (September): 53–60.

Landy, M. K., Roberts, M. J. and Thomas, S. R. (1990) *The Environmental Protection Agency: Asking the Wrong Questions*, New York: Oxford University Press.

Leonard, H. J., Yudelman, M., Stryker, J. D., Browder, J. O., DeBoer, A. J., Campbell, T. and Jolly, A. (1989) *Environment and the Poor: Development Strategies for a Common Agenda*, New Brunswick: Transaction Books.

McCarthy, J. E. (1991) 'Waste reduction and packaging in Europe', *Resource Recycling* (July): 56–63.

Moberg, D. (1991) 'Garbage: the city's blue-bag recycling program stinks', *Chicago Reader* (20 September): 1, 20–29.

Morris, J. and Dickey, L. W. (1991) 'Three 80s for the 90s will cut waste in half', *Resource Recycling* (March): 111–117.

Murphy, R. (1994) *Rationality and Nature: A Sociological Inquiry into a Changing Relationship*, Boulder, CO, San Francisco and Oxford: Westview Press.

Pellow, D. N., Schnaiberg, A. and Weinberg, A. S. (1995) 'Pragmatic corporate cultures: insights from a recycling enterprise', *Greener Management International* 12 (October): 95–110.

Rabasca, L. (1993) 'Recycling in 1993 ebbs and flows', *Waste Age's Recycling Times* (28 December): 1–12.

Redclift, M. (1984) *Development and the Environmental Crisis: Red or Green Alternatives?*, New York: Methuen.

—— (1986) 'Redefining the environmental "crisis" in the South', in J. Weston (ed.) *Red and Green: The New Politics of the Environment*, London: Pluto Press.

—— (1987) *Sustainable Development: Exploring the Contradictions*, New York: Methuen.

Reddy, A. K. N. (1979) *Technology, Development and the Environment: A Reappraisal*, New York: United Nations Environment Programme.

Rudel, T. K. and Horowitz, B. (1993) *Tropical Deforestation: Small Farmers and Land Clearing in the Ecuadorian Amazon*, New York: Columbia University Press.

Schnaiberg, A. (1975) 'Social syntheses of the socio-environmental dialectic: the role of distributional impacts', *Social Science Quarterly* 56 (June): 5–20.

—— (1977) 'Obstacles to environmental research by scientists and technologists: a social structural analysis', *Social Problems* 24 (5): 500–520.

——— (1980) *The Environment: From Surplus to Scarcity*, New York: Oxford University Press.

——— (1982) 'Did you ever meet a payroll? Contradictions in the structure of the appropriate technology movement', *Humboldt Journal of Social Relations* 9(2) (Spring–Summer): 38–62.

——— (1983a) 'Soft energy and hard labour? Structural restraints on the transition to appropriate technology', in G. F. Summers (ed.) *Technology and Social Change in Rural Areas*, Boulder, CO: Westview Press.

——— (1983b) 'Redistributive goals versus distributive politics: social equity limits in environmental and appropriate technology movements', *Sociological Inquiry* 53(2/3) (Spring): 200–219.

——— (1992a) 'Recycling vs. remanufacturing: redistributive realities', working paper WP–92–15, Center for Urban Affairs and Policy Research, Northwestern University, Spring.

——— (1992b) 'The recycling shell game: multinational economic organization vs. local political ineffectuality', working paper WP–92–16, Center for Urban Affairs and Policy Research, Northwestern University, Spring.

——— (1993) 'Paradoxes and contradictions: a contextual framework for "How I learned to reject recycling"', paper presented at the meetings of the American Sociological Association, Miami Beach, FL, August 1993.

——— (1994) 'The political economy of environmental problems: consciousness, coordination, and conflict', in L. Freese (ed.) *Advances in Human Ecology*, vol. 3: 23–64.

Schnaiberg, A. and Gould, K. A. (1994) *Environment and Society: The Enduring Conflict*, New York: St Martin's Press.

Schumacher, E. F. (1973) *Small is Beautiful: Economics as if People Mattered*, New York: Harper & Row.

Socolow, R. H., Andrews, C. and Berkhout, F. (eds) (1994) *Industrial Ecology and Global Change*, Cambridge and New York: Cambridge University Press.

Stretton, H. (1976) *Capitalism, Socialism, and the Environment*, Cambridge: Cambridge University Press.

Swanson, S. (1991) 'Recycling grows into a way of life', *Chicago Tribune* (16 June): s. 1.1.

Szasz, A. (1994) *Ecopopulism: Toxic Waste and the Movement for Environmental Justice*, Minneapolis and London: University of Minnesota Press.

Tibbs, H. (1993a) *Industrial Ecology: An Environmental Agenda for Industry*, Emeryville, CA: Global Business Network.

——— (1993b) 'The ethical management of global technology', paper prepared for the annual meetings of the American Sociological Association, Miami Beach, FL, August 1993.

UNIDO (1979) United Nations International Development Organization, *Monographs on Appropriate Industrial Technology* nos. 3, 4, 6, 8 and 9. New York: United Nations.

United States National Commission on the Environment (1993) *Choosing a Sustainable Future: A Report of the National Commission on the Environment*, Washington, DC, and Covelo, CA: Island Press.

Walley, N. and Whitehead, B. (1994) 'It's not easy being green', *Harvard Business Review* (May–June): 46–52.

Weinberg, A. S., Pellow, D. N. and Schnaiberg, A. (1996) 'Sustainable development as a sociologically defensible concept: from foxes and rovers to citizen-workers', in L. Freese (ed.) *Advances in Human Ecology*, vol. 5: 261–302.

Weinberg, A. S., Schnaiberg, A, and Gould, K. A. (1995) 'Recycling: conserving resources or accelerating the treadmill of production?', in L. Freese (ed.) *Advances in Human Ecology*, vol. 4: 173–205.

Part II

The practice of sustainable development

4 The evolution of European Union environmental policy

From growth to sustainable development?

Susan Baker

The European Union (EU) is committed to a policy of sustainable development in an attempt to reconcile its historical commitment to economic development with its new concern to protect the environment. This Chapter examines whether this new commitment can in practice help to reconcile economic and environmental interests within the Union, including the factors that operate against such a reconciliation. The Chapter examines only those factors that are related to the Union as a whole, as opposed to specific policy sectors, member-states or regions, all of which are addressed by other contributions to this volume.

The EU's commitment to sustainable development has occurred at a number of different levels, which for convenience can be grouped into two categories: formal, legal and declaratory statements; and policy programmes. We begin with the formal position of the Union with respect to sustainable development.

SUSTAINABLE DEVELOPMENT IN THE EU – THE FORMAL DIMENSION

Background

In 1972 the heads of state of the European Community (EC) first declared their intention of addressing the problems associated with the increasing degradation of Europe's natural environment (Baker 1993). An important influence behind this declaration was the Commission's realization that individual member-states' own environmental protection policy could conflict with the goals of competition policy (Baker 1993). That economic considerations were one of the primary reasons for the Union's involvement in environmental protection policy is not surprising, given the original *raison d'être* of the Union. It is nevertheless important to note because it reminds us that historically the Union has based its environmental protection policy not so much on a belief in the legitimacy of environmental protection as such but rather on the assumption that environmental protection measures have economic and, particularly, trade consequences (Baker 1993). Yet despite the centrality of economic growth a new, albeit subordinate, imperative of environmental protection did evolve. This new commitment to environmental protection was to become a source of policy tension within the EU and between 1972 and 1992 the Community had difficulties in reconciling its environmental and economic interests (Baker 1993: 8–11). In 1992 the EC made a renewed attempt to reconcile these interests, as is evident in the Fifth Action Programme on the Environment and later in the Maastricht Treaty.

The legal dimension

In December 1988 the EC heads of government stated, in a Declaration on the Environment, that 'sustainable development must be one of the over-riding objectives of all Community policies' (CEC 1992b). However, at the Rome Summit two years later the heads of government replaced the term 'sustainable development' with a commitment to environmental protection in order to ensure 'sustainable growth', and it was this formulation that was subsequently to make its way into the Maastricht Treaty. The Treaty, however, also speaks about promoting economic and social progress which is sustainable (CEC 1992a: 7). To complicate the matter further, the Treaty's section dealing with development co-operation requires Union policy to foster 'the sustainable economic and social development of the developing countries' – which at first sight appears to mean the Union applies the concept of sustainable development to the developing countries while applying 'sustainable growth' to the Union.

We thus have a rather confusing situation, whereby the Maastricht Treaty speaks of 'sustainable progress', 'sustainable growth' and 'sustainable development'. The meaning of these formulations remains unclear. It could be argued that the multiple terminology is accidental. However, for a number of reasons this is not an entirely satisfactory answer. First, the Maastricht Treaty was the outcome of complex, protracted and politically sensitive bargaining among member-states. It is unlikely that in such negotiations vagueness in wording or inconsistency in terminology would pass unnoticed. Second, when the formulation 'sustainable growth' appeared in the first draft of the Maastricht Treaty under the Luxembourg Presidency in April 1991 there was some (unsuccessful) pressure to revert to the original term 'sustainable development' (Verhoeve *et al.* 1992). The variety of terms used is therefore far from arbitrary.

The use of different terminology is of significance for policy in two ways. First, it means greater flexibility, and thus the possibility of greater inconsistency, in the development of future EU environmental policy. Second, it could be argued that the Union believes that it can adopt its old strategy of economic development based on growth and onto which environmental considerations can be grafted, whereas the future of the developing world must lie in a more integrated approach based on sustainable development, which may involve foregoing growth in order to achieve environmental harmony. This raises the worrying possibility that the Maastricht Treaty enshrines double standards with respect to how it envisages the operationalization of the Brundtland challenge. Third, it gives rise to uncertainty with respect to policy objectives. The separation of sustainability from the broad concept of development and its linkage with growth impose limitations on policy. 'Growth' usually refers to the narrow economic sphere, to increased economic activity, especially in production and consumption. 'Development', like the word 'progress', normally has wider connotations than growth, and can include social and political reform as well as economic redistribution, all of which may or may not be accompanied by growth. 'Sustainable growth' as a policy goal would seem to uncouple environmental management from the more radical social, economic and political changes envisaged by the Brundtland Report. Fuller investigation of the policy significance of the EU's commitment to sustainable development is required, a task that needs to be undertaken in the context of consideration of the other principles of EU environmental policy, including those enshrined in EU treaties (such as the principle of subsidiarity; see Chapter 5).

PUTTING SUSTAINABLE DEVELOPMENT INTO PRACTICE

Incremental policy-making: from the First to the Fourth Action Programmes on the Environment

Declaratory statements are just one step in the making of policy: policy programmes have to be formulated and implemented. The Action Programmes form the main means whereby EU environmental commitments are translated into policy, of which there have been five to date. It is the Fifth Action Programme on the Environment that provided the most explicit commitment by the Union to the policy of sustainable development. However, we must guard against the mistake of believing that this commitment was sui generis: it is a development of the four previous programmes. This is consistent with the fact that policy-making in the EU is predominantly incremental, and therefore the shift to sustainable development is unlikely to be the result of a radical new departure in policy thinking. Furthermore, the commitment to sustainable development adopted in the Fifth Action Programme is framed within the context of, and limited by, the previous four programmes. Looking back over these programmes will enable us to identify the context within which the Union's commitment to sustainable development is situated and the limitations imposed upon it.

The First Action Programme (1973–1976) defined the basic principles of Community environmental policy, including that the best environmental policy consists in the prevention of pollution; that prevention is compatible with economic and social development; that exploitation of natural resources must be avoided; and finally, that natural resources are an asset that should be used and not abused (CEC 1973; Johnson and Corcelle 1989: 11–12). These principles have become key elements of the framework within which Union sustainable development policy is situated.

The Second Action Programme covered the years 1977–1981. This was basically a continuation and expansion of the actions carried out in the First Action Programme (CEC 1977). A central concern of the Third Community Action Programme (1982–1986) was the integration of environmental considerations into other policy areas (CEC 1982). Weale has argued that concern was due to the recognition that many environmental problems arise from activities in other economic sectors (Weale and Williams 1992: 45). The Commission had another reason to call for integration, believing that integration is 'the lynch-pin in the process of establishing social and economic development patterns' (CEC 1992b: v).

The belief that environmental protection can be the source of economic development links integration with 'ecological modernization', an ideology which, as we will discuss in greater detail below, represents one way in which the EU is operationalizing the principle of sustainable development. Environmental policy integration was also endorsed by the Brundtland Report. However, despite the importance of integration and the formal stress placed upon it, integration policy has been faltering and haphazard, without serious resonance in the central policy activities of the EU (Weale and Williams 1992: 49). Policy-makers have failed to clarify what is involved in integration, and as a consequence those concerned to advance the idea have typically had a range of rather disparate problems in mind (Weale and Williams 1992: 46). This claim by Weale is strengthened by the fact that the Fifth Action Programme remains vague about how integration is to be achieved in practice, although the Commission is currently examining this.

Integrating environmental considerations into other policy areas is politically and administratively difficult and is inhibited by specific features of the EU policy-making process. For example, within the EU there has been a strong tendency for sectoral organizations to pursue sectoral objectives and to treat their impact on other sectors as side-effects, to be taken into account only if they are compelled to do so. According to Brundtland, many of the environmental and developmental problems that confront us have their roots in this sectoral fragmentation of responsibility (WCED 1987: 63). The rigidity of EU institutions makes the task of overcoming fragmentation difficult. Those with responsibility for other policy areas will be likely to resent what they see as the 'intrusion' of policy-makers into their traditional areas of competence. Furthermore, relationships and vested interests within EU policy communities, particularly those that are based on sectoral interests can become unsettled when new sets of environmental considerations are introduced. Environmental considerations are also likely to be seen as having restrictive consequences for economic activity. To add to these difficulties, an existing policy might not easily incorporate environmental concerns, requiring instead radical policy changes. This may prove to be the case as the Commission tries to incorporate environmental considerations into its transport and agricultural policies.

The Commission has become acutely aware of its failure to put the principle of integration into practice. While it has changed few of its administrative procedures, in June 1993 it nonetheless issued an internal Communication advising the Directorates-General (DG) on the practical implications of integration, including pointing out the necessity of designating an official within each DG to ensure that legislative proposals take account of environmental factors within a framework of sustainable development and also to create a co-ordinating unit within DG XI (Grayson and Hobson 1994: 6). It has also published a number of documents relating to integration in specific areas, including the urban environment and transport (Verhoeve *et al.* 1992). Some limited screening of projects funded from the Structural Funds has also been introduced, but these remain unsatisfactory.

The Fourth Action Programme covered the period 1987–1992. Its starting-point was the acceptance of the ideology of 'ecological modernization', a complex idea which holds that environmental protection is not in competition with, but rather an essential precondition for, growth and development (Weale and Williams 1992: 47). Ecological modernization is based on the belief that economic and other public policies that ignore harmful environmental effects on the grounds of cost do not in the end avoid these costs but merely displace them across space or time. In adopting this ideology the Commission stated its belief that future economic development could be linked with obtaining competitiveness through higher standards of pollution control and the production of environmentally safer products and processes. Thus policies for economic development and policies for the protection of the environment came to be seen as complementary rather than as rivals (CEC 1986: 4).

The ideology of ecological modernization has serious limitations in that it grounds environmental protection policy not in the recognition of the intrinsic worth of the environment but in the argument that it makes sound economic sense to invest in clean air, water purification and soil protection. As was discussed in the Introduction to this book, from the point of view of many environmentalists this is flawed thinking. However, the adoption of this philosophy by the EU is logical, as it fits with the overall economic *raison d'être* of the Union. Its importance lies in the fact that it allows the Union to justify its simultaneous pursuit of a rigorous programme of economic growth based on the completion of the internal market and of an ever-expanding environmental protection policy. Whether this will ultimately lead to a future that is sustainable, even in the weakest sense of the word, remains in doubt.

Sustainable development and the Fifth Action Programme

The Fifth Action Programme on the Environment and Sustainable Development covers the period from 1996–1997. A number of factors influenced this Programme, including, first, the publication of the 'Report on the State of the Environment' (EC 1992), which indicated a slow but relentless deterioration in the general state of the environment of the Union. Second, there was an acknowledgement that existing environmental policy was incapable of dealing with the burdens that the deepening of the integration process will pose for natural resources and the environment (CEC 1992a: 3). The final factor was the belief of the Commission that the Programme would enable the Union to play a leadership role in relation to international efforts to promote sustainable development.

What is especially noticeable in the Fifth Action Programme is the centrality given to breaking the perception that there is a trade-off between environmental protection and economic development. As we have seen, the priority of the Fourth Action Programme was to make the link between the economy and the environment primarily in the industrial sector, through promoting the policy of ecological modern-ization. The Fifth Action Programme links environmental protection with the wider concept of sustainable development, to be operational-ized across all economic sectors and policy areas (Europe Environment 1992). Five target sectors have been identified for special attention in the Programme: industry, energy, transport, agriculture and tourism. This approach is firmly rooted in the anthropocentric belief in the management of the natural environment. Here the reconciliation of environmental and economic interests is achieved through the reduc-tion of the environmental to the economic. This approach runs the risk of reducing the concept of sustainable development to a question of 'feasibility': a production or consumption pattern is judged to be sustainable in so far as sufficient resources are available to continue similar production and consumption in the future. Sustainable devel-opment, not least within Brundtland, is a wider socio-political concept than this.

As in the Maastricht Treaty, the Fifth Action Programme also used the novel formulation of linking sustainable development with growth, stating that environmental protection was aimed at providing 'optimal conditions' for socio-economic well-being and growth for the present and future generations (CEC 1992a: 5). This involves moving the Union onto a 'critical path' of sustainable development which will:

- maintain the overall quality of life;
- maintain continuing access to natural resources;
- avoid lasting environmental damage (CEC 1992a: 18).

This path appears to endorse a weak model of sustainable develop-ment, as is also evident from an examination of the Programme's policy objectives. These includes optimum reuse and recycling of the materials used in production and consumption, rationalization of production and consumption energy (CEC 1992a: 4). Yet – and this is crucial – while the Programme hoped to reduce wasteful consumption, it envisaged that this could be done at the same time as increasing productivity. There was no attempt to confront the fact that the Union's inhabitants currently consume a disproportionate share of the world's resources; nor are issues of redistribution discussed, an absence especially noticeable when account is taken of the assurances made that the implementation of sustainable development policy will not be at the expense of other Union priorities.

The image of the path is important in the Fifth Action Programme because it facilitates recognition that sustainable development will not be achieved in a period as short as that covered by its Programme. The Commission sees the Fifth Action Programme as one step in a longer-term campaign (CEC 1992a: 4). However, the mismatch between the time horizon of the Programme and that envisaged for a shift to sustainable development may well give rise to problems of policy consistency and coherence across time and to implementation deficits.

Efforts are made in the Programme to pre-empt future implementation difficulties, including setting out performance targets for the period up to the year 2000. However, these objectives and targets are weak in that they do not constitute legal obligations, and by the Commission's own admission some of the targets lack precision. Implementation is also to be helped by the broadening of what had hitherto been a narrow emphasis on administrative and regulatory policy instruments (CEC 1992b: 23). As was seen in the Introduction, the broader mix of instruments envisaged by the Fifth Action Programme will add market-based instruments, horizontal supporting instruments and financial support mechanisms. The Commission hopes that the introduction of this wider range of instruments and its associated greater reliance on market forces, will stimulate behavioural changes (CEC 1992a: 19). The use of an extended range of instruments is also intended to create a new interplay between the main groups of social actors (government, enterprise, public) and the principal economic sectors (CEC 1992a: 26).

The inclusion of the social partners is in keeping with the Commission's new emphasis on what it refers to as 'shared responsibility'. This is also consistent with Brundtland's argument that sustainable development needs community knowledge and support, which entails greater public participation in the decisions that effect the environment (WCED 1987: 63; see also Chapter 11).

To summarize, the Action Programmes are in part an attempt to reconcile the Union's growing concern with environmental protection and its historic commitment to economic growth. The task of the rest of this Chapter is to examine the factors that will shape the future success of the EU in achieving reconciliation between economic and environmental interests through the use of policies based on the concept of sustainable development.

FACTORS SHAPING THE ACHIEVEMENT OF SUSTAINABLE DEVELOPMENT WITHIN THE EU

Democracy and accountability in complex policy-making processes

The primacy of the Council of Ministers and of the European Council in policy-making, given that these institutions are not directly elected by the citizens of the EU as a whole, has raised serious questions about democracy and democratic accountability within the EU (Baker 1996). The democratic deficit in the EU has a direct bearing upon EU environmental policy. It has hampered public debate about environmental policy measures and has meant that decisions on EC regulations are shrouded in the secrecy of the Council (van der Straaten 1992: 72). But the limitations of the democratic nature of the EU are of particular relevance when applied to the policy of sustainable development, because the success of this policy is dependent upon the elaboration of a new interface between top-down and bottom-up policy input.

From a top-down perspective, it is becoming evident that the state (or supra-state bodies) has a crucial role to play in the shift to sustainable development, not least with respect to strategic planning and overseeing necessary institutional adjustments. The state must also co-ordinate the integration of environmental considerations into other policy sectors and ensure policy coherence across the local, regional, national and international levels. Thus it can be argued that a strong state is a necessary (although not a sufficient) condition for sustainable development. However, a strong state may not necessarily be – and indeed often is not – a democratic state.

Sustainable development also requires a decentralization of policy activities, especially to the regional and local levels. A cornerstone of Brundtland's argument is that sustainable development requires effective citizen participation in decision-making (WCED 1987: 65). The widening of the scope of bottom-up involvement, from its initial participation in implementation to the increased demand for and rising expectations about involvement in all stages of the policy-making process, is especially noticeable since the Rio Earth Summit and the initiation of the Agenda 21 process. Bottom-up involvement is now seen as a defining feature of sustainable development, rather than as a mere means to its implementation, and is regarded as necessary to ensure that policy is legitimized and that it takes account of the needs, cultural diversity and economic aspirations of those involved.

The success of the shift to sustainable development within the EU will depend upon how the imperatives of centralization and the development of a strong state on the one hand and bottom-up policy involvement on the other can be combined and the tensions between them resolved. This is likely to be a particularly difficult task for the EU, given its democratic deficit, institutional inflexibility and complex intergovernmental nature (Baker 1996; Lodge 1989: 69; Judge 1993: 38). The task faced by the Union in undergoing democratic reform, for example by institutionalizing accountability, is a difficult one. Familiar mechanisms of political accountability may not be sophisticated or flexible enough to operate effectively in the EU context, especially in view of the complex mixture of quasi-federalist, intergovernmental and supranational organizational structures that exist within it and the tension that arises over which of these regimes shall eventually triumph. Resolving the issue of accountability requires agreement about the fundamental nature of the Union and its future development, coupled with a clear understanding of how to structure its institutions in such as way as effectively to attain and express that European ideal. Such clarity of purpose is absent from the EU at present.

Openness of the policy process

The EU policy-making process does not involve only formal policy-making structures; policy is also the outcome of consultation with interest groups. Environmental policy is a relatively new policy area for the Union, and thus in many ways it is more open than some of the older, more established policy sectors, with their more institutionalized policy communities (Baker 1993; Mazey and Richardson 1994). Nevertheless, the environmental policy process has been criticized for its weak policy outcomes, undoubtedly a legacy of the historical requirement that all Union environmental policy be the result of unanimous voting procedures. This has meant in effect that both radical environmental interests and the interests of more environmentally committed member-states have not been reflected in final policy outcomes. Ensuring the openness of the policy process is a crucial element in the shift to sustainable development, which, if successful, offers the possibility of a new and fruitful partnership between environmental, economic and political interests.

The post-Maastricht commitment to the twin principles of partnership and subsidiarity could play an important role in facilitating policy openness. It could be argued that this 'federalization' of the Union is one way of filling the democratic deficit, as it allows increased local and regional participation in policy formulation and implementation. However, there are tensions relating to the interpretation given to these principles and to actual practice (Baker 1996). Nevertheless the commitment may, in the future, provide opportunities for regional, local and environmental interests to have a greater say in the shaping of the decision-making process of the Union, the manner in which the commitment to sustainable development is translated into policy and, ultimately, the way in which sustainable development is implemented.

Further developments have also occurred. As part of its new strategy of involving economic and social partners in the policy process, and the development of a new 'bottom-up' policy style, in 1992 the Commission proposed the establishment of three ad-hoc 'dialogue groups': a 'general consultative forum', made up of functional representatives, non-governmental organizations (NGOs), regional and local authorities; an 'implementation network' of representatives of relevant national authorities and of the Commission; and an 'environmental policy review group', comprising representatives of the Commission and the member-states at Directorate-General level (CEC 1992a: 9). The Fifth Action Programme is also eager to encourage the involvement of NGOs in the process of environmental awareness building (CEC 1992a: 27). The establishment of these new structures is welcome, especially the emphasis on policy partnership, but it is as yet too early to assess their effectiveness in compensating for the democratic deficit.

The incremental nature of the policy process

Policy-making within the EU is characterized by incrementalism, with policy undertaken in a step-by-step movement. Environmental policy is no exception, as we have seen in the examination of the incremental expansion in the range and depth of coverage expressed in the environmental Action Programmes. This policy style has important implications for environmental policy because it inhibits the process of change when the demand is for either radically new policies or policies that conflict with existing practice. If a policy has low visibility, fits with prevailing values and involves narrow concerns its chances of success are greater than if it is highly visible, controversial and wide-ranging. This enables us to make a useful, if not entirely hard and fast, distinction between two types of environmental policies:

1 Policies that have as their goal the management of environmental quality within the context of existing economic, political and social

policy and that require marginal, incremental adjustment to the features of those policies.

2 Policies that have more radical goals, such as the reorganization of consumption patterns, the redefinition of what constitutes economic activity, the redistribution and radical altering of Western use of resources and the reform of existing political and military structures.

This distinction is useful in that it helps us to understand why some policy recommendations by interest groups are incorporated into the environmental policy of the EU and why others have little success in policy output terms. It can be a factor explaining the lack of access of a wide range of environmental interests to the EU policy-making process. It can also help explain why the EU has adopted a weak understanding of sustainable development. Incrementalism makes the chances of successful translation of the commitment to sustainable development into actual policy dependent upon the extent to which the required policy changes can be fitted with existing policy commitments. Policy proposals that fit with the strategy of environmental quality management stand a greater chance of acceptance, while policies that fit more closely with the second, more radical, pattern have little, if any, chance of success. The concept of sustainable development has been interpreted by the Union (and its member-states) to fit within the confines of managerial as opposed to radical policy solutions.

Within the EU, weak sustainable development stands a reasonable chance of successful implementation, given the planning framework provided by the Fifth Action Programme, the commitment to achieving policy integration, the new resources made available under the Cohesion Funds and the establishment of new structures for ensuring bottom-up input into policy-making. However, whether this 'truncated' version of sustainable development will enable the Union to ensure that it can meet the needs of the present generation without compromising the ability of future generations to meet their own needs remains in doubt.

Institutions' adaptability and capacity

The European Commission's Directorate-General XI with responsibility for Environment, Nuclear Safety and Civil Protection (DG XI) is weak and has historically suffered from staff and budget shortages in comparison with other departments (Liberatore 1991: 296). The shift to sustainable development requires institutional development and adaptation (Hanf *et al.* 1993). Some institutional changes have already occurred or are occurring within the Commission. The budget of DG XI, for example, has been increased and a number of institutional modifications made (Inlogov 1994: 6). However, although it is growing in importance, the environmental portfolio of the Commission is still relatively junior, whereas those Directorate-Generals responsible for the development of the single-market programme – that is, finance and industry – remain at the traditional centre of the Commission's activities (Weale and Williams 1992: 58). Further, the European Environmental Agency has been established, and is expected to provide *horizontal supporting instruments*, including improved scientific data, to enable the EU both to formulate new environmental policies and to appraise the effectiveness of its existing policies.

Policy instruments and implementation

Despite the fact that the Action Programmes appear quite comprehensive in their range of concerns, very few instruments have been used by the Union to put these Programmes into effect. The most frequently used legal instrument for environmental policy is the Directive, although since the Fifth Action Programme consideration has also been given to developing a range of fiscal and economic tools. Directives are binding regarding the results to be achieved and the time allowed to achieve them, leaving the choice of form and method of implementation to the national authorities. Directives facilitate member-state discretion but have been seen as a factor contributing to the implementation deficit in environmental policy.

The implementation deficit is of major significance for the shift to sustainable development because it limits the number of concrete instances where the reconciliation of economic and environmental interests is actually being attempted. It also makes us more aware that acceptance of the principle of sustainable development is but one step in a more complex process. Sustainable development policy has to be implemented and this will occur under different patterns of economic and social development and with varying degrees of commitment from the member-states.

Other policy priorities

Implementation of the commitment to sustainable development has also to occur within existing policy parameters, especially within the context of the Union's commitment to the completion of the internal market. According to Weale, the internal-market programme provides us with one of the most striking examples of the implementation deficit of the Union with respect to environmental policy in general and the integration of environmental considerations into other policy considerations in particular (Weale and Williams 1992: 49). The new imperative of environmental protection may, for some time, continue to exist in an uncomfortable relationship with the Union's and member-states' historical commitment to economic growth.

CONCLUSION

Sustainable development is not a simple concept nor is it implemented in a vacuum; rather it forms part of a complex policy aimed at reconciling two seemingly contradictory processes: economic development and environmental protection. Within the EU sustainable development is a contested concept, as well as being implemented in a contested and already crowded policy terrain. Its success as a policy goal will depend on the ability of EU actors to forge a new interface between older policy interests and new policy concerns, between the existing top-down policy style and the new bottom-up policy imperatives, and between the traditional institutional structures and public administration procedures and the new calls for institutional adaptation and flexibility.

A number of factors are shaping how this synthesis will evolve: first, there are the political and economic priorities of the EU; second, there is the necessity of balancing national, sub-national and sectoral interests; third, there is the choice of instruments used to stimulate genuine changes in human behaviour. The EU places emphasis on voluntary and market forces to achieve this behavioural change, underestimating the more proactive role it may have to play itself. Given the emphasis on market-led change, behavioural modification is more likely to be confined to those changes that can be reconciled with current quality-of-life priorities. Such adjustments may prove insufficient to achieve the shift to sustainable development.

Shifting the economies of western Europe on to a sustainable development path is a difficult task and the potential for conflict at the political level should not be underestimated. Policies promoting sustainable development involve making individuals and organizations fully aware of, and accountable for, the environmental costs of their actions. This will have a significant impact on quality of life and/or profitability and is almost certain to be deeply unpopular among both producers and consumers. Nor should the difficulties surrounding the integration of sustainable development policy into other policy sectors be underestimated. Yet the EU has a significant role to play in shaping sustainable development. The tragedy may be that the EU, a world leader, may well encourage others to replace the original concept of sustainable development with a weaker and highly truncated version of sustainable development.

REFERENCES

Baker, S. (1993) 'The environmental policy of the European Community: a critical review', *Kent Journal of International Relations* 7(1) (Summer).

—— (1994) 'La politica medioambiental y las regiones periférica de la Comunidad Europea' [Environmental policy and peripheral regions of the EC], in N. Arenilla, J. Loughlin and T. Toonen (eds) *La Europa de las regiones: una perspectiva intergubernamental* [Europe of the Regions: An Intergovernmental Perspective], Granada: Granada University Press.

—— (1996) 'Environmental policy in the European Union: institutional dilemmas and democratic practice', in W. Lafferty, and J. Meadowcroft (eds) *Environment and Democracy*, Cheltenham: Edward Elgar.

CEC (1973) Commission of the European Communities, 'First Programme of Action on the Environment', *Official Journal of the European Communities* 16, C112, 20.12.73.

—— (1977) 'Second Programme of Action on the Environment (1982–86)', *Official Journal of the European Communities* 20, C134, 13.6.77.

—— (1982) 'Third Programme of Action on the Environment', *Official Journal of the European Communities* 26, C46, 12.2.82.

—— (1986) *The State of the Environment in the European Community*, Brussels: EUR 10633.

—— (1992a) *Towards Sustainability: A European Community Programme of Policy and Action in Relation to the Environment and Sustainable Development*, Brussels COM (92) 23 Final, 11.

—— (1992b) *Report from the Commission of the European Communities to the United Nations Conference on the Environment*, Brussels: March, SEC (91) 2448 final.

EC (1992) *The State of the Environment in the European Community: An Overview*, Com (92) 23, vol. III.

Europe Environment (1992) 'EEC: Fifth Action Programme for the Environment and Sustainable Development', supplement to *Europe Environment* 386 (5 May).

Grayson, L. and Hobson, M. (1994) 'Sustainability', *Inglogov Informs* 4 (Birmingham: University of Birmingham, Institute of Local Government Studies).

Hanf, K., Czarnecki, C. A. and Philip, M. E. (1993) 'Towards sustainable development in Africa: managing the environment–economy link', working paper, Erasmus University of Rotterdam.

Ingolov, (1994) 'On Sustainability', issue 1, vol. 4, Institute of Local Government Studies, University of Birmingham.

Johnson, S. P., and Corcelle, G. (1989) *The Environmental Policy of the European Community*, London: Graham & Trotman.

Judge, D. (1993) (ed.) *A Green Dimension for the European Community*, London: Frank Cass.

Liberatore, A. (1991) 'Problems of transnational policymaking: environmental policy in the European Community', *European Journal of Political Research*, 19(2 and 3): 281–305.

Lodge, J. (ed.) (1989) *The European Community and the Challenge of the Future*, London: Pinter.

Mazey, S. and Richardson, J. (1994) 'Policy co-ordination in Brussels: environmental and regional policy', in S. Baker, K. Milton and S. Yearley (eds) *Protecting the Periphery: Environmental Policy in Peripheral Regions of the European Union*, London: Frank Cass.

van der Straaten, J. (1992) 'A sound European environmental policy: challenges, possibilities and barriers', in D. Judge (ed.) *A Green Dimension for the European Community*, London: Frank Cass.

Verhoeve, B., Bennett, G. and Wilkinson, D. (1992) *Maastricht and the Environment*, London: Institute for European Environmental Affairs.

WCED (1987) *Our Common Future*, Oxford: Oxford University Press.

Weale, A. and Williams, A. (1992) 'Between economy and ecology? The single market and the integration of environmental policy', in D. Judge (ed.) *A Green Dimension for the European Community*, London: Frank Cass.

5 The integration of sustainable development objectives into EU policy-making

Barriers and prospects

Angela Liberatore

Integration is emerging as a basic principle and objective of EU environmental policy. It requires that environmental factors are taken into account in the formulation and implementation of all sectoral policies. Integration also involves a cross-sectoral dimension since environmental problems such as climate change, biodiversity and water management necessitate tackling the multiple causes and sources of pollutant emissions and natural resource mismanagement across sectors.

The relevance of integration for moving towards sustainable development is straightforward: if environmental factors are not taken into consideration in the formulation and implementation of the policies that regulate economic activities and other forms of social organization, a new model of development that can be environmentally and socially sustained in the long term cannot be achieved. In turn, it is to be expected that environmental policy will be changed as a result of the increasing interaction between the previously rather separate policy agendas of environmental protection, economic growth and activities with major economic as well as environmental impacts such as agriculture and transport. An important aspect to be considered is the fact that integration can result either in the strengthening of environmental considerations and priorities or in their dilution within other policies.

This contribution attempts to discuss current notions and practices of integration in the EU, including their relationship with the concept of – and EU commitments to – sustainable development. In the first section of this Chapter an examination is undertaken of the factors that contributed to the emergence of integration as an EU environmental policy principle and goal. Then the main dimensions of integration are discussed and some indicators proposed. Finally, constraints and opportunities are analysed.

INTEGRATION AS A GUIDING POLICY PRINCIPLE

Key policy developments always include the formulation and use of guiding principles. Such principles are not simply a matter of rhetoric: they reflect certain policy priorities and in turn influence them. Therefore a brief account of the guiding principles of EU environmental policy can be a useful background for understanding integration in the EU context.

Environmental policy principles

Early developments in environmental policy in the Organization for Economic Cooperation and Development (OECD) and the EC in the early 1970s included an emphasis on the 'polluter pays' principle as a means of allocating the costs of environmental protection in a way that would not produce distortion of competition. This reflected the EC and OECD concerns, which continue to be very important, for the trade and broader economic implications of environmental measures (Liberatore 1992; Weale 1993). More recently, in the 1980s, the precautionary principle emerged as a guiding principle of EC environmental policy and international environmental agreements. It is aimed at guiding decision-making in conditions of uncertainty regarding events and processes that might involve serious and irreversible damage (O'Riordan and Cameron 1994).

Starting with the EC's Third Environmental Action Programme, adopted in 1983 and strengthened in the Fourth and Fifth Environmental Action Programmes (adopted in 1987 and 1993, respectively), the need to integrate environmental considerations into the formulation and implementation of all sectoral policies became both a guiding policy principle and a policy goal in the EU. The Third Environmental Action Programme stated that the Community should seek to integrate environmental concerns into the policy development of certain economic activities (CEC 1983: s. 1.8); the Fourth Action Programme devoted a whole section to integration (CEC 1987: s. 2.3); and integration is the core of the Fifth Programme *Towards Sustainability* (CEC 1993a). The principle of integration is also provided for in the Maastricht Treaty, where it is stated that the environmental protection requirements must be integrated into the definition and implementation of other Community policies (Maastricht Treaty, art. 130R (2)). Why did these developments take place?

Factors which contributed to the emergence of the integration principle

Among the factors that have been influential in the emergence of integration as a guiding EU policy principle, the following deserve special attention:

- the links between economic integration and environment protection;
- the increasing influence of the discourse on sustainable development;
- the influence of policy developments within certain member-states;
- the process of institution-building within the EU.

Integral to the policies on environmental protection was the process of economic integration (completion of the internal market), which raised substantial concerns over the environmental impact of the integrative process. Such concerns had previously been voiced by environmental NGOs, and were now clearly expressed by a task force of experts appointed by the Commission's Directorate-General for the Environment (DG XI), in a widely circulated report on the environment and the internal market (CEC 1989). The report argued that no serious consideration had been given to the fact that while the removal of physical, technical and tax barriers would certainly improve intra-Community trade, it was also likely to have serious negative environmental impacts, such as an increase in pollutant emissions from the transport sector if no counter-measures were taken. It recommended, therefore, that action be taken in the form of monitoring the use of the Structural Funds and encouraging investments in cleaner technologies, with special regard to key sectors such as energy and transport.

The implications of environmental protection for the process of economic integration have been constantly in focus in DG XI, as shown by the preamble of many environmental directives, where the need to harmonize legislation in order to avoid distortion of competition is stressed. The possibility of improving competitiveness by means of cleaner technologies, energy efficiency, internalization of environmental externalities and other environmentally beneficial measures was also discussed in the European Commission's White Paper on *Growth, Competitiveness and Employment* (CEC 1994a: ch. 10) and in a study commissioned by DG XI on *Potential Benefits of Integration of Environmental and Economic Policies* (DRI *et al.* 1994). In other words, the integration of environmental concerns into EU policy-making and the process of European economic integration are reciprocally linked.

The recent debate on administrative and legislative simplification and deregulation in the EU has contributed to an even stronger emphasis on the need to justify any environmental protection measure in terms of its compatibility with measures aimed at increasing economic competitiveness. The experts' report on the simplification of legislative and administrative procedures (CEC 1995b), the so-called Molitor Report, dedicated a full Chapter to environmental regulation and recommended that future legislation explicitly take into account the constraints which such regulations impose on the private sector. Leaving aside the specifics of the report, its overall influence in assessing environmental protection in terms of its consequences on economic competitiveness cannot be underestimated.

The relationship between environmental protection and the economy was also at the core of another important element that fostered the emergence of the integration principle in the EU context: the increasing influence of the discourse on sustainable development. Such influence is reflected in the title of the Fifth Environmental Action Programme, *Towards Sustainability*, and in the call for a new model of development briefly made at the Copenhagen Council of Ministers of June 1993 (CEC 1995a) and elaborated in the Commission's White Paper on *Growth, Competitiveness and Employment*. The EU further committed itself to finding ways of implementing Agenda 21 – which resulted from the United Nations Conference on Environment and Development (UNCED) held in Rio in 1992. In this regard, the Lisbon Council of 1992 adopted an eight-point plan to implement the commitments made in Rio (CEC 1995a: 10). The plan included the ratification of the Climate and Biodiversity Conventions, the development of national plans to implement Agenda 21 and support for the establishment of the Commission for Sustainable Development (CSD). In practice, the Conventions were ratified and national plans adopted in most, but not all, of the EU member-states by mid-1995, while the European Commission regularly reports to the CSD on progress made in the EU.

As far as the operationalization of the concept of sustainable development is concerned, diversity is the order of the day, since the concept can be interpreted in many different ways. However, given that the most influential definitions of sustainable development involve aspects that are difficult to measure, it is perhaps not surprising that the operationalization of the concept is far from uncontroversial. Particular problems have been associated with the issues of inter-generational equity, the notion of carrying capacity and the question of whether it is possible to substitute natural capital with human-made capital (Pearce *et al.* 1993). In spite of the differences and open questions, however, most people agree that sustainable development involves significant changes in the economy in order to improve environmental quality and human welfare in a long-term perspective. Integration can thus be regarded as an attempt to operationalize sustainable development in the sense that it can identify the activities where changes are primarily needed and foster changes that are both environmentally benign and socially equitable in a long-term perspective, taking into account present economic and political constraints.

A further factor which has contributed to the establishment of the idea that environmental implications should have been taken into consideration in all EU sectoral policies has been the acceptance of the integration idea within some member-states. The need to foster both 'external integration' (that is, integration of environmental aspects into all relevant government policies) and 'internal integration' (that is, integration of the various instruments to be used to tackle a specific problem) was mentioned in the Dutch National Environmental Policy Plan of 1989 (Ministry of Housing, Physical Planning and Environment 1989) and was pushed by the Dutch government on to the EU agenda. In 1990, on the initiative of the Irish Presidency, the Dublin Council of Ministers issued the 'environmental imperative' declaration that stated that environmental considerations must be fully and effectively integrated into transport, energy, infrastructure and other policy areas. Two years later, at the beginning of its own Presidency of the Council, the British Government announced its intention of advancing the integration of the environmental protection requirements into other Community policies (Baldock *et al.* 1992). Given the importance of inputs from member-states for the development of EU policies, the fact that the principle of integration had been officially endorsed by one country in its own environmental plan and was 'sponsored' by other governments as well proved instrumental to its establishment at EU level. The agreement reached among member-states over the endorsement of the principle is reflected in the reference to integration in the Maastricht Treaty.

Finally, the process of institution-building within the EU has been shaping the emergence and use of the principle of integration. The Community was established in 1957 as an *economic* regional organization with competence mainly in the field of trade, and over the years has expanded its competence into several other policy domains. With regard to environmental protection, it took some fifteen years for a competence to be developed – the first EC Environmental Action Programme was adopted in 1973 – and a further fifteen for officially recognized status to be achieved (in 1987 with the Single European Act). Since then, the Community has enacted extensive environmental regulation (Kraemer 1992) and established organizational structures, namely DG XI and the European Environmental Agency.

Within this context, the emphasis on the need to integrate environmental considerations into all relevant sectoral policies can be regarded very differently. For example, it can be seen as a tool for weakening environmental policy by diluting rather than integrating environmental factors into other policies. In this respect, resistance from sectors of national or EU administrations to the 'interference' of environmental policy in other policies, and the tendency to need to justify all environmental measures in terms of their additional benefits in to competitiveness and employment, can lead to such dilution.

The tension between strengthening and dilution is also shaped by the debate on subsidiarity. According to the Maastricht Treaty:

> In areas which do not fall within its exclusive competence, the Community shall take action, in accordance with the principle of subsidiarity, only if and in so far as the objectives of the proposed action cannot be sufficiently achieved by the member-states and can therefore, by reason of the scale or effects of the proposed action, be better achieved by the Community.
>
> (Maastricht Treaty, art. 3b)

Similarly, with regard to the environment, the Single European Act of 1986 had already stated that 'The Community shall take action with regard to the field of the environment to the extent to which the objective can be better obtained at the Community level' (art. 130R).

The interpretation of the subsidiarity principle is thus far from unequivocal: the principle can be used either to protect member-states' prerogatives against undue Community interference or to allow the EU to act when supranational action is necessary (Dehousse 1992). Concerning the environmental field, it is difficult to distinguish clearly between the European environment and national or regional environment due to the trans-boundary nature of many pollution and resource depletion problems. Furthermore, defining how to 'better' pursue environmental quality is a complex process where political and economic interests, scientific evidence and societal perceptions interact (Axelrod 1994; Kraemer 1992). The matter becomes even more complex when ones tries to match subsidiarity, sustainable development and integration. European institutions' attempts to integrate environmental considerations into sectoral policies, such as energy or transport, or across sectors, including coastal zones or the urban environment, may clash with national or sub-national competences and lead to resistance to EU action on the grounds of subsidiarity. It is not yet possible to assess the consequences of the subsidiarity debate on the process of institution-building in the field of the environment and on the integration of sustainable development objectives into EU policy-making. Nevertheless, it is safe to say that even in the case of problems whose global nature is agreed, and which are thus seen as requiring EU action on the basis of the required scale and effect of the action to be taken, the choice of targets and instruments may still be in dispute: the choice is going to be influenced by the way subsidiarity will be interpreted and used by member-states and EU institutions.

DIMENSIONS OF INTEGRATION: FROM THEORY TO PRACTICE

Integration involves several dimensions: first, a sectoral dimension (that is, the sectors where and across which the integration of environmental considerations should be achieved); second, an issue dimension (that is, where environmental issues are tackled by applying the integration principle); third, a spatial and a temporal dimension (sectors and issues are both located in space and time, but some are more diffused or are economically and socially more important than others in certain countries and regions, and some are more urgent than others); fourth, an organizational dimension (that is, the relations between the various institutions responsible for environment-related matters); fifth, a 'toolkit' dimension (that is, the instruments to be developed to achieve integration); and, sixth, a distributive and ethical dimension (the integration of environmental concerns may be easier and/or more beneficial to certain sectors, groups or regions than others, involving issues such as burden-sharing and compensations. The following discussion illustrates the respective importance and the interrelatedness of these dimensions.

Sectors

The sectoral dimension is the one mainly focused on in the Fifth Environmental Action Plan, which identifies five main target sectors: agriculture, energy, industry, transport and tourism. Furthermore, the European Parliament issued several Res olutions to support the integration of environmental considerations into agriculture, transport and the Structural Funds (CEC 1986, 1991, 1993b). Various initiatives have been launched that might contribute to the promotion of sustainable development by integrating environmental factors into the above-mentioned sectoral policies. Table 5.1 summarizes some of the main initiatives by sector.

Table 5.1 Main EU initiatives integrating environmental considerations (by sector)

Sector	Main initiatives
Agriculture	Assessment of environmental impact of measures financed under agriculture funds
	Possibility of transferring set-aside obligations to environmentally sensitive areas
	Agri-environmental measures
Energy	Programmes: SAVE, ALTENER, THERMIE, JOULE
	Proposal for a CO_2/energy tax
Industry	Eco-audit and eco-label schemes
	Proposal for a directive on integrated pollution prevention and control
Tourism	Promotion of 'sustainable tourism' to assist tourism
Transport	'Auto-oil' programme
	Directive on the charging of transport infrastructure costs to lorries

Source: EU Fifth Environmental Action Programme

Many of the measures listed in Table 5.1 and planned in the Fifth Environmental Action Plan have already been launched, and a few are currently being implemented (such as agri-environmental measures, eco-audit, SAVE and other energy programmes). However, some important measures intended to integrate environmental considerations into sectoral policies have yet to be adopted. Concerning the transport sector, for example, environmental considerations played only a very marginal role in the planning of the Trans-European Network for Transport and a proposal for the limitation of CO_2 emissions from cars has proved very controversial. Also with regard to CO_2 emissions, but in relation to the energy sector, the long-debated proposal on a CO_2/energy tax was radically transformed and led the Essen Council of Ministers of December 1994 to merely 'take note' of the Commission's 'intention to submit guidelines' to enable each member-state to apply a CO_2/energy tax on the basis of common parameters if it so desired (CEC 1995b: 143). There is thus mixed evidence with regard to actual success in integrating environmental considerations into key sectoral policies, although proposals are being formulated within EU institutions and by environmental NGOs (see CNE *et al.* 1995) to improve integration during the process of revision of the Maastricht Treaty.

Issues

As indicated by the case of measures to reduce CO_2 emissions, another important dimension of integration of environmental factors into policy-making is the need to address specific issues. For example, in order to tackle climate change it is necessary to develop strategies and instruments that aim to reduce greenhouse gases across various sectors, including energy, transport, agriculture and industry. The same applies to other issues.

Table 5.2 summarizes the main interactions between some key sectors and two global environmental issues (climate change and ozone layer depletion) via the relevant emissions. It shows that several sectors need to be addressed in order to tackle the same issue and that, at the same time, actions taken to reduce certain emissions across sectors can contribute to the solution of more than one problem. This leads to the conclusion that integration cannot be only sectoral but needs to be cross-sectoral as well if issues such as the ones above are to be dealt with.

Table 5.2 Sector contributions (emissions) to climate change and ozone layer depletion

Sector	Emissions	Issue
energy	CO_2	climate change
industry		ozone layer depletion
transport		
industry	CFCs	ozone layer depletion
		climate change
agriculture	CH_4	climate change
energy		
waste		

Concerning Table 5.2, it would be impossible to design even such a simple table without developing an understanding of the links and feedbacks between the sources of emissions and other forms of pressure on the environment, the environmental changes due to these pressures, and the impacts on economy and society due to environmental change. Scientific evidence and uncertainty are powerful arguments in the policy debate (Majone 1989), particularly in the discussion between policy-makers and target sectors, and scientific evidence itself (including socio-economic assessments) can lead to the identification of the main sources of environmental degradation and of the most vulnerable ecosystems, thus shaping the debate on policy options. But at the same time, science alone is insufficient to overcome resistance from target sectors or social groups that might be affected by environmental measures. Distributive aspects (discussed below) must be addressed.

Space and time

Different economic activities can produce synergistic effects on a very localized environment as well as on the global environment. Some ecosystems are ecologically more vulnerable than others and certain regions or cities are socially more vulnerable than others (due to high rates of unemployment or other socio-economic conditions). Also, as a consequence of different degrees of socio-economic vulnerability, different social groups may have different views and stakes with regard to the utilization of the same natural resources within and across the EU and beyond. At the same time, as will be discussed below, the sphere of competence of authorities in charge of environmental protection or environmentally relevant matters does not always match with the boundaries of the affected environment. Thus the integration of environmental factors into all areas of policy-making requires that attention be paid to the interactions between different spaces: the geographical space of the affected environment, the economic space of the activities that have an impact on the environment, the institutional space of the relevant authorities and policy instruments, and also the cultural space of the values of, and interactions between, different social groups within and across nations.

Time is also a crucial dimension, and resource, of policy-making in general and of integration in particular. Mismatch between the timing of ecosystem deterioration or rehabilitation, of political decision-making, of scientific research, of economic investments and of changes in societal attitudes and behaviour, are frequently observed in the field of environment protection and represent potential barriers to the achievement of sustainable development. A different sense of urgency shapes the action of different individuals and organizations with regard to the tackling of environmental issues and other problems. Integrating sustainable development objectives into all sectors of policy-making and economic activities requires the capacity to find, and the possibility of finding, a balance between the different timing of environmental and development processes as perceived by the relevant social actors.

Organization

As mentioned earlier, the territorial competences of authorities in charge of environment protection and other environmentally relevant matters do not always match with the affected environment or the sources of environmental damage. Several combinations are possible. First, local authorities may want to enact legislation on urban pollution or other local matters but lack the fiscal competence and resources to implement them since these competences are centralized at the national level. Second, national authorities may have competences on environmental protection matters but be unable to address trans-boundary problems. Third, supranational or international authorities may be granted the power to issue environmental legislation but not the competence or the practical instruments to foster compliance or guarantee implementation.

The principle of subsidiarity is very important in this respect, but it is only partly suited to address the problem of the mismatch between levels of authority and levels of environmental pressure and damage. Ambiguities related to the interpretation of what is the best level of action are often used to reinforce national sovereignty in the face of EU competences, or vice versa. Issue orientation can complement subsidiarity and enhance the identification and implementation of organizational forms of policy integration or inter-policy co-operation (Knoepfel 1995) at each – and across – all relevant levels: between local and national authorities and between different Ministers of the same country; between them and the corresponding authorities of other countries; and between them and the EU institutions. Cases such as the international actions taken to protect the Mediterranean and the Baltic Sea prove that such inter-policy co-operation within and beyond the EU is feasible. They also show, however, that effective integration of sustainable development objectives into all sectoral policies cannot be achieved through organizational design alone. Specific instruments aimed at facilitating integration by favouring dialogue between various stakeholders, exchanging information on implementation problems, pooling technical resources and allowing the adaptation of previous policies in the face of technical and socio-economic change are also needed. Initiatives launched within the framework of the Fifth Environmental Action Programme, such as the General Consultative Forum on the Environment, the Implementation Network and the Policy Review Group are useful steps in this direction.

Instruments

The opposition between direct regulation and economic instruments tended to dominate the debate on environmental policy instruments in the mid-1980s. More recently the need to broaden the range of policy instruments, rather than substituting one with another, has been stressed. Such broadening – a pillar of the Fifth Environmental Action Programme – includes the adoption of authority instruments (regulation), incentive instruments (including economic instruments and voluntary agreements), capacity instruments (information, education, research) and participatory/consultative fora. Packages of instruments have been suggested to address specific issues. Regarding climate change, for instance, a package including the decision to stabilize EU CO_2 emissions, the fostering of energy efficiency through research and development and financial incentives and the proposals of a CO_2/energy tax (also measures to reduce CO_2 emissions from cars) has been formulated.

As a result of learning from the difficulties and failures in the implementation of national and EU environmental legislation, economic instruments have been adopted in several EU member-states and formulated at the European level. However, implementation difficulties (beside difficulties related to their enactment) have also been encountered with regard to economic instruments, as a result of which it would be unsound to contrast 'hard-to-implement legislation' with 'self-enforcing economic instruments'. A closer look at implementation difficulties shows that several factors hamper the use of policy instruments. These include administrative capacity, technological developments and distributive implications. The relevance of these factors differs for different policy instruments. For instance, administrative capacity, including technical and economic resources, monitoring and control competences, influences not only the way legislation is implemented but also whether taxes or charges are actually paid. Distributive aspects of policy instruments, aspects that are at the core of the perception that there exists an environment/development trade-off, deserve special attention when discussing the integration of sustainable development objectives into sectoral policies.

Distributive elements

Burden-sharing (that is, sharing the economic and social costs of environmental protection or other measures) and its less-often used positive counterpart benefit-sharing (resulting from improved environmental quality and other quality of life improvements) are crucial for the operationalization and integration of sustainable development objectives into policy-making. In fact, the EU has already recognized the importance of addressing distributive issues when dealing with such different matters as agriculture subsidies, fisheries quotas and the size and allocation of the Structural Funds as well as environmental problems. The debate on the Large Combustion Plant Directive, aimed at addressing the acidification problem by controlling SO_2 emissions from industrial sources, is a case in point: agreement on that directive could only be reached by addressing distributive issues through a 'bubble' approach wherein European targets were to be reached on the basis of different national targets corresponding to different levels of economic development and environmental vulnerability (Haigh 1989). The issue of burden-sharing also shaped the formulation of the CO_2/energy-tax proposal (Liberatore 1995) and is likely to influence further developments in EU environmental policy. Since the costs and benefits of integrating environmental factors into sectoral policies are usually unequally distributed within and across sectors, countries and social groups, resistance to integration can only be overcome if solutions to distributive dilemmas are found.

INTEGRATION VERSUS DILUTION

The concept of integration assumes a form of reciprocity. It presupposes that the different components have similar importance and weight. If one of the components is much weaker, it is likely to be diluted into, rather than being integrated with, the others. With regard to the policy process, this means that if one policy area is much weaker than others, its objectives and instruments risk dilution rather than integration. Of course, saying that a policy is weaker or stronger than others is a relative judgement and depends on the evaluation criteria used. If one measures the relative strength of policies in terms of budget or personnel, it will be obvious that EU environmental policy is one of the weakest policies; but if one considers policy outputs such as legislation and the development of new competences and institutions, then EU environmental policy will appear rather influential. These aspects co-exist and indicate that the integration of environmental factors into sectoral policies is an open challenge.

A measurement of the degree of integration or dilution (or no relationship at all) goes beyond the scope of this contribution. However, some indicators of integration can be suggested to facilitate future assessments of success or failure in achieving integration. Indicators of integration include the following: first, whether and to what degree (frequency, scope, depth) environmental impact assessments (EIA) are conducted during the planning of activities, *ex-post-facto* or never; second, whether consultations between different local, national and EU authorities having competences on environment and environment-related matters are frequent, unusual or lacking, and whether these consultations are just symbolic or whether forms of co-decision emerge; third, whether compatibility with environmental legislation is assessed when issuing legislation in other fields; fourth, whether evaluation of policy, research and economic performance includes the evaluation of the environmental consequences of policies, research and economic activities; and, finally, whether funding is made available for sustainable development initiatives in each sector. Table 5.3 summarizes the way these integration indicators can be used to evaluate the integration, dilution or non-relationship of environmental and sustainable development policy objectives (X) and other sectoral policies (Y).

Table 5.3   Indicators of integration between environmental/sustainable development objectives and sectoral policies

Integration indicator	Integration between X and Y	Dilution of X in Y	No relation between X and Y
EIA	frequent, in-depth, ex-ante	occasional superficial, ex-post-facto	no EIA
consultations	frequent, 'co-decision'	occasional, 'symbolic'	no consultation
compatibility of legislation	systematically assessed	occasionally assessed	not assessed
performance evaluation	systematically includes environmental aspects	occasionally includes environmental aspects	does not include environmental aspects
funding	substantial	marginal	no funding

CONSTRAINTS ON INTEGRATION

The main constraints on, or even barriers to, integration include prevailing short-term perspectives, lack of vision with regard to the possible consequences of continuing unsustainable development paths, lack of capacity and difficulties in handling distributive issues.

Short-term perspectives lead to discounting the future in economic, political and even psychological terms. Electoral campaigns, companies/investments or shopping habits tend to discount not only the distant future of unknown future generations, but even the near future of present generations. When discussing the integration of sustainable development objectives into policies as diverse as agriculture, energy or tourism, the risk of diluting integration over time is high due to the strong tendency to focus on short-term perspectives in all fields of economic production and in consumption behaviour.

Lack of vision refers to the difficulty of appreciating the link between present behaviour and future conditions and the relationships – including cumulative effects – between different types of human pressures on the environment. It also refers to the difficulty of redefining problems and options in the light of technological, socio-economic and ecological changes. While they are often accused of being 'just plans', the Fifth Environmental Action Programme, Agenda 21 and the various national plans for sustainable development may provide visions which can guide more specific actions.

Insufficient capacity can hamper *any* vision becoming reality. Different kinds of capacity must be taken into account with regard to the integration of environmental factors into the various policy sectors and across sectors, including administrative, institutional, technical, scientific and economic capacity. Capacity is a relative and dynamic factor: it can be learned and improved over time. However, back-ground conditions or vested interests can impede institutional development, the utilization of aspects of scientific evidence and the availability or otherwise of technological or financial resources. This is crucial in handling asymmetries, and the related distributive problems, between different social groups and countries in the EU, and beyond Europe as well.

Distributive problems within and across sectors, social groups and countries can generate conflicts that endanger the very notion of sustainable development and the possibility of integration. Under-estimating those conflicts or postponing the handling of distributive problems can lead to difficulties in reaching agreement on the definition of issues and on the instruments needed to address them.

OPPORTUNITIES FOR INTEGRATION

On the basis of current policy developments, some opportunities can be identified to foster the integration of sustainable development objectives into policy-making. They include the development of concepts and procedures for shared responsibility, diffusion of mutual-gain approaches and instances of policy learning.

Shared, but differentiated, responsibility refers to the need to take into account the responsibility of various actors in damaging and in protecting the environment and the involvement of all the stakeholders in policy formulation and implementation. Shared responsibility is an emerging principle of EU environmental policy. During UNCED, representatives of developing countries and several NGOs emphasized the phrase '*differentiated* responsibility' to account for the current diversity within and between countries in the use and depletion of natural resources and in the availability of means to protect the environment. Means to implement the idea of shared, but differentiated, responsibility include consultative fora, provision for technology sharing/transfer, mechanisms to allocate the costs of environmental protection on the basis of the 'polluter pays' principle, taking into account different levels of economic development and information diffusion to enable all relevant stakeholders to take part in the process of policy formulation, and so on. Some of these instruments are being used in the EU and in the broader international context.

One of the difficulties involved in putting the idea of shared, but differentiated, responsibility into practice is the required shift in the perception and behaviour of some of the stakeholders who are used to a relationship of conflict with other stakeholders and find it hard to regard them as 'partners'. As pointed out in studies on conflict resolution in the field of the environment, acknowledging the different interests and views rather than attempting to understate them is an important prerequisite to understanding the causes of the conflicts and to allowing dialogue and co-operation (Susskind 1994). Integrating sustainable development objectives into all policy domains involves the ability and willingness of different stakeholders within each sector, and across sectors and locations, to co-operate while having different positions and responsibilities. Initiatives such as the Business Council for Sustainable Development and the European Partners for the Environment, including business, NGOs and governmental representatives, indicate that some organizations are willing to move in such a direction.

Mutual gains and win–win approaches attempt to facilitate co-operative problem-solving by identifying options that involve benefits for all or most parties. In the current EU debate on sustainable development, emphasis is often put on the so-called 'double dividend', that is, the possibility of improving environmental quality and at the same time improving international competitiveness and increasing employment. Measures aimed at improving energy efficiency, for example, are regarded as leading to reciprocal advantages for energy users (who consume and pay less), producers of energy-efficient technologies and those in charge of and/or interested in environmental protection. Demand-side and supply-side measures in the field of transport could lead to a modal shift that in turn would benefit users and providers of public transport (the latter including public companies as well as train and/or bus producer industries) besides contributing to improving environmental quality. It must be noted that while certain sectors, social groups or countries may find mutual gains, there can still be some losers. In other words, looking for mutual-gain solutions does not mean that they always exist and for everybody; rather, the possibility exists of identifying options that could otherwise be neglected and thus unnecessarily increase the costs of the dramatic changes required by the implementation of sustainable development.

Policy learning refers to the ability of policy-makers to draw lessons from their own previous experience, from the experience of others (in other policy sectors, institutions or countries, for example) and from technological and scientific progress, and to apply these lessons in the formulation and implementation of new policies or in the modification of current policies. Basic requirements for learning are the circulation of information, the ability to reflect on and evaluate past events and performance, and the existence of background conditions that allow pluralism concerning potential sources of lessons. Integrating sustainable development objectives into sectoral policies involves the possibility of learning from previous experience with regard to both environmental policy and other relevant policies, whether in the EU or its member-states, or even in countries and organizations outside Europe.

Certainly, an effort to learn from experience can be found in the review process that led to the publication of the Commission's Interim Review on the implementation of the Fifth Environmental Action Programme (CEC 1994b). More specific instances of policy learning can be found in the Fifth Environmental Action Programme's emphasis on the need to broaden the range of policy instruments given previous experience, including failures, in implementing environmental regulation, and the emergence of the integration principle. The latter represents an attempt to overcome the shortcomings of the strictly sectoral approach of early EC environmental policy that treated separately the various environmental sectors, such as air, water and soil, by addressing the economic activities that cause environmental degradation. In turn, integration can be regarded as involving a two-way learning process: integrating environmental considerations into all sectors of policy-making involves changes in these sectors, but also in the way environmental goals and instruments are set and implemented.

CONCLUSIONS

The integration of environmental and sustainable development objectives into all areas of EU policy-making is a challenging task. Institutional arrangements, economic interests and models, political strategies and cultural values are at stake, and profound changes are needed to implement such a task. While being officially endorsed in policy and legal documents, including the Maastricht Treaty, integration is facing various barriers that could lead to the dilution rather than the integration of sustainable development objectives into EU sectoral policies and across sectors. At the same time, opportunities can also be identified, including the exploration of the interrelationship and potential mutual gains between environmental and development objectives. Whether the EU will expand and deepen its role in the broader European and international context of sustainable development will depend on its ability to value these opportunities and move towards a new, rather than simply larger, model of development.

REFERENCES

Axelrod, R. (1994) 'Subsidiarity and environmental policy in the European Community', *International Environmental Affairs* 6(2): 115–132.

Baldock, D. *et al.* (1992) *The Integration of Environmental Protection Requirements into the Definition and Implementation of other EC Policies*, London: IEEP.

CEC (1983) 'Council resolution adopting the Third Environmental Action Programme', *Official Journal of the European Communities*, C46, 17.2.83.

—— (1986) 'EP resolution on agriculture and the environment', *Official Journal of the European Communities*, C68, 24.3.86.

—— (1987) 'Council resolution adopting the Fourth Environmental Action Programme', *Official Journal of the European Communities*, C70, 18.3.87.

—— (1989) *Report on the Environment and the Internal Market*, Brussels: European Commission, DG XI.

—— (1991) 'EP resolution on transport and the environment', *Official Journal of the European Communities*, C267, 14.10.91.

—— (1993a) *Towards Sustainability: A European Community Programme of Policy and Action in Relation to the Environment and Sustainable Development*, Luxembourg: Office for Official Publications of the European Communities.

—— (1993b) 'EP resolution on the incorporation of environmental considerations in the Structural Funds', *Official Journal of the European Communities*, C42, 15.2.93.

—— (1994a) White Paper, *Growth, Competitiveness and Employment: The Challenges and Ways Forward into the 21st Century*, Luxembourg: Office for Official Publications of the European Communities.

—— (1994b) *Interim Review of Implementation of the European Community Programme of Policy and Action in Relation to the Environment and Sustainable Development 'Towards Sustainability'*, CIM (94) 453 final, Brussels.

—— (1995a) *The European Councils: Conclusions of the Presidency 1992–1994*, Brussels: European Commission, DG X.

—— (1995b) *Report of the Group of Independent Experts on Legislative and Administrative Simplification*, COM (95) 288 final.

CNE (Climate Network Europe), EEB (European Environment Bureau), T & E (Transport & Environment), FoE (Friends of the Earth), Greenpeace, WWF (World Wildlife Fund) (1995) *Greening of the Treaty II: Sustainable Development in a Democratic Union: Proposals for the 1996 Intergovernmental Conference*, Utrecht: Stichting Natur en Milieu.

Dehousse, R. (1992) *Does Subsidiarity Really Matter?*, EUI Working Paper, no. 92/32, Florence: European University Institute.

DRI *et al.* (1994) *Potential Benefits of Integration of Environmental and Economic Policies. An Incentive-based Approach to Policy Integration*, Luxembourg: Graham & Trotmand/Office for Official Publications of the European Communities.

Haigh, N. (1989) *EEC Environmental Policy and Great Britain*, 2nd edn, Harlow: Longman.

Knoepfel, P. (1995) 'New institutional arrangements for a new generation of environmental policy instruments: intra- and inter-policy cooperation', in B. Dente (ed.) *Environmental Policy in Search of New Instruments*, Dordrecht: Kluwer Academic Publishers.

Kraemer, L. (1992) *EEC Treaty and Environmental Protection*, London: Sweet & Maxwell.

Liberatore, A. (1992) 'Towards sustainability? Economic integration and environment protection in the European Community', *Current Politics and Economics of Europe* 2(4): 275–287.

—— (1995) 'Arguments, assumptions and the choice of policy instruments. The case of the debate on the CO_2/energy tax in the European Community', in B. Dente (ed.) *Environmental Policy in Search of New Instruments*, Dordrecht: Kluwer Academic Publishers.

Majone, G. (1989) *Evidence, Argument and Persuasion in the Policy Process*, New Haven, CT, and London: Yale University Press.

Ministry of Housing, Physical Planning and Environment (1989) *National Environmental Policy Plan*, The Hague.

O'Riordan, T. and Cameron, J. (eds) (1994) *Interpreting the Precautionary Principle*, London: Earthscan.

Pearce, D. *et al.* (1993) *Blueprint 3: Measuring Sustainable Development*, London: Earthscan.
Susskind, L. (1994) *Environmental Diplomacy*, New York and Oxford: Oxford University Press.
Weale, A. (1993) 'Ecological modernization and the integration of European environmental policy', in J. Liefferink *et al.* (eds) *European Integration and Environmental Policy*, London: Belhaven Press.

6 Sustainable development in Mediterranean Europe?

Interactions between European, national and sub-national levels[1]

Geoffrey Pridham and Dimitrios Konstadakopulos

Protecting the environment cannot really be achieved unless an environmental dimension becomes integrated into other policy sectors and in particular into economic policy. That is the basic message of sustainable development, as defined by the European Union in its Fifth Environmental Action Programme (EAP) and the Maastricht Treaty. This ambitious aim has demanding implications for policy-making, requiring constant strategic planning and concerted effort by a variety of different actors. As such, sustainable development presents a formidable challenge to the countries of Mediterranean Europe given their reputation for policy ineffectiveness and political corruption, as well as for administrative lethargy and defective policy co-ordination. Ultimately, sustainable development has systemic implications in the operation of environmental policy, for its consequences are not only administrative, political and economic but also social and cultural.

The Mediterranean member-states of the EU are all countries in which the state has been overdeveloped and has played a dominant role in the economy, with consequently close links between political concerns and economic interests. Furthermore, the prevalence of consumerist values in these recently modernized countries presents a powerful obstacle to the spread of environmental values (Pridham 1994: 81). The outcome has been, at best, an ambivalent response on their part to environmental problems in recent years, a period which has seen increased intervention by international organizations, above all by the European Union, in this field (La Spina and Sciortino 1993: 217). In all probability sustainable development will at best have only a slow and very gradual impact in redirecting and reprioritizing the environmental policies of these states. Concentrating on the Southern members, however, does allow us to measure the realistic chances of the EU as a whole pushing for sustainable development.

This Chapter therefore seeks to show how far the states of Mediterranean Europe have responded to the concept of sustainable development and also the different problems of applying it in policy practice. In view of their envisaged difficulties in adapting to this rather new policy approach, we will focus on the policy patterns that have defined and shaped their environmental agendas over the past few years and whether or not these favour the emergence of sustainable development. The Rio Summit (1992) recognized the supranational (EU) and the sub-national as two levels of crucial importance in moving towards forms of sustainable development. We also look, therefore, at the policy processes and institutional procedures of the three countries in question. The section 'Environmental policy evolution and policy thinking in the European context' (pp. 128–137) is concerned essentially with how far the three countries of the South are willing to meet the challenge of sustainable development; while the sections 'Institutional constraints and policy performance' (pp. 137–142) and 'Below the state: the role of sub-national authorities' (pp. 143–148) focus on their ability to do so.

ENVIRONMENTAL POLICY EVOLUTION AND POLICY THINKING IN THE EUROPEAN CONTEXT

Policy patterns and priorities

The generally low priority often accorded to environmental policy in the past by the governments of these countries is not entirely surprising since they – Italy being a partial exception – arrived late on the environmental policy scene compared with the more developed and politically advanced countries of northern Europe. Evidence is either explicit in public statements from key government leaders and relevant portfolio holders or implicit in the high priority accorded policy interests commonly seen as in conflict with environmental concerns, notably developmental and especially public works (Pridham 1994: 86).

In Italy, for example, the policy approach has traditionally been dominated by response to crisis or emergency, leading invariably to a flurry of hasty legislation via decree. As a result, environmental legislation has become quite extensive and very sectoral and specialist, producing a complexity of its own, but this does not necessarily indicate policy priority. Introducing the first national report on the state of the environment in Italy in 1989, Giorgio Ruffolo, Minister of the Environment, criticized his country's obsession with the gross national product and its 'basic cultural resistance to accepting the idea of sustainable development': 'Environmentalist policy is conceived still, to a large degree, as something external, peripheral and sectoral with respect to the production and consumption processes' (Ministero dell'Ambiente 1989: 37).

Similarly, in Spain the overriding concern has been high unemployment, thus making it difficult to break traditional thinking about the environment and employment generation as being antagonistic (Ministerio de Obras Públicas y Urbanismo 1989b: 220). In Madrid, the possibility of a new direction in environmental policy has also been inhibited by a policy style that has tended to be closed and cumbersomely bureaucratic without effective channels for consultation with interests involved, including environmental (Aguilar 1991: 1). This outlook and practice have clearly strengthened resistance to ideas of sustainable development in policy thinking, as revealed in the early 1990s at the European level when Spain virulently opposed the notion of introducing a carbon tax, concerned about the possible effects on her industrial interests (*Financial Times*, 28 January 1992). At about the same time Greece resisted European Commission proposals on restricting the use of CFCs, these being widely used in poorer Southern states where alternative technology is expensive (*Independent*, 22 February 1992).

At best, we are looking at incremental rather than rational styles in these countries, with a marked tendency for policy to be reactive and not proactive. In Greece, serious measures first began to be taken in the early 1980s, but after a couple of years interest declined, particularly once the PASOK government reprioritized developmental over environmental concerns. Greek government interest has varied over time, affected by the extent of the visibility of certain environmental problems, their relevance for party-political debate and the competitive significance of other policy priorities (Pridham *et al.* 1995: 256–262). Like Italy, Greece has a profusion of environmental measures – and the same is true of Spain if we include regional legislation. The predominant characteristic of Greek legislation has been the regulatory approach, using restrictions, limitations, licensing and the setting of standards. This profusion of measures has resulted in intense sectoralism in Greece and an absence of coherence, which became very apparent during the process of harmonization with EU directives in the 1980s (Pridham *et al.* 1995: 255).

Such a background of fragmented legislation in these countries presents special problems for the adoption of bolder approaches such as the Single European Act's emphasis on integrated pollution control and the preference for the precautionary principle and preventive action in the Maastricht Treaty. For instance, legislative fragmentation affects implementation when it is delegated to lower levels, which can exercise considerable discretion in the way policies are interpreted and acted upon. This implies that alternative views of sustainable development may well emerge and determine policy outcome.

Nevertheless, the European Union has increasingly become the primary motive force behind environmental policy activity and policy change in southern Europe. The stimulus to environmental legislation from Brussels is even true of Italy, a longstanding member-state, noted for 'the absolute prevalence of rules which owe their inspiration to the EC rather than the national level' (Capria 1991: 1). The clear predominance of the European motive behind national environmental legislation is above all evident in the case of Spain, which joined the EU only in 1986, five years behind Greece. The government in Madrid spent the first few years applying a whole backlog of EC environmental laws, basically for the political reasons of wanting to participate fully in Europe (Ministerio de Obras Públicas y Urbanismo 1989a: 245). As a high official of the Ministry of Public Works (environmental policy department) explained:

> we approved en bloc all the Community directives on the environment without any time or other reservation . . . as we said to ourselves, we would not study the economic cost: it was necessary to approve it and then we will see, and that caused us much effort . . . now it is a matter of knowing the economic cost of measures . . . [we did this] because politically it was important to enter the Common Market . . . our only possibility of stability and political change was the Common Market.
>
> (Ros Vicent, Madrid, October 1992)

This was a clear case of political will being able to push through environmental agreements.

At the same time, the EU has also been regarded in the South as an attractive source of funding for developmental programmes. Greece, notably, was instrumental in launching the Integrated Mediterranean Programmes (IMPs) in the mid-1980s. The IMPs, however, identified the environmental action as merely a subsidiary activity to be achieved largely through other sectoral programmes. Only from the early 1990s has the principle of integrating environmental with developmental concerns begun to influence EU programmes, including special ones aimed at assisting the Southern states such as the Environmental Regional Programme (ENVIREG), the Mediterranean Strategy and

Action Plan (MEDSPA), not to mention the Cohesion Fund. But the effects of these programmes have been very limited so far. In Spain's case, as admitted above, no thought was given in advance to what adopting so much environmental legislation entailed. In the past few years Madrid has adopted a hard-nosed emphasis on material interests, most noticeable in Spanish threats over the agreement on the Cohesion Fund. While the Fund includes investment in environmental infrastructure in the South, Spanish interest has decidedly been in the opportunities this offers for development. The deadlines set by EMU have focused the attention of governments in the South on such matters as convergence criteria and further economic growth. In Athens, growing concern over Greece's ability to keep pace with European economic and monetary targets has tended to reduce the attention paid to the environment.

Finally, attitudes in the South over EU environmental policy have been somewhat coloured by a certain anti-Northern feeling, although this is diffused and cannot be said to dominate policy approaches. There is a sense that European environmental policy is essentially Northern in outlook, and specifically German in its emphasis on uniform standards. For instance, the strict German packaging-recycling scheme became a highly controversial benchmark for the rest of the EU. Of the three Mediterranean countries, such feeling has been most marked in Spain, reinforced by the view that European policy neglects the particular sectoral interests of the South in the environment. One Spanish official described it as:

> a policy which has concentrated more on problems of industrial pollution and measures to combat it, than on programmes on the assessment, protection and recovery of soil, flora and fauna, and making proper use of resources to avoid the progressive impoverishment and waste of nature.
>
> (cited in Baldock and Long 1987: 59)

Such differences over environmental priorities carry a potential for divergent ideas when it comes to applying sustainable development in practice.

Sustainable development and policy thinking in Mediterranean Europe

Recent policy patterns in the three Southern countries cast much doubt over the prospects for sustainable development there. And yet there is also a distinct tendency for international pressures to be very significant, if not at times decisive. Moreover, in the last couple of years, various signs of policy innovation and movement have occurred in parallel to and partly as a consequence of the Rio Summit and more energetic discussion at EU level of the need for sustainable development.

That the Rio Summit has given momentum to new policy thinking in the South seems fairly clear, although no doubt there is an element of paying official lip service to ideas which have become fashionable. The Greek government's national report for Rio made suitable reference to concepts like the 'standstill principle', 'abatement at source', the 'polluter and user pays' principle, the precautionary principle, application of best practicable means, and the integration of environmental aspects into sectoral policies (Ministry of the Environment, Physical Planning and Public Works 1991: 127). In Madrid – again taking government statements – there has been a rather more vigorous response to Rio. The Spanish government acknowledged that the Earth Summit of Rio obliges it to 'redesign its model of development, to explain it and discuss it with all social and economic actors in every forum, in the form of a national strategy for the environment and sustainable development' (Ministerio de Obras Públicas, Transportes y Medio Ambiente 1993: 27).

Whether a value change is underway in government policies is not really clear. Rather, the evidence is at this stage ambiguous as to how far ideas of sustainable development have begun to percolate through policy-making circles at the national level. A survey of elite interviews in Spain during 1992–1994 shows that the concept of sustainable development was mentioned more often in those carried out in spring 1994 than in those carried out in autumn 1992. In Madrid, a high official in the Ministry of Public Works, Transport and Environment (water quality subdepartment) said he had been hearing the concept of sustainable development around the corridors of power for 'some years' and that 'the influence of Brussels has furthered this concept at the national level' (Gonzalez Nicolas, Madrid, April 1994). He indicated that a few key officials in the Ministry were important here, including one soon afterwards appointed as head of the new European Environmental Agency. Another high official in the department of environmental policy in the same Ministry took a more sceptical line. He recognized that the idea of sustainable development was very present in government circles, but 'at the theoretical level', for 'all are talking about sustainable development' within the national government, also in regional governments as well as in conferences on the environment – a tendency evident since Rio – but the problem was no effective action (Ros Vicent, Madrid, April 1994). Similarly, in Greece an official with long experience in a government planning institute noted with respect to sustainable development that 'people [in government circles] are informed, they know what it is; people have this kind of consciousness and there are some heroic efforts to care for the environment, to allocate funds, but when you come to implementation, when you come to management . . . then everything breaks down' (Katochianou, Athens, November 1992).

From responses in elite interviews it was not at all clear that high officials had a considered understanding of sustainable development and its full implications; and in not a few cases they resorted to very pragmatic and rather modest interpretations of how it might be reflected in policy. What can nevertheless be noted is that Rio gave some impetus to the notion of sustainable development in southern Europe. This was a hopeful sign for the EU commitment to it, so far as these countries were concerned. But whether sensitivity to international trends in the South produced more than rhetorical enthusiasm remained to be seen.

An emerging strategy in environmental policy?

Relevant responses to sustainable development might be categorized as either strategic (macro-responses), involving a deliberate movement towards sustainable development in national environmental policy; or partial or very sectoral but in sympathy with sustainable objectives (micro-responses). We are concerned here with the former, but will consider the latter below in the section entitled 'Below the state' (pp. 143–148).

The effort made in Italy at the start of the 1990s to act strategically was the first serious example in southern Europe to break with the pattern of a largely reactive response to the environment. Ruffolo became insistent on shifting to a preventive approach and developed three- and even ten-year programmes to back up his intention. He also argued for increasing environmental expenditure, for enlarging environmental legislation and for Italy to take a more activist line at the international level to confront problems of ozone depletion and the greenhouse effect (Ministero dell'Ambiente 1992: preamble). The Italian government began soon afterwards to think about eco-taxes and to promote recycling schemes and voluntary agreements with major industrial groups (Lewanski 1993: 13). This fitted with the argument, made in the Fifth EAP, that sustainable development required 'a broader mix of instruments' and not just regulatory methods.

'Ecological taxes' appear to have had an important role in the strategy of the Italian Ministry of Environment. The first such tax was levied on plastic shopping bags in 1989 and it caused a 34 per cent decrease in their use (Liberatore and Lewanski 1990: 40). The Italian, Greek and Spanish governments have embarked on various economic instruments, including incentives to use clean fuels such as lead-free petrol. Greece imposed a fuel tax and the proceeds go to an environmental fund. Tax relief was offered when purchasing a new car with anti-pollution technology meeting EU standards, and additional tax relief was available when a clean car was bought and an old car was withdrawn from circulation (Pelecasi and Skourtos 1992: 101–104). While redistribution may occur through funds transferred to pollution control equipment, such taxes have a bias towards short-term solutions and they do not create incentives for a change in modal choice in the transport sector.

More interventionist approaches to environmental policy-making by the three Mediterranean member-states, based on the Fifth EAP and assisted by EU funds, are starting to emerge. First, they are becoming less reactive and more proactive, with an emphasis on long-term planning. Broadly speaking, sustainable development may be seen as involving setting targets for key environmental indicators and then influencing economic activity to meet those targets. Here, planning requires a high degree of state intervention and co-ordination. This was highlighted in the first three-year environmental management programme in Italy, while, following the second programme, special planning and development programmes were instituted for the Mezzogiorno (to enhance environmental protection infrastructures) because of developmental differences between certain Italian regions (OECD 1994: 93). There have been some efforts, although only recently, to improve policy co-ordination across different levels of government, notably in Spain.

Second, a more strategic approach looking at the environmental implications of sectoral policies has begun to emerge. To make sustainable development workable, governments will need to co-ordinate policies for specific sectors of the economy. In Spain there are now various interministerial bodies to facilitate a coherent policy, such as the Economic and Social Commission, which deals with all economic and environmental issues, and the National Climate Commission, which, with the participation of various ministries, is responsible, for example, for making sure that energy policy is not contrary to forestry policy and vice versa (Mingot, Madrid, October 1992). This change is also evident in government action at the EU level. For example, the Greek government during its EU Presidency in 1994 promoted long-term thinking on two environmental issues: management of coastal areas; and tourism and the environment. Tourism is immensely important for the Greek economy and for that reason the Greeks are keen on the notion of sustainable tourism. They convened an informal Council of Ministers meeting to discuss this special subject in May of that year (Kourteli, Brussels, April 1994).

Third, a start has been made on integrating spatial economic planning, land-use planning and environmental protection. For example, Spain has since 1982, and particularly after the adoption of the Law for the Coasts in 1988, regenerated many kilometres of beaches and promenades, stopped building in coastal areas and protected the littoral environment, which became particularly degraded during the 1970s (Osorio, Madrid, April 1994). The Law of the Coasts is considered to be one of the most advanced pieces of legislation in the EU for the protection of coastal areas. In Greece, the Minister of the Environment, Physical Planning and Public Works from 1993 included among his priorities for the environment the creation of a National Land Registry, an issue that had eluded the Greek state for 150 years, Greece and Albania being the only European countries without a National Land Registry (*To Vima*, 31 July 1994).

The relationship between economic and environmental interests has begun to change, albeit slowly. Changes have been most evident in Italy, where large industry is now taking a positive line towards the environment, after having, in the past, been implicated in a series of industrial accidents such as at Seveso. Such major firms as Ferruzzi-Montedison, Fiat, ENI and ENEL have invested considerable amounts in environmental protection and several large firms publish annual reports on this (OECD 1994: 106). The significant small and medium-sized enterprise sector has, however, been slow to adapt – in Italy as in the other countries. Change is also noticeable in Spain. According to an official of the Madrid region:

> although still there is conflict, all business associations are collaborating to a great extent; they are having exhibitions, conferences where the amount of participating companies is very high and all of them now hold environmental meetings, company executives register on courses incorporating environmental education etc. There is a radical change and companies now incorporate the environment in their economic policies.
>
> (Hortas Perez, Madrid, April 1994)

Other evidence suggests that this is indeed true, but that it is so far a limited tendency. Nevertheless, if there is a change in mentality on behalf of industry it is caused by two factors: first, state regulations oblige companies to comply with environmental legislation; and, second, commercial considerations have an influence, as increasingly consumers prefer products which respect the environment (Hortas Perez, Madrid, April 1994). Similarly, the Greek Minister of Industry has argued that competitiveness should be based on production methods friendly to the environment, for ensuring a high level of environmental protection improves chances for economic competitiveness (*To Vima*, 10 July 1994).

Small companies are helped by economic programmes geared towards small and medium-sized enterprises, in the form of subsidies, in order to improve their environmental infrastructures. In the Region of Madrid subsidies are awarded after environmental auditing has taken place (Hortas Perez, Madrid, April 1994). Such environmental auditing is not compulsory, but has been practised by the Region of Madrid since 1989. Although it is expensive, nevertheless up to the end of 1992 over 100 industrial units had been audited (García *et al.* 1994: 315). There are some signs of change in the mentality of Spanish industry, especially from the subsidiaries of British, German and Dutch companies. 'Such companies are the motors of change for Spanish industry . . . and is so because these international companies have different experiences in other countries' (Alvarez, Madrid, October 1992). Altogether, this evidence may be seen as pointing to a certain growth in ecological modernization.

Apparently, industries can be persuaded to act to prevent environmental degradation only when their economic interests are shown to be directly threatened. As García, Lerma and Santos put it in their study of nine European countries:

> In all countries of the study the picture is the same: the environment becomes an issue for industry through the combination of regulations adopted by the administration, the pressures from the environmental movement and from the attention paid to the pollution by the mass communication media.
>
> (García *et al.* 1994: 194)

We turn to these latter pressures in the next section.

The evidence discussed above of changing attitudes towards sustainable development among political and economic actors is significant in itself. It represents a qualitative departure from the common if not exclusive thinking in policy circles in these countries in the mid-1980s. But the signs are that this new thinking is not yet widespread and is probably not firmly rooted. It can in any case be misleading to attribute much meaning to statements of policy-makers per se, for there is, among other things, a tactical element involved. Government circles in these countries show, to differing degrees (especially in Greece), a sensitivity to international opinion and an inclination to please Brussels.

At the same time, too much emphasis should not be placed on elite attitudes as autonomous. Adopting Putnam's notion of a 'pulling' environment and 'pushing' attitude (Putnam 1973: 3), we include within the first the pressures from the EU and the international economy for a more eco-friendly approach. Then the possibility arises for interaction with national elites and some scope for change, all the more since in these three countries there are not, as there are in one or two other member-states, ideological reservations about increased European integration. If such outside pressures combine with growing acceptance of sustainable ideas among economic and social actors, then some reinforcement of the limited and slow policy innovations of these past couple of years is likely.

INSTITUTIONAL CONSTRAINTS AND POLICY PERFORMANCE

We now turn to the capacity of the Southern countries for moving towards sustainable development, looking first at the national levels and in the next section at the sub-national authorities. We focus on the structural problems of environmental management and relate these to system effectiveness and political commitment.

The record of these three member-states in carrying out European legislation is, while varied, not such as to encourage confidence in their ability to measure up to more demanding policies of sustainable development. Italy had consistently for many years the worst record of all EU countries in incorporating legislation from Brussels, although parliamentary procedural reform in 1991 produced a major improvement. Spain has, on the other hand, boasted an implementation rate comparable to that of the Northern countries, while Greece has been rather better at formal than practical implementation. By far the most serious problem for the Southern countries has indeed been practical implementation. They may be identified as a difficult case in the light of the number of referrals for infringements made to the European Court of Justice (Pridham and Cini 1993).

Institutional structures and procedures

Ultimately, much depends on the administrative and political competence of individual member-states in carrying through legislation in
the EU. Despite having been granted a stronger legal role in the environmental field, the Union still has weak powers of co-ordination at
the levels of incorporation, implementation and enforcement. As was
noted in the mid-1980s, 'the primary competences are vested in
member-states . . . the political and administrative systems of member-
states are so diverse that great variations in the incorporation,
implementation and enforcement of environmental directives necessarily result' (Rehbinder and Stewart 1985: 232). For this reason, the
EU process cannot realistically be confined to action simply within the
formal European institutions:

> rather it embraces a network of relationships and contacts among
> national policy-makers in the different member-states . . . can be
> analysed only as the tip of a much larger iceberg formed by the
> domestic contexts that set constraints on each member government.
>
> (Wallace 1977: 33–34).

This lesson must also be pertinent to sustainable development and the
possibilities for applying it in individual countries.

The Southern member-states fall into the less concentrated mode of
administration. The creation of environmental ministries (Italy 1986)
or large ministries which include 'environment' in their title (Greece
1980, Spain belatedly in 1993) has not substantially changed the
picture of fragmentation of environmental responsibilities between a
range of different ministries. Furthermore, the environment ministries
in the South tend to be noticeably smaller than their counterparts in
the Northern member-states, thus reflecting their limited bureaucratic
weight in the different capitals. That is particularly significant, for in
two of the three Southern countries responsibility for the environment
is combined with public works. In countries that are so concerned
about their economic development – and are also known for their
widespread clientelist practices – there may be a special reason why
environmental administration may be held back from expansion or
subjected to reform (Weale *et al.* 1994).

Difficulties stemming from institutional fragmentation may be
neutralized to some degree by effective co-ordination between
ministries involved in the same policy area. But it is here that the
Southern states have been notably deficient. Such co-ordination is
potentially crucial when we look ahead to the prospects for integration

between environmental and other policy concerns, let alone between various ministries involved (often sectorally) in the environmental field. Ministerial rivalry and bureaucratic lethargy have proved powerful. The experience of interministerial committees has been discouraging, for example in Italy, and this did not improve with the establishment there of a special environment ministry. Greece introduced a co-ordination mechanism under the Framework Law of 1986, but this has remained largely a dead letter. There the procedure for adopting European legislation is slow and cumbersome, involving officials from different ministries (Scoullos and Kaberi 1989: 1–2). Of late, there have been some institutional innovations in Spain to improve centre–periphery co-ordination of environmental affairs, but their effectiveness remains to be tested.

Policy infrastructure (policy facilities and expertise resources) strengthens the competence of policy-makers and the chances of effective policy application and innovation. This is particularly true in the environmental field, where, more than in most areas, decisions can depend a great deal on accurate specialist advice. In this respect, the southern European countries are clearly behind the Northern ones, and this dichotomy has had a profound effect on their ability to carry through EU legislation to the point of enforcement. Monitoring facilities exist, but they are often rudimentary and not always reliable. Italy now has quite an extensive system of monitoring, but the problem of reliable data remains (Pridham 1994: 89–90). Some improvements have occurred, notably in Spain, where EU membership was instrumental in the development of a system of data collection as a precondition for policy planning (Pridham 1994: 89). The difficulty has been exacerbated by the absence of effective planning or even of some planning ethos, notably in Greece, where this deficiency has contributed to environmental degradation arising from the application of EU developmental programmes (Pridham 1994: 89).

The scientific problem of establishing cause and effect means that it is difficult to establish responsibility for the externalities produced by polluting activities. It is sometimes seen as better not to act for fear of the uncertainty of effects. This may lead to policy paralysis or, more dangerously, to a tendency to ignore or discount the future risks of present action. In Greece the introduction of cars with catalytic converters has been a controversial issue for some time. Many scientists were reluctant to endorse their use because of the effect on human health (causing cancer) and on the environment from the release of precious metals from cars with catalytic converters (Eleftherotypia, 18 March 1992). The Minister of Health asked the Supreme Scientific

Council to decide on this issue. It recommended that the advantage of clean cars outweighed possible health risks. Nevertheless, it made it clear that more research was necessary in order to decide whether emissions from the new cars were causing cancer or not (Eleftheros Typos, 20 September 1992). There is the additional problem that interpretation of evidence provides ample scope for manipulation and conflict between interests, which inhibits policies promoting sustainable development.

Political commitment and environmental policy

We are concerned here with the kind of political pressures that may serve to strengthen policy commitment in the environmental area, and influence consensus or even concerted action in favour of sustainable development. We look at a series of actors and tendencies that are relevant.

The main political parties in these three countries have tended not to lend a high priority to environmental concerns, save on an ad-hoc basis and usually for electoral motives, when a particular environmental issue is visible or an environmental crisis has occurred. The rise and challenge of Green parties usually compels established parties to give more continual attention to the environment. But their impact has been much weaker in southern than in northern Europe, except in Italy for a time. One fairly recent study of the Italian environment commented that 'the country's main political forces still regard environmental protection as external, peripheral or only partially relevant to the production–distribution–consumption function of society' (Alexander 1991: 106). The systemic crisis which has recently undermined Italy's old parties has not, by and large, benefited environmental concerns.

The Mediterranean member-states have seen a rise in the number of environmental campaign groups over time. It is estimated that approximately 700 of them are based in Spain, probably the same number in Italy and 80 in Greece. Such non-governmental organizations (NGOs) encompass an enormous diversity, ranging from small, localized groups, through national bodies, up to international organizations. They are increasingly significant in drawing attention to problems, mobilizing opinion and lobbying for specific policies. Such groups vary in their organization and culture, and in their strategies and techniques for achieving influence. The most influential groups – such as Friends of the Earth (FoE), the World Wildlife Fund (WWF) or Greenpeace – have built up global networks, are represented in Brussels, have developed alternative expertise and displayed skilful use of the media. At present the FoE's European network is working mainly 'in formulating sustainable, and balanced development, and promoting active partici- pation, together with environment education and information' (Amigos de la Tierra, spring 1994). Meanwhile, the WWF is gaining a reputation as a respected critic of some of the EU's developmental policies, especially its Structural Funds.

However, the impact of the NGOs on government policy has, in these countries, been rather limited. The closed process of environ- mental policy-making in Spain and Greece particularly has left little scope for the lobbying of policy-makers. In Italy, there has been some consultation with government, most noticeably when a particular minister was willing. Environmental groups in these countries have tended to be deeply distrustful of decision-making processes, as over environmental impact assessment, on the grounds that government departments and agencies manipulate supposedly impartial procedures to get the results they want. Environmental groups in the South have, with a few exceptions (e.g. Lega Ambiente in Italy), been generally more passive than those in the Northern countries. However, an opportunity has been opened up at the European level, for the Commission has come to rely considerably on environmental organiza- tions for concrete information on environmental defaults in member-states.

The relative passivity of these groups relates to the usually low profile of the environment in the media and among public priorities. Sensationalist news items during emergencies have most characterized the popular press, this tending to underline the reactive approach in policy. The quality press has usually reported intermittently, though sometimes informatively. Since the mid-1980s there has been a distinct growth in regular press coverage on environmental matters outside emergencies in Italy, but not in the other two countries. As a whole, television has been more neglectful of environmental matters than the quality press. There has in all these countries been a mild growth in public awareness of or sensitivity to environmental issues, although the kind of widespread cultural attachment to environmental matters more commonly found in Scandinavia, Germany and the Netherlands generally does not feature in Mediterranean Europe. Only in Italy has this developed to some extent, and then primarily in the northern regions (Alexander 1991: 105). In fact, localism is very marked in these countries, suggesting a distinct link between territory and environ- mental awareness (Pridham 1994: 96).

Materialistic objections to sustainable development are fairly obvious, but criticism from vested interests tends to be directed at specific policies or actions that bear directly on firms' operations and profits rather than sustainable development as a principle. One severe problem facing the Southern countries is that of the environmental costs in applying European directives. It is this question that led Spain, for instance, to block an extension of majority voting on environmental matters in the Council of Ministers. Industry can hardly be discussed without mentioning its generally close relationship with the state in these countries. This has been pronounced in Greece, where industry has traditionally been cosseted by the widespread belief that the state rather than the private sector should carry the onus of environmental protection. However, Greek governments of whatever party have avoided strict environmental controls for private producers on the grounds that these would hinder industrial development – thus hardly encouraging the private sector to adapt to new environmental demands (Pridham *et al.* 1995: 249). Relations between industry and government have in Spain traditionally not been close in the policy process. However, experience within the EU has helped to overcome this absence of dialogue in the environmental field. The Ministry of Public Works in early 1994 created a Consultative Council for the Environment which includes a wide range of organizations from the worlds of industry and science as well as environmental groups. This is seen as a step towards integrating economic and environmental concerns, the Council's purpose being to elaborate and pursue policies on sustainable development (Ministerio de Obras Públicas, Transportes y Medio Ambiente 1994: 3–4).

Clearly, the countries of Mediterranean Europe have a long way to go before they are in a viable position to carry through and promote ambitious programmes of sustainable development. Some policy-makers and large companies have begun to pioneer relevant policies, but there remain serious problems of environmental management. As a precondition, political and environmental organizations need to become more committed and effective in lobbying for eco-friendly solutions, while a growing public concern over the environment would provide an added pressure for increased readiness by policy-makers to embark on new approaches. As it stands at present, the most continuous form of pressure is coming from abroad, and especially Brussels.

BELOW THE STATE: THE ROLE OF SUB-NATIONAL AUTHORITIES

The debate over sovereignty and subsidiarity has focused on the power of the nation-state. What has often been neglected in analyses of environmental management is the sub-national level, meaning local and, where they exist, regional authorities. It is, for instance, at the sub-national level that environmental movements are particularly strong and effective in the Southern countries. Conservation groups, often linking up with established NGOs, have done much to arrest the tide of destruction of landscapes, habitats and species; they have campaigned against polluting and hazardous activities; and they have promoted the case for more sustainable forms of development.

Furthermore, the strong local dimension to environmental awareness in Mediterranean Europe suggests a potential here for sustainable ideas to be transmitted into action. This is relevant to developing 'bottom-up' as well as 'top-down' approaches in environmental protection, as advocated by the Fifth EAP. At the same time, there are structural difficulties in environmental management that need to be addressed.

Sub-national authorities and the environment

One of the distinguishing features of the Italian and Spanish constitutional systems is the decentralization of power through regional authorities. Italy contains twenty regions, with five of them traditionally 'special' regions with extra constitutional powers. The regional structures in Italy have been identified as one of the main causes of delay in implementing European legislation. In his statement for the 1989 report on the state of the environment, Ruffolo noted that 'the decentralised structure of the Italian state, with vast competences in the environmental field attributed to the regions, provinces and municipalities has checked and slowed down the process of our legislation' (Ministero dell'Ambiente 1989: 22).

Spain, following the enactment of the Constitution of 1978, is a state with an extensive regional distribution of power, based on the principle of political territorial pluralism. The country is divided into seventeen autonomous communities (regions) with varying degrees of autonomy and some differences in legislative powers, leading in the environmental field to a diversity of competences (Ministerio de Obras Públicas y Transportes 1992: 14). This greatly inhibits a coherent and efficient policy approach, as the state level is primarily responsible for the enactment of basic environmental legislation, leaving much scope for the regions and local authorities. The regions have, for instance, wide powers in land planning and the management of environmental protection. In Greece, regions exist but they do not have constitutional powers over environmental protection, although they are involved with the EU environmental programmes. Greek local authorities are solely responsible for such matters as the drinking water supply, sewage networks, and the collection and disposal of solid waste (Ntalakou 1992: 6).

Despite these structural complexities, the concept of sustainable development seems to have far greater chances of success at the local or even regional level than at the national or international level. For there the scale is smaller, the pace of life is slower, and reality is simpler and easier to understand. As a national party functionary responsible for environmental matters in Spain put it:

> Spain is a country little enamoured with institutions. There is a history of little respect towards the institutions, so the messages that come from the institutions are seen as remote . . . environmental messages that are sent out by the [national] administration, such as laws on water with a strong environmental content, all the legislation of the EU – the citizen sees this as a bit distant and does not internalise it. Now, what he does internalise . . . is what is most directly related to him. In this sense, the town halls play a very important role in environmental management because the results are visible. For example, the collection of rubbish and waste, the matter of water in Madrid, the canalisation of rivers, etc.
>
> (Angel Del Castillo, Madrid, October 1992)

Different regions and also cities in Italy and Spain especially, together with some island communities in Greece, have developed fairly advanced approaches to environmental protection along the lines of sustainable development. One of the most environmentally active regions in Spain is the Autonomous Region of Madrid, which through its environmental agency was the first region there to adopt the concept of sustainable development and to develop feasibility studies for the five sectors of the Fifth EPA, together with all the local organizations that are connected with the environment (Horta Perez, Madrid, April 1994).

Notwithstanding the brutal invasion of mass media, local communities still have an appreciable cultural infrastructure, enabling them to cultivate new ideas and new attitudes to life (Laskaris 1993: 37). Greek culture incorporates a traditional form of local government, which, influenced by the church, emphasizes co-operation, consensus-building and balance. These features provide a potentially strong foundation for sustainable development initiatives. Participation by key individuals, particularly at the local community level, is seen as an important means of achieving these objectives. As the national organizer of one environmental organization in Greece put it:

> it is the person such as the mayor, and also there is a number of small groups of people such as local associations, cultural groups, environmental groups or a combination of all these which take care of their cultural centre. And at the same time they deal with environmental matters and sometimes they put pressure on their local government.
>
> (Kyriazi (HELMEPA), Athens, November 1992)

In Greece, local authorities have shown an increase in environmental initiatives since the beginning of the 1990s – essentially since the European Year of the Environment campaign of 1987, which in Greece assumed a very localistic focus. An official of the Athens Ministry of Merchant Marine remarked that local port authorities (129 of them) were in most cases far more committed to environmental protection than central government departments, for public pressure is more effective at the local level (Doumanis, Athens, November 1992). However, local governments in Greece have neither the human resources and knowledge nor the administrative power of most other European countries, although from 1 January 1995 new legislation granted more competences to prefectures and local authorities. Nevertheless, there are some local communities like that of the island of Kefalonia, where all the island's municipalities have combined to operate an efficient rubbish collection and disposal system and a public transport service. In contrast, the island of Mykonos is an area of highly developed commercial tourism with problems of illicit house building and illegally developed hotels which it has no way of controlling (Katochianou, Athens, November 1992). It is obvious what could happen in islands with weak restrictions and protection measures.

Local communities are more than ever linked with and dependent upon the national level, through a complicated system of economic, political, administrative, educational and functional relations. This is as true of Italy as it is of Greece, while Spain has achieved significant decentralization of education policy. Education is important, for it is adapted to the needs of the broader system of production.

The diversity of sub-national structures and procedures in these three countries raises the question of the optimum level for practising sustainable development, presumably where communities are able to adapt it to the peculiarities that they alone really know well (Laskaris 1993: 38). For example, in Spain it has been found that the ideal size of a town in Catalonia with good quality of life from an environmental point of view is around 10,000 inhabitants. Below that level one can encounter a lack of services and above that level one starts to experience managerial problems which exacerbate environmental problems (Puigdollers, Barcelona, October 1992).

Clearly, then, the nature and powers of sub-national structures do matter in allowing potential sustainable development to develop in the countries of Mediterranean Europe. At the same time, the relationship between 'bottom-up' efforts and pressures and 'top-down' direction of environmental policy needs to be clarified. Evidently, policy-makers must be clear about what they want to sustain, who receives the benefits and who bears the costs of the push towards sustainable development.

The case of tourism

At the sub-national level the idea of sustainable development, specifically in tourism, has, however, begun to take off in policy thinking, albeit in a variety of regions rather than as a widespread phenomenon (Pridham 1994: 88). Tourism is a major economic sector in all the three Mediterranean countries and is, by all forecasts, expected to grow dramatically in the next few decades. Increasingly, the impacts of tourism on the environment has become a serious concern. The quest for quick profit has often overcome other considerations, and has led to mass tourism.

However, tourism has recently become revitalized as a strategy of national, regional and local development. Emerging tendencies are visible, as new patterns of tourism reveal. There is increasing evidence that environmental quality is regarded as a necessary condition for tourism. A recent study (1993) by the Greek Centre of Development Studies, Athens, noted that 'many tourists now insist on a clean environment, as well as the type of tourism which highlights the environmental aspects of the area', and that 'this demand has forced tourist areas to take measures to improve the environment and to develop programmes and services which will promote environmental forms of tourism – it is striking that many tourists claim they would not go to areas with any kind of environmental problem' (Tsartas 1993: 387). Alternative, rural, interior or eco-tourism are types of tourism which, involving local communities in the process, can be an instrument for sustainable development. They involve a controlled form of urban development, not in terms of megaprojects, but rather in terms of manageable miniprojects.

In recent years some local and also regional authorities in (northern) Italy and Spain (notably Catalonia and the Balearics) have begun to respond to the same need. Since 1975 the Greek National Tourist Organization has implemented a programme for the preservation and development of traditional settlements in Greece. The aim of the programme (1975–1992) was to allow conservation of cultural heritage, and also to promote a tourist development which was environmentally friendly, following modern ecological considerations (Greek National Tourism Organization 1991: 4). According to Spanish officials, the initiative for sustainable tourism was taken by the autonomous communities themselves, such as the Balearics, Canaries, Valencia and Catalonia. This included studies to assess the viability of sustainable development, projection of demand and supply for their own tourist markets, and how to adapt the tourist product to present tourist demand.

The change of policy towards sustainable development in the Balearics, for instance, was caused by various factors. The number of tourists reached saturation point and a change in demand occurred as tourists started to expect more environmental quality. Bad publicity a few years ago helped to stimulate that process, as well as a change in the attitude of the local population (Diez de Rivera, Madrid, October 1992). Another element was highlighted by an official of the Catalan regional government:

> The Balearic islands are one of the places with the most active environmental movements in Spain. There is something very important in the Balearic islands in relation to the rest of Spain: the best cultural associations; they are traditionally accustomed to working in groups, to being united.
>
> (Puigdollers, Barcelona, October 1992)

So far – and it is perhaps too soon to judge – such initiatives have usually fallen short of ambitious aims, and they have been limited territorially. That is because not all the following conditions have been satisfied: a heavy dependence of local economic interest on tourism being threatened by growing environmental degradation; the political will or initiative of local authorities; an existing or potential environmental awareness among local populations, strengthened by cultural traditions and local pride; national government as a facilitator (through legislation, investment and support mechanisms); and international organizations, especially the EU, becoming increasingly important as facilitator and stimulus to environmental education. Nevertheless, sub-national engagement in sustainable development ideas and practices in tourism is a recent tendency, and one which raises a significant question, for it appears that the countries of Mediterranean Europe have begun to select this sector (one of those identified in the Fifth EAP) as an area of priority in the pursuit of sustainable development. Given prognoses of tourism growth in these countries, the significance of this should not in any way be underrated.

The European Union has only recently begun to become involved in tourism policy, but a potential may lie here as sub-national authorities have over the past few years increasingly turned to Brussels for its development programmes, as a partner in policy dialogue and as a channel for increasing their own political visibility. However, in the long run it is likely to be the economic motive that will prove the key determinant in pushing forward projects of sustainable development at the local level, particularly when, as in the case of tourism, environmental degradation presents a direct threat to economic interests.

CONCLUSION

Over the last few years, sustainable development has become established as a concept of policy-making in the Southern EU member-states. The need for greater integration of the environment into all areas of policy-making has come to be recognized by national policy-making elites. Also, the governments of all three countries have at different levels begun to take note of growing pressures from the public and environmental groups. But it is pressure from the EU, where the concept of sustainable development has been prominent, that looks like being crucial, at least in the light of policy patterns up to now. The precedent set by the considerable impact of European legislation and the openness of these countries to international influence are hopeful signs for eventual progress towards sustainable development.

Just as Japanese governments use foreign, especially American, pressure as a pretext for unpalatable domestic policy, so Italy, Spain and Greece have used the strictures of the European Union. In other words, environmental policies must be of the type prescribed by the EU, because the EU says so; and – a powerful argument in the South – because structural funds come from the EU too. At the same time, there is clearly some inconsistency in EU policy. The construction of new motorways, of which a large proportion have been and are being built in these countries so that they can be incorporated more success-fully into the system of large production, is inconsistent with the concept of sustainable development. But, on balance, what should worry us, however, is any serious weakening of pressure from the EU on the environmental front, especially so far as the Southern member-states are concerned.

Although the concept of sustainable development is reasonably well established on the policy agenda, it is not evident that this is under-stood clearly or even uniformly by policy-makers in these countries. Furthermore, the integration of the environment into all sectors and levels of policy-making is proving to be patchy, slow and small-scale. The weight of past policy traditions and procedural patterns is consid-erable, with a predominantly reactive style of approach, institutional fragmentation and the absence of concerted action (save locally). All these features cast doubt over the prospects for sustainable develop-ment in Mediterranean Europe.

However, there are fairly recent signs that paint a more optimistic scenario for the future, although much also depends on the state of the international economy. Efforts at policy innovation during the 1990s, at national as well as local levels, have – together with a gradual adop-tion of strategic thinking and planning – represented a departure from conventional environmental policy in the direction of sustainable development. But it is above all in one sector – tourism, so dear to the interests of these countries – that the traditional perception of a trade-off between environmental protection and economic development has been most completely changed.

Prevailing systems of decision-making in many countries tend to separate economic, social and environmental factors at policy, plan-ning and management levels. This influences the actions of all groups in society, including governments, industry and individuals, and it has important implications for efficient and sustainable development. An adjustment or even a fundamental reshaping of decision-making, taking into account country-specific conditions, may be necessary if the environment and development are to be put at the centre of economic and political decision-making (UNCED 1992: 87). The chal-lenge here to traditional procedures and habits of behaviour in Mediterranean Europe is considerable.

NOTE

1 This chapter draws on the four-year research project 'Environmental Standards and the Politics of Expertise in Europe', funded by the Single Market Programme of the Economic and Social Research Council (ESRC).

Discussion concentrates on the three southern European countries of Italy, Spain and Greece covered in this project.

REFERENCES

Aguilar, S. (1991) 'Policy styles and policy sector influence in pollution control policies', paper presented at the ECPR Joint Sessions of Workshops, University of Essex, UK.

Alexander, D. (1991) 'Pollution, policies and politics: the Italian environment', in F. Sabetti and R. Catanzaro (eds) *Italian Politics: A Review*, London: Pinter.

Amigos de la Tierra (1994) interview, Madrid.

Baldock, D. and Long, T. (1987) *The Mediterranean Environment Under Pressure: The Influence of the CAP on Spain and Portugal and the 'IMPs' in France, Greece and Italy*, London: Institute for European Environmental Policy.

Capria, A. (1991) 'Formulation and implementation of environmental policy in Italy', paper presented at the 12th International Congress of Social Policy, Paris, 8–12 October.

Castillo, A. del (1992) interview, Madrid: PSOE.

Doumanis, D. (1992) interview, Athens: Ministry of Merchant Marine.

García, E., Lerma, I. and Santos, A. (1994) 'Medio ambiente y relaciones industriales: un análisis en el contexto europeo', in E. García, I. Lerma, and A. Santos (eds) *Ecología, relaciones industriales y empresa*, Bilbao: Fundación BBV.

Gonzalez, N. (1994) interview, Madrid: Ministerio de Obras Publicas, Transporte y Medio Ambiente.

Greek National Tourism Organization (1991) *Preservation and Development of Traditional Settlements in Greece*, Athens: Greek National Tourist Organization.

Katochianu, D. (1992) interview, Athens: Center of Planning and Economic Research (KEPE).

Kourtelli, C. (1994) interview, Brussels: COROPER.

Kyriazi, V. (1992) interview, Athens: HELMEPA.

La Spina, A. and Sciortino, G. (1993) 'Common agenda, Southern rules: European integration and environmental change in the Mediterranean states', in D. Liefferink *et al.* (eds) *European Integration and Environmental Policy*, London: Belhaven Press.

Laskaris, C. (1993) 'Environmental crisis: a world social and educational problem', in C. Laskaris *et al.* (eds) *Environmental Crisis*, (in Greek), Athens: Synchroni Epochi.

Lewanski, R. (1993) 'Environmental policy in Italy: from the regions to the EEC, a multiple tier policy game', paper presented at the ECPR Joint Sessions of Workshops, University of Leiden, the Netherlands.

Liberatore, A. and Lewanski, R. (1990) 'The evolution of Italian environmental policy', *Environment* 32(5): 10–40.

Mingot, F. (1992) interview, Madrid: CIEMAT.

Ministerio de Obras Públicas, Transportes y Medio Ambiente (1993) *Medio ambiente en España 1992*, Madrid: Ministerio de Obras Públicas, Transportes y Medio Ambiente.

Ministerio de Obras Públicas, Transportes y Medio Ambiente (1994) *Información de medio ambiente* (March): 3–4.

Ministerio de Obras Públicas y Transportes (1992) *Medio ambiente en España 1991*, Madrid: Ministerio de Obras Públicas Transportes.

Ministerio de Obras Públicas y Urbanismo (1989a) *El derecho ambiental y sus principios rectores*, Madrid: Ministerio de Obras Públicas y Urbanismo.

Ministerio de Obras Públicas y Urbanismo (1989b) *Medio ambiente en España 1988*, Madrid: Ministerio de Obras Públicas y Urbanismo.

Ministero dell'Ambiente (1989) *Nota aggiuntiva del ministro Giorgio Ruffolo*, Rome: Ministero dell'Ambiente.

Ministero dell'Ambiente (1992) *Relazione sullo stato dell'ambiente*, Rome: Ministero dell'Ambiente.

Ministry of the Environment, Physical Planning and Public Works (1991) *National Report of Greece 1992*, Athens: Ministry of the Environment, Physical Planning and Public Works.

Ntalakou, V. (1992) 'Legal aspects of environmental protection and the contribution of local self-government', mimeo (in Greek), University of the Aegean.

OECD (1994) *Environmental Performance Review: Italy*, Paris: OECD.

Osorio, J. (1994) interview, Madrid: Ministry of Public Works, Transport and Environment.

Pelecasi, K. and Scourtos, M. (1992) *Atmospheric Pollution in Greece* (in Greek), Athens: Papazisi.

Perez, H. Hortas (1994) interview, Madrid: Agencia Medio Ambiente.

Pridham, G. (1994) 'National environmental policy-making in the European framework: Spain, Greece and Italy in comparison', *Regional Politics and Policy* 4(1): 80–101.

Pridham, G. and Cini, M. (1993) 'Enforcing environmental standards in the European Community: is there a Southern problem?', paper presented to the COST-7 Conference, 'Setting, Operating and Enforcement of Environmental Standards', Maastricht, 3 December 1993.

Pridham, G., Verney, S. and Konstadakopulos, D. (1995) 'Environmental policy in Greece: evolution, structures and process', *Environmental Politics* 4(2): 244–270.

Puigdollers, J. (1992) interview, Barcelona: Departamento de Medio Ambiente, Generalitat.

Putman, R. (1973) *Beliefs of Politicians: Ideology, Conflict and Democracy in Britain and Italy*, New Haven, CT: Yale University Press.

Rehbinder, E. and Stewart, R. (1985) *Environmental Protection Policy* vol. 2, Berlin: Walter de Gruyter.

Ros Vicent, J. (1992) interview, Madrid: Ministerio de Obras Publicas, Transporte y Medio Ambiente.

Scoullos, M. and Kaberi, H. (1989) *The Implementation of the EEC Environmental Legislation in Greece*, Athens: Ellini Etairia.

Tsartas, P. (1993) 'Touristic development: environmental, economic and social effects', in Laskaris *et al.* (eds) *Environmental Crisis*, (in Greek), Athens: Synchroni Epochi.

UNCED (1992) *Earth Summit '92*, London: Regency Press.

Wallace, H. (1977) 'National bulls in the Community china shop', in H. Wallace, C. Webb and W. Wallace (eds) *Policy-Making in the European Communities*, Chichester: John Wiley.

Weale, A., Pridham, G., Williams, A. and Porter, M. (forthcoming) 'Administrative organisation and environmental policy: structural convergence or national distinctiveness in six European states?'.

7 Policy networks, local discourses and the implementation of sustainable development

Yvonne Rydin

URBAN SUSTAINABILITY AND THE LOCAL POLICY PROCESS

It is now taken as read that the implementation of sustainable development would imply policy action at the local level and that, particularly in the case of the heavily urbanized countries of Europe, this means a distinctive urban focus. This view is given recognition in the Local Agenda 21 process arising out of the UNCED summits and reports and the establishment of a roving United Nations (UN) Commission on Sustainable Development. It is also reflected in numerous EU publications, including the *Green Book* on the urban environment (CEC 1990) and the Fifth Environmental Action Programme on the Environment, *Towards Sustainability* (CEC 1992b), among others.

But while the significance of the local level is recognized, there is much less clarity regarding how implementation at the local level is to be achieved. A form of hierarchical planning is often invoked, explicitly or implicitly, in which principles and definitions are established at higher tiers and more detail is added as one descends through successive tiers of government. According to this way of thinking, the policy documents at the UN level set the context for EU policy, which in turn drives national-level policy before feeding through to regional and local strategies. An example of this approach operating is in relation to water quality. Here the EU sets out desired standards for water quality in directives. As is the nature of EU directives, these have to be put into effect via a national policy instrument and, in this case, the British Secretary of State for the Environment (the Cabinet minister with overall responsibility for the Department of the Environment; DoE) issues statutory instruments incorporating these quality standards. The water companies in England and Wales are then legally required to meet these standards. (Since water privatization, local government plays no role here.)

But this kind of straightforward top-down approach is not the norm. In the case of air quality, for example, while the EU has equivalent quality standards, they have not spawned a similar mandatory system of enforcement; this is largely because it is not possible to identify a distinct set of actors who can be held responsible for air quality in the way that water companies can be held responsible for water quality. Therefore policy links are more complex. In the British case, the Department of Environment has issued an *Air Quality Management Strategy* (Department of the Environment 1995); this requires local authorities to prepare their own local strategies. But the problems of implementation and enforcement remain, so that one finds local government actively lobbying central government for more powers to achieve the goals of the national and local strategies. In the British case, the problems are compounded by the limited formal powers of local government units and the dictum of ultra vires, which constrains their actions.

So also in the case of sustainable development, the simple application of the hierarchy is not possible. The pronouncements at UN and EU level have generated a British national strategy (Department of the Environment 1994) and the Local Agenda 21 process is resulting in strategies being produced in local boroughs and councils. There are some top-down links, as with the requirement from central government for all land-use development plans prepared by local government to take account of the goal of sustainable development, outlined in *Planning Policy Guidance No. 12* (Department of the Environment 1992). But the promise of local implementation of a national and international agenda remains elusive. Here the problems of diffuse and often unidentifiable responsible actors and of inadequate local government powers are compounded by the inherent ambiguities of the concepts of 'sustainable development', 'sustainability' and 'urban sustainability'. These concepts are used in many different ways in different contexts and are inherently contestable, though disagreements on use are often glossed over in policy and academic discussion (Greig 1993). For all these reasons the notion of top-down implementation of a sustainable development strategy at the urban level is inappropriate. It is not profitable to search for the ideal definition of sustainable development in an urban context, against which to measure policy practice or the correct hierarchy of policy measures for defining organizational roles; rather one should see the debate about this as part of the local policy process out of which decisions may arise which mitigate to a greater or lesser degree the environmental impacts of our urbanized way of life. This involves an exploration of how 'mutual adjustment' over sustainable development issues occurs. Lindblom uses the concept of mutual adjustment to cover 'all forms of highly multilateral exercises of influence and power, including but by no means limited to bargaining' (Lindblom 1990: 240). It is through such interactive processes that policy for urban sustainability becomes defined and redefined, and responsible actors become identified (or not). It is also in such processes that economic, political and other resources are brought to bear.

Therefore attention needs to be paid to the distinctive characteristics of the local area, exploring the ambiguities of local policy for sustainable development in urban areas and the ways such ambiguities relate to local policy networks and the structures of economic interests. This Chapter undertakes such a task for two case-study cities in Britain. It considers the extent to which the success of environmental arguments at the city level depends on the economic structure of the city and how readily environmental arguments can be fitted with the prevailing economic rationale for the city. It looks at the extent to which conflicts between specific environmental policy initiatives and economic policy goals arise, and how such conflicts are managed differently depending on whether local policy-making is directed towards the purely city level rather than regional or national concerns. And it pays attention to the role of the local environmental movement, its size and activism, and the extent to which it has opportunities for involvement in local policy across the range of issues, not just 'green' issues.

The paper draws on research undertaken during 1992–1994 with a grant from DG XII of the European Commission under its Socio-Economic Aspects of the Environment Research Programme (contract no. EV5V-CT92-0150). This research project was based in Britain and Italy, and in each country an interdisciplinary team of researchers was brought together, comprising geographers, planners, political scientists, architects, social psychologists and rhetoricians.[1] The brief of the project was to examine the cultural and economic conditions of decision-making for the sustainable city with a view to examining how the local policy process around the issue of sustainable development was constrained by the structures of economic interests and the cultural form that policy debate took. The empirical work was based in four case-study cities: Edinburgh and Leicester in Britain, and Bologna and Firenze in Italy. The concern was with policies for sustainable development at the urban level, but, to operationalize this concern, more specific policy areas were identified for examination. These were traffic restraint (CEC 1992a; Barde and Button 1990; Engwicht 1992), retail location (Owens and Cope 1992; Ecotech etc. 1993; Sherlock 1990) and green-space management.

The methodology for the project as thus defined was based on substantial background documentary research but also, in the case of the British case studies, centrally on a series of in-depth, unstructured but focused interviews with key policy actors in the cities. Key actors were identified through initial recommendation and then a snow-balling process. The verbatim transcripts of these interviews were then analysed through close reading and use of a qualitative data analysis software package (Nudist). The Italian case studies (which will be reported in Mazza and Rydin 1997) involved more extensive documentary research and a more curtailed interview programme. The following discussion focuses on the British case studies, Edinburgh and Leicester. First, the economic structure of the two cities is explained; then the political activity around the three policy themes is explored, focusing on the existence of policy networks; and, finally, links are made with the communicative dimension of policy and the nature of policy discourse in the two cities.

ECONOMIC INTERESTS IN THE CASE-STUDY CITIES

Leicester is a medium-sized city in the East Midlands with a population of 278,000 at the time of the 1990 census. It covers a total area 46 sq. km with a central core of 1.1 sq. km. It bears some of the physical evidence of a medieval settlement but is predominantly based on a nineteenth-century urban heritage surrounded by, and in areas redeveloped by, postwar expansion. The core industry in the nineteenth and early twentieth centuries was textiles and, despite recent job losses, it still is one of the major employers in the city: in 1987 Leicester County Council estimated that 12 per cent of Leicester's industrial structure was accounted for by the textiles industry; to this could be added another 6 per cent accounted for by leather, footwear and clothing firms. The economy of the city has diversified and another major employer is the category of distribution, hotel, catering and repairs (18 per cent of the city's industrial structure), with distribution in particular benefiting from the city's location just to the east of a major junction on the M1 north–south route with connections on to the M69 to Birmingham and the West Midlands (and then onto northwestern and southwestern motorway routes).

Services have generally expanded but the major growth industries of banking/insurance/finance, tourism, transport and communications are underrepresented in the Leicester economy. Neither is it in the high-tech growth 'banana' or 'crescent' that drove much economic activity in the 1980s. As a result there is an evident concern with the economic development prospects of Leicester, as discussed below. This is not to suggest that the city has the problems of a peripheral region suffering the decline of economic restructuring. Rather the city appears economically weak by comparison with some of its neighbours in the region, such as Nottingham. This is based as much on a comparison of the retail and leisure facilities available to residents of, and visitors to, the cities as on the underlying pattern of job opportunities. Hence the concern to enhance Leicester's position in the regional hierarchy has focused on encouraging town centre redevelopment in the form of new shopping facilities such as the specialist shopping centre of St Martins, which opened in the late 1980s, the 500,000 sq. ft Shires enclosed shopping centre opened in 1992 and proposals for refurbishing the 1970s Haymarket Shopping Centre. These are all grouped around the central core of the city close to the large covered market, the old Exchange and the Town Hall.

Another feature of Leicester's economy is the large number of small firms. Many of these are owned by and/or employ the significant proportion of Leicester's population that is of Asian origin; 25 per cent of the city's population are from ethnic minorities (that is, within the city council area, which excludes many of the surrounding suburbs). It has been argued that this small-firm structure gives Leicester a degree of resilience in times of economic recession, but it also contributes to a low-wage economy.

Edinburgh, by contrast, is the second largest city in Scotland and its de facto capital, with a population of 420,000 at the time of the 1990 census. The total area extends to 260 sq. km but with a very concentrated central core of only 1.1 sq. km. It has a long illustrious history, still evident in its built heritage with its medieval Old Town, the eighteenth-century Georgian-style New Town and surrounding urban development of the nineteenth and twentieth centuries. It has a spectacular geology, with three volcanic peaks in the centre, one surmounted by the castle, a series of hills and ridges on the outskirts, notably the Pentland Hills, and then the Scottish Highlands and the Southern Uplands beyond. A 40,000 acre green belt protects the urban fringe from development and there is much attractive open space within the city.

As might be expected, tourism is a major contributor to the Edinburgh economy. In 1991 British tourists spent about £147 million per annum and overseas tourists another £133 million. The festivals that occur in the summer alone contribute over £70 million to the economy. Retailing, both tourist- and resident-oriented, is also a major sector, with Edinburgh's shops accounting for the fourth largest expenditure for cities in the UK. The established shopping area of Princes Street and its surroundings is complemented by covered shopping in the St James' Centre and the Waverly Centre, both at the end of Princes Street. Other centres are found at Cameron Toll to the west of the city centre and the new South Gyle centre, which opened in 1993 on the western periphery.

In addition, there is a wide range of other service-sector employers. Edinburgh is Britain's second largest financial and administrative centre, after London, and had approximately 1.6 million sq. m of office floorspace in 1991, with another 0.75 million sq. m in the pipeline. Banking/insurance/finance, the legal profession, central and local government administration, medicine and higher education are all represented in the economy, creating a strong economic base and employment prospects which attract and hold middle-class residents. In contrast to the social structure of many British cities, there is substantial higher-income residence in the central areas of the city, with many lower-income estates found on the periphery. While areas of deprivation can be found throughout the city, the economic opportunities for Edinburgh residents have been maintained by the growing service sector and the relatively stable manufacturing base due to more recent growth in the electronic and engineering sectors.

This, therefore, provides the structure of economic interests with which local political activity meshes. The next section moves on to consider the nature of this political activity where environmental issues are concerned. In doing so it discusses the relevance of the policy network concept.

POLICY NETWORKS AND DECISION-MAKING IN THE CITIES

There is a major difference in the way that decision-making on environmental issues occurs in the two case-study cities due to the existence of a formal networking arrangement in Leicester based around the Environment City organization. Leicester was designated as the first Environment City in 1990 and has had its designation reconfirmed for a further five years. The original designation was very much part of the process of setting up the whole Environment City Programme; key movers were the Leicester Ecology Trust (now known as Environ) and the city council. The designation is now awarded by the Wildlife Trusts (formerly the Royal Society for Nature Conservation – RSNC) under sponsorship from British Telecom. Cities have to bid for the title by submitting a programme that shows not so much work already done but mechanisms for achieving environmental improvements in the future. A key element of such a programme is the ability to demonstrate the involvement of all three sectors: the local authorities, the business community and voluntary organizations. The award carries no funds but enables the city to use the title 'Environment City' and ensures involvement in a growing city-based network that the Wildlife Trusts are developing.

The way in which Environment City works is through developing environmentally based networking throughout the city. Leicester is fairly typical in that the Environment City organization has set up a number of specialist working groups on selected topics such as transport, energy and so on. These working groups consist of experts or relevant policy actors from the three sectors. While these groups may just, in the words of one interviewee, bring together 'like-minded people' who already know each other, the mechanism reinforces links and enables discussion of issues and tactics which would not otherwise occur in existing fora. There are no funds available for directly supporting environmental policy or levering in support from other bodies, but the discussions can suggest ways to redirect funds, provide arguments and strategies for releasing funds from existing budgets, and identify new, untapped sources. In these ways it is hoped that the Environment City mechanism will promote environmental policy. However, there is little evidence that such networking can alter decision-making, where fundamental conflicts over resources and policy direction persist; it is, rather, a useful mechanism for facilitating policy formulation and implementation at the margin.

Furthermore, the activity of such a networking organization must be seen in relation to the prevailing organization of civil society in the cities and, in particular, to the nature of the local environment movement. In Leicester, the Environment City organization was a significant actor because it brought together other organizations who were already influential. It could then act as a continuing support and specifically bolster those organizations representing environmental concerns. This role is indicated by the central position that Environment City (now Environ) held in the network of linkages between the organizations interviewed. This was assessed using detailed analysis of the transcribed interviews to reveal the extent to which organizations referred to other organizations in each city. This analysis identified a number of key points. First, local authorities are, as might be excepted, key actors in the local policy networks. In both Leicester and Edinburgh the city council and the county or regional council were the top two in the lists of the number of total references and the number of organizations referring to them. Second, in Leicester the third significant organization referred to was the Environment City body; in Edinburgh this role was taken by a long-established NGO closely associated with maintaining Edinburgh's historic heritage, the Cockburn Association. Third, the total number of cross-references in Leicester was significantly greater than in Edinburgh – twice as many references for the same number of interviews.

This latter phenomenon can be explored further by grouping the individual organizations into larger categories and examining the interaction between them, as illustrated in Figures 7.1 and 7.2. This suggests further features of the policy process in the two cities. It confirms the significance of local authorities as reference points to both of the key groupings of economic and business interests and environmental groups. (The other category refers to the police, press and higher education institutions.) References to local authorities were always at least three times as numerous as the references by local authorities to the organizations in the other groupings. It also emphasizes the significance of the environmental organizations in Leicester. Reference to environmental groups outnumbers reference to economic and business interests by two to one in Leicester, whereas the numbers for the two groupings were roughly equal in Edinburgh – but 68 per cent of these references to Leicester environmental groups were by other bodies within the environmental lobby; the figure for Edinburgh was only 40 per cent. This suggests that the environmental movement is very active in Leicester *as a movement*. The Environment City organization was a significant source and object of these cross-references, and this emphasizes that it plays an important role both in reflecting the nature of the movement and in acting as a continuing support. As well as this broad-brush analysis of linkages on environmental issues at the urban level, more specific forms of interaction were found in the decision-making on three selected policy issues.

On the issue of retail location, policy development in Leicester has been centrally shaped by the impact of a long planning battle over proposals to build a regional shopping centre at Junction 21 of the M1 motorway, which was felt to be a threat to the city centre. A series of public inquiries and associated negotiations galvanized many actors within the city to form a coalition against the development and in

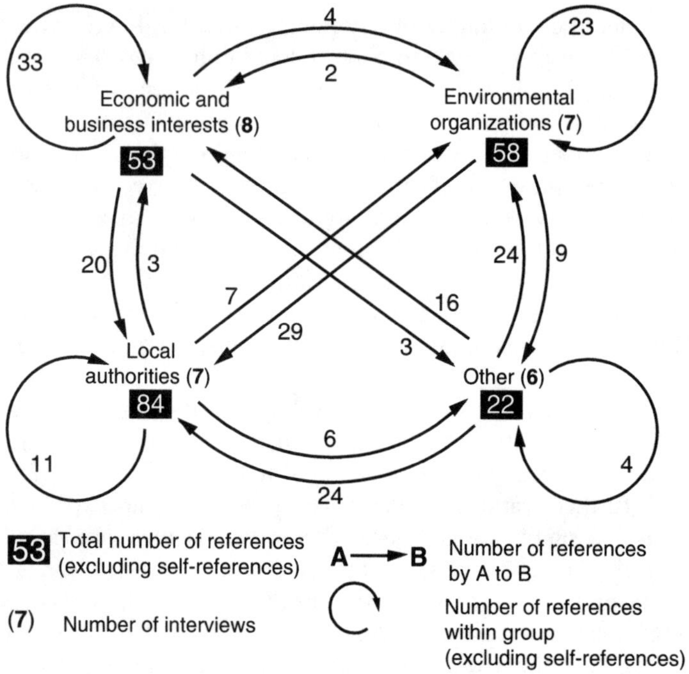

Figure 7.1 Edinburgh

favour of concentrating future development in the central area. This coalition broadly comprises the county and city councils, both officers and politicians, local business and central-area landowners, together with business interests from outside the locality who have come, albeit temporarily, to be active in the city, for example developers. As a result there is little evidence of conflicts between the tiers of local government; structure and local plan policies on retail location have been formulated to complement and reinforce each other. This coalition can rely on and is reinforced by the broader consensus across policy communities that economic development is the dominant policy goal. The city council in particular has taken a leading role in promoting this consensus and pursuing policy to achieve the economic development goal. Continuity in the political leadership of the council, through the person of the Council Leader, has assisted this, as has the interchange of officers between the city and county councils. Formal and informal contacts between the city council and the chamber of commerce reinforce this position. The representative of the chamber interviewed emphasized that it was not possible for the city council to satisfy all its members all the time, but it was generally accepted by

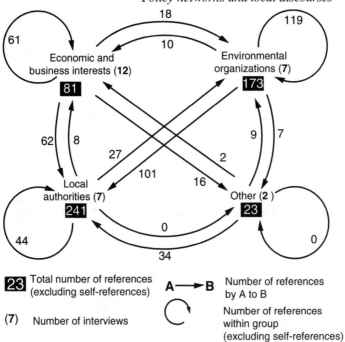

Figure 7.2 Leicester

chamber members that the city was following a policy of local economic development that they agreed with.

This contrasts with the situation in Edinburgh. While the economic performance of the city centre remains central to all key decisions on retail location, there is not the same active coalition of interests in support of a general consensus on boosting the local economy. This is related to the lack of a closely integrated network of actors around the goal of city-centre promotion. The chamber of commerce does not enjoy a close relationship with the district; the radical nature of the past Labour administrations in the district council appears to have soured relations. Furthermore, the representation of the business community by lobby groups is quite fragmented: for example, there are separate Princes Street and George Street Associations.

Another example of the failure of an integrated growth coalition operating in Edinburgh is provided by the limited life of the Edinburgh Vision project. This sought to bring various parties together to develop a coherent vision for the city and promote both the city and policies for city enhancement. It appears that the participating organizations of Lothian and Edinburgh Enterprise Ltd (LEEL; the local enterprise company), the local authorities and the chamber of commerce could see little benefit in continuing the project and establishing the network on a firm footing. Rather, city-centre interests have pursued their own individual rationales. For example, the district council's support of the South Gyle project was based on its ownership of the site and its financial interest in the development, as well as the policy notion that the centre was 'overshopped'; in pursing this project the district found itself in opposition to the region and to some surrounding districts concerned about the generation of traffic and the impact on other retail centres such as Livingstone New Town.

In the case of traffic restraint, the way in which responsibilities are divided between the local authorities is important. In Leicester there was a division of responsibility between the city and the county, with the city council acting on the county council's behalf on certain matters. This resulted in a mixture of conflict and negotiation over transport-related issues between the councils. Both councils expressed some frustration where they were dependent on the other for an aspect of policy, and the Environment City Transport Specialist Working Group could play a useful role in providing a forum for discussion between actors in both councils outside their usual organizational setting. The active role given to the city council, together with its pledged support of the central area as the locus for economic activity, also allowed economic interests to penetrate decision-making on transport. In Leicester the involvement of the city council in promoting new retail development in the city centre resulted in corporatist forms of decision-making on associated transport issues. Thus the detailed planning of the pedestrian priority zone and traffic management in the centre was being directed by the needs of the new Shires retail development, as expressed through close and frequent discussion between the city council and the developers (who had retained ownership of the shopping centre). Similarly, parking policy was driven by an assumed need to provide for the city-centre development, with commercial interests involved in this decision-making process.

In Edinburgh, by contrast, all transport and traffic responsibilities were retained by the region, leaving the district council with little involvement in general or specific issues which affect traffic and travel in the city. This can help explain the limited extent of pedestrianization initiatives, though resistance from retailers concerned about any change is also a factor, as is the assumed preference of the population for on-street parking. Conflicts between the city and the region arise but regional-level decisions effectively prevail. In the case of the proposals for a north–south metro and a southern suburban rail route, the region favoured the former proposal and refused to support the latter despite the district's preference for implementing the rail route on the basis of lower cost and a belief that it was more likely to happen. The region's preferences prevented the rail proposal going forward and kept the metro plan in discussion. The dominance of the regional council means that other key actors are primarily directed towards the region in their policy involvement; Edinburgh Spokes, the cycling NGO, works mainly with a designated unit in the regional council and bypasses the district level.

And the supraregional level, in the form of the Scottish Office (a central-government ministry), was also influential. The Office's support for the second Forth Road has drawn local actors into debate with the Scottish Office. One interviewee expressed the opinion that local government reorganization in Lothian would be used by the Scottish Office to take more transport functions away from the local level and consolidate its own position. Rail is another area where power over local transport is significantly influenced by decisions made outside the local government arena; the plans for privatizing Scotrail (the public-sector railway-service provider) has implications for local and regional rail networks in and around Edinburgh and yet local government has no input. So the organizational power of the regional and national level in Edinburgh often exceeded that of local government even on apparently localized issues.

The green-spaces issue stands apart from the others in two senses. First, it is the policy area where the environmental groups have the most access and influence, even implementing much policy in detail. Second, there were very similar patterns in the two cities. There was a common pattern of wider involvement of groups, both environmental and community-based, and less connection to the economic interests of dominant groups in the city. Much of the policy activity occurred at the very localized, site-specific level, where there was often detailed negotiation between local authorities, landowners and community interests in the site. Protected from the assumption of economic significance, green-space policy therefore had a more open political character.

How is this detailed empirical evidence to be characterized and, in particular, is a policy network analysis useful here? Rhodes, a leading exponent of the usefulness of the network concept, defines it as follows: 'a cluster or complex of organizations connected to each other by resource dependencies and distinguished from other clusters or complexes by breaks in the structure of resource dependencies' (Rhodes and Marsh 1992: 182). But, beyond this, the area is typified by the 'proliferation' of definition and typologies. In an attempt to overcome this, Rhodes and Marsh propose a clearer distinction between a 'policy community' and an 'issue network', with 'policy network' reserved as the generic term. A policy community comprises a limited number of participants, a dominant professional or economic interest, frequent interaction, consistency over time, consensus, exchange relationships based on resources, bargaining, hierarchical relations within participating organizations and the potential for a positive-sum game (whereby joint action by two or more parties can generate additional benefits, which can then be shared by the parties) arising from the balance of power between participants. An issue network, by contrast, involves consultation not shared decision-making, competition, fluctuating interaction over time, conflict rather than consensus and unequal power relations. From this it is clear that the quick map of political activity in relation to these three policy issues in two cities reveals neither only one policy community nor only one issue network.

The traffic issue in both cities supported a fairly close-knit group of decision-makers which may be termed a policy community. Similarly, the retail location issue was strongly related to the coalition of interests in support of the city centre, another policy community. The sense of a potential positive-sum game is strong in all these cases. However, the more diffuse concern with retail issues in Edinburgh suggests an essentially latent policy network, while the more open and variable networks surrounding green-space issues in both cities can be characterized as an issue network. On top of this, the Environment City organization represents an attempt at a broader form of issue network around sustainable development or rather, perhaps, a network of issue networks. This attempt raises an interesting question, for, as Rhodes and Marsh acknowledge, policy networks of all kinds exist to routinize relationships, to promote continuity and stability (Rhodes and Marsh 1992: 196). And, further, those with a dominant professional or economic interest are most resistant to change. Hence, the attempt to create a sustainable development issue network over and above an existing urban pattern of issue networks and policy communities (which will be dominated by professional and economic interests) will face severe difficulties.

Dowding (1995) has criticized some uses of the policy networks concept (or metaphor) as essentially descriptive and too focused on the characteristics of the network bearers rather than the linkages of the networks themselves. He has therefore called for greater attention to the use of resources in bargaining games and to the way in which the advocacy coalition literature deals with preference and beliefs. One useful insight he draws attention to is:

> how fragmented and separate groups . . . are able to act concertably to yield more power than the sum of each member. Similarly, breaking up governance structures into differentiated quasi-governmental organisations within newly created policy communities can cause overall power loss.
>
> (Dowding 1995: 31)

This suggests a possible way forward out of the inertia created by existing policy communities. Where economic or professional interests dominate to the detriment of an environmental perspective, breaking up existing patterns to spread responsibilities will diminish the power of those interests; specifically, policy responsibility should be dispersed not concentrated. However, to ensure environmental concerns are then taken on board, new structures for bringing together agencies and the representatives of these environmental concerns should be created to create a new positive-sum scenario. It would seem, therefore, that the success of an initiative such as Environment City is dependent on breaking up to some extent the underlying policy communities and then transforming the sustainable development issue network into a policy community by providing resources and activating resource dependencies.

The policy network literature is therefore of some help in understanding the nature of political decision-making found in the case-study cities. But it also points to a neglected dimension. Although not explicitly recognized as such, the factors identified by the policy network approach have a cultural, a communicative, dimension. The issues of consensus, shared understandings and a common perspective are repeatedly raised in the literature. Advocacy coalitions are explicitly concerned with belief systems, both core beliefs and policy beliefs about how to protect those core beliefs. Dowding identifies key resources as knowledge or information, legitimate authority, conditional and unconditional incentives to affect preference formation and the identification of interests, and, lastly, reputation (Dowding *et al.* 1995). These resources are all fundamentally imbued with a communicative dimension. They have to be talked about and argued about before they become effective (*pace* Majone 1989; Stone 1989; Hajer 1989; Hood and Jackson 1991; Throgmorton 1991; Fischer and Forester 1993; Hillier 1993). This suggests that a further slice of the analysis of these case studies should concern the nature of the policy discourses in the cities, which in turn reflects back to a issue raised at the beginning, the inherent ambiguities of sustainable development and need to explore how the term is constructed locally.

POLICY DISCOURSES IN THE CITIES

The distinctive economic structures and the distinctive politics of the environment of the two cities are associated with quite distinct dominant policy discourses, as evidenced by the views, arguments and language of key policy-makers in the three identified policy areas of traffic restraint, retail location and green-space management.

In Leicester, concern with the economic position of the city compared to its neighbours is reflected in a 'Leicester Boosterism' discourse based in a broad consensus across the policy-makers interviewed. Although it exaggerates somewhat both the current economic situation in the city and the potential for change, this is nevertheless a dynamic discourse emphasizing and encouraging change. It involves a search for measures which will promote Leicester as a location for development, investment and other consumption activity. It requires action by policy-makers to promote the city in these terms and, given the inevitable resource constraints, it results in an emphasis on city marketing and on the use of property-led regeneration and flagship projects also evident in other cities (Burgess 1981; Ashworth and Voogd 1990; Healey *et al.* 1992).

The Leicester Boosterism discourse tends to dominate much discussion in the city, in so far as it is allowed to set prior goals for policy; the promotion of the city is a necessary element in most policy ideas. This does not always lead to other arguments being sidelined in favour of arguments for economic development. In the case of environmental arguments, it is interesting to note that the ambiguities of many of the key terms such as 'sustainability', 'environmental quality' and even 'amenity' enabled environmental arguments to be subsumed within the dominant discourse. This was evident in relation to both retail location issues and traffic restraint. Following the battles over Centre 21 (the proposed regional shopping centre mentioned above), the local authorities and other key policy-makers pursued a policy which emphasized the city centre as the preferred location for new and enhanced retail development. The recent shopping developments permitted in the central area and the active role that the local authorities, particularly the city council, have played in facilitating these developments is indicative of this policy preference. It has now been possible to ally various environmental and sustainability arguments to support the pre-existing policy. These principally relate to the identified need to maintain the viability of city centres, identified in the EU *Green Book* (CEC 1990) and DoE guidance (Department of the Environment 1993), thereby reducing cross-commuting between settlements and travel to outlying centres for retailing and employment. This is further associated with encouraging higher-density settlements and more concentrated urban forms.

However, this elision of economic and environmental arguments raises certain questions. Focusing retail facilities in the city centre may maximize their accessibility to Leicester residents and avoid cross-commuting between areas of the city in search of particular goods or suppliers. However, it will only reduce transport-based emissions if consideration is also given to the mode and technology by which residents visit the centre: cycling, bus, light rapid transit, electric vehicle or car. While public transport 'solutions' are often included within the policy debate, it is notable that city-centre development precedes any transport modifications and that the plans of developers presuppose provision for the car-borne shopper. Furthermore, the goal of raising Leicester within the urban hierarchy involves attracting shoppers from across the region more generally, which may actually increase the total amount of travel for retailing purposes. Though north–south and east–west conventional rail links are available, most city-centre developments have been to the west of the current prime pitch in Gallowtree Gate, while the railway station is to the east and the two are separated by considerable secondary shopping and the ring road (though there is a pedestrian underpass). There has been little consideration of how promotion of the city, and in particular the city centre, actually meshes with the goal of travel reduction, or at least transport-based emissions reduction. Rather, the discourse is driven by the *assumed* benefits of maintaining retail facilities in the centre rather than on the extreme periphery.

Similarly, the debate on traffic has been linked to the Leicester Boosterism discourse. This has involved defining the traffic problem in terms of congestion and the impact that such congestion has on the attractiveness of the centre to visitors and shoppers, and thus to developers and investors. Traffic restraint, in the form of altering road layouts and full or partial pedestrianization, is thus a solution to congestion *and* a means of improving the image and experience of the city. Light rapid transit systems can also be seen as tackling congestion and, given their comparative novelty, as a form of urban marketing. Environmental arguments are here again harnessed to reinforce arguments for such policy measures.

The general arguments for reducing car travel are supplemented by localized concerns about air pollution. Traffic-free areas are experienced as having a better air quality *and* improving the amenities of the city centre. However, as Leicester has found out, semi-pedestrianization – particularly with free access for buses – creates neither a safe, pleasant nor a low-pollution area for shoppers and visitors. Furthermore, a focus on traffic restraint and its impacts in the localized area of the city centre will not address the broader sustainable development concerns over patterns of travel. Given the policy preference for promoting the city centre, the problem remains of how people are to get to the city centre. Traffic restraints in the centre could ease congestion and local air quality there, but what of the amount of traffic involved in reaching the city or edge-of-centre periphery? Should parking around the centre be increased, with visitors then moving into the traffic-free areas by foot? Is more road investment needed to ease access to these parking areas? Or should parking be restricted and access along radial routes continue to be hindered to try and deter visitors from using the car and encourage them to transfer to some form of public transport? These difficult questions remain unresolved in the discourse which meshes city-centre promotion, reduction of traffic congestion in the centre and both local and global environmental concerns.

Meanwhile, the discussion of policy for green-space management remains somewhat divorced from the dominant Leicester Boosterism discourse. The nature of the relationship depends on the location of the green spaces in question. Where they are to be found in the city centre the management of these spaces becomes attached to the concern with city promotion and the main rationale of management is enhanced amenity. However, in Leicester many green spaces are in the suburbs or urban periphery, or in abandoned former industrial sites outside the core. Here there is the possibility for green spaces to be seen as multifunctional: amenity ranking alongside recreation, production (as in allotments) and, importantly, ecological value. Given an active local environmental movement and one key mover, in the form of the Leicester Ecology Trust, considerable effort was put into detailing the ecological value of various green spaces, and this data, in the form of an ecological survey, is now a key input into decision-making on specific sites. Similarly, recreational use of open (not always green) spaces, promoted by various community groups, has been taken on board by the city council, resulting in a policy protecting such spaces in areas of 'open space deprivation'. The green-space policy debate has therefore developed in more diverse ways, more open to environmental and community-based concerns, because it is seen as peripheral to the concerns of economic development in the city.

In Edinburgh, again a dominant policy discourse can be discerned, but this contrasts markedly with the case of Leicester. Policy debate in the Scottish city is based not on the perceived need to attract more development and investment, but on the generally held view that Edinburgh is sufficiently wealthy and that the city centre, at least, is on the verge of overdevelopment. Hence there is a willingness to divert development pressures. In particular, there is concern that the historic urban heritage should be conserved, exemplified in a 'Historic Edinburgh' discourse. This is a conservationist, even preservationist, discourse primarily opposed to change, unlike the Leicester Boosterism discourse. It is associated with a general satisfaction with the urban environment expressed by key policy-makers and a recognition of the uniqueness of that environment. It is also, perhaps, typical of a capital city, where the commitment to the physical urban heritage comes to represent the commitment to government institutions located there: hence the sensitivity of development proposals affecting seats of government or the monarchy. Furthermore, it relates closely to the importance of tourism in the local economy: the preservation of Historic Edinburgh is essential to the tourist trade.

Hence, in the discussions on retail location there is general support for diverting some retail pressure to edge-of-city locations, as in the South Gyle centre. The Historic Edinburgh position also supports a selective diversion of retailing in which specialist and high-value comparison shopping is retained in the centre, with more everyday facilities being pushed out. The tourist base of the economy also recommends this strategy, since specialist shopping is more appropriate to the historic experience being sold to tourists. This again contrasts with Leicester, where the range of shopping is kept within the centre and the large market itself caters for many everyday needs. (In both cities there were, of course, small district shopping centres and supermarkets for these everyday needs also.)

There is little explicit harnessing of environmental arguments in these arguments about retail facilities in Edinburgh. It is seen as being essentially a matter of providing for demand within the limits of Edinburgh's heritage. Yet, with its reasonably large city-centre population, Edinburgh is more akin to many continental cities, where there would be scope for providing shopping facilities within ready walking distance of residential areas, thus mirroring the pedestrian-dominated, mixed land-use cities described in many of the polemics about urban sustainable development, and indeed in the EU *Green Book*. However, the spatial split between specialist and everyday shopping promoted by the Historic Edinburgh strategy works against achieving this ideal.

While the central shopping areas of Edinburgh are close to the main railway stations and the bus service is generally considered to be a good one, there has been little consideration of how the emerging patterns of retailing could best be served by the public transport system. The new South Gyle shopping centre was designed to be fed primarily by car traffic, and localized congestion was exacerbated during the early weeks of its opening. Discussion continues over local road improvements to ease such congestion. Less concrete discussion is occurring over how public transport improvements could serve the site. Indeed, the various suggestions for public transport initiatives – north–south metro and reopening a railway line to give a south-circular suburban route – are focused more on easing the problems of commuters to the city, reflecting the prominent position of Edinburgh as an employer in the regional economy.

The traffic restraint discussion is, as in Leicester, focused on a definition of the problem in terms of congestion. In comparison with other cities, traffic congestion seems relatively modest, but a strong concern with traffic delays and parking problems was expressed by several key actors interviewed. This concern relates to the need of three specific groups: the middle-class residents of the central area; the office-users, who expect to be able to access the city and park by their offices in the centre; and the tourists, although provision for this group was resented by some, it was largely justified in terms of not depriving residents and existing occupiers of their use of roads and parking space. Convenience for the presumed 'owners' of road space, the existing residents and occupiers of Edinburgh, is the key criterion against which the problems of traffic and parking were judged, thus preventing any serious consideration of solutions in terms of traffic restraint and pedestrianization. Given that amenities are protected by other aspects of the Historic Edinburgh project, traffic restraint is not used to this end.

The environmental arguments about transport and traffic across the city are not foregrounded. This is not to say that there is no appreciation of the environmental aspects of travel patterns. Rather, this appreciation is occurring over a broader range of spatial scales than in Leicester. There are small-scale initiatives: as in Leicester, the local cycling NGO is active in promoting cycleways, and moves towards establishing a network have, indeed, gone further in Edinburgh. However, at the other end, there are major regional transport changes which engage the energies of local authorities and NGOs alike. A focus of debate has been the Joint Authorities Transport and Environment Study (JATES) (Halcrow Fox 1990). This was commissioned by the regional council to consider a number of transport scenarios, including the impact of road pricing on traffic flows. While congestion and cost were the major criteria against which the options were judged, there was at least an implicit consideration of environmental consequences. NGOs, including the Scottish Wildlife Trust, have therefore been involved in representations on JATES and the associated policy discussions. Between these levels of localized initiatives and responses to regional proposals there is little scope to consider how local and global environmental impacts arise from city-level changes in land-use patterns. Again, the locus of Edinburgh as a quasi-capital focuses many NGOs on acting at a regional or national level rather than remaining city-focused, and the actions of the Scottish Office in some ways can override the actions of regional and city councils in developing local policy. Thus local policy discourse becomes more fragmented and environmental concerns have to be integrated into policy debate at many different levels. Leicester offers a more unified and perhaps coherent discourse at the city level.

The broader regional and national focus of Edinburgh NGOs also affects the discussion of green-space management, with some Edinburgh-based NGOs having an involvement in projects and policy developments well beyond the city. This is reflected in a broader level of discussion of environmental issues more akin to London-based NGOs; again, they are less exclusively city-focused. But there are a number of locally based initiatives as in Leicester and, again as in Leicester, these are discussed in many terms: amenity, recreation, production and ecology. Depending on location and the relation of the green space to built features of the city, the discussions of green-space management have a closer or more remote relation to the Historic Edinburgh discourse. For example, the Edinburgh Green Belt Trust concentrates on restoring spaces and buildings within them primarily to preserve features of historic importance and maintain their contribution to the heritage of Edinburgh. The Green Machine is a project focused more on spaces in peripheral estates where the emphasis was on community involvement in restoration, continued management and use of the spaces for a variety of purposes. Elsewhere sites of ecological importance are managed and protected for reasons of nature conservation; the Scottish Wildlife Trust is involved in such cases. As in Leicester, this most obviously 'green' policy issue is able to retain some distance from dominant policy discourses in the city, reflecting also the operation of an issue network rather than a tightly defined policy community. This discussion shows the ways in which sustainable development in urban areas becomes differentially defined in different local areas and the ways in which the ambiguities of the term become interpreted in various local policy areas.

This active exploration of the term by the actors in the local policy process is an integral element of the operation of local policy networks. And an understanding of the resulting discourses provides a key to understanding local political activity and its relationship with economic interests. Language can be a resource in policy change but it can also act as a constraint, a resource in the mouths of those who benefit from the status quo. Understanding current usage can help distinguish pressures for change from resistance to change.

CONCLUSION

This Chapter has sought to show the benefits of a qualitative approach to research on local environmental policy, in particular an approach which incorporates a discussion of local policy discourses alongside that of economic interests and political participation in policy. It has shown in two case studies that the structures of economic interests, policy discourse and policy networks are closely related.

In Leicester we found a relatively weak economic structure and a closely integrated set of city-level networks of policy actors. This was reflected in a consensus on local economic development focused on the city centre, a consensus cemented by resistance to past threats from out-of-town development. An active environment movement was influential in incorporating environmental arguments and criteria into a wide variety of policy areas, but not necessarily in such a way as to overcome the presumption in favour of economic development policy goals; rather, environmental arguments could be subsumed within economic arguments.

In Edinburgh we found a strong economic base and no consensus on attracting more development to the centre, but rather a consensus on diverting some of the pressures away from the centre. The consensus in favour of preserving the historic heritage of the city reinforced this view. This consensus did not find form in a strong coalition of policy actors; rather, there was a fragmented and weak pattern of networking. The purely city-level focus was also missing since there were strong pulls towards considering issues at the regional and even the national level. Environmental discussion was also pulled towards a broader range of spatial scales than just the urban one. For these reasons environmental arguments were less integrated into decision-making across the spectrum of issues, except where they could be reflected as part of the pervasive concern with the historic heritage of Edinburgh.

This suggests that moves to secure the implementation of sustainable development at the urban level need to take cognizance of the pattern of economic interests in the city, the extent to which these are cemented into local decision-making through policy communities, and the possibility that the norms and values of these interests may be reflected in local policy discourse. Advancing the environmentalist agenda involves a challenge to economic interests, so that local policy for environmental goals requires support through changes in political organization and patterns of communication. Creating new patterns of urban governance in which environmental issues drive networking and offering resources for environmental interests to bargain with are two paths forward. But attention also needs to be paid to the language of policy to ensure that environmental arguments are not subsumed beneath economic ones and that a fuller range of rationales for environmental policy action are given a hearing.

NOTE

1 The members of the British team were Alison Greig (now at Surrey County Council), Michael Hebbert (now at the University of Manchester), Sonia Livingstone (LSE), Peter Lunt (University College London), George Myerson (King's College London) and the author.

REFERENCES

Ashworth, G. J. and Voogd, H. (1990) *Selling the City: Marketing Approaches in Public Sector Urban Planning*, London: Belhaven.

Barde, J.-P. and Button, K. (1990) *Transport Policy and the Environment*, London: Earthscan.

Burgess, J. (1981) 'Selling places: environmental images for the executive', *Regional Studies* 16(1): 1–17.

CEC (1990) *Green Paper on Urban Environment*, COM(90)218, Brussels: CEC.

—— (1992a) *Green Paper on the Impact of Transport on the Environment*, COM(92)46, Brussels: CEC.

—— (1992b) *Towards Sustainability: A European Community Programme of Policy and Action in Relation to the Environment and Sustainable Development*, COM(92)23, Brussels: CEC.

Department of the Environment (1992) *Development Plans and Regional Planning Guidance: Planning Policy Guidance No. 12*, London: HMSO.

—— (1993) *Town Centres and Retail Development: Planning Policy Guidance No. 6*, London: HMSO.

—— (1994) *Sustainable Development: The UK Strategy*, London: HMSO, Cmnd 2426.

—— (1995) *Air Quality Management Strategy*, London: HMSO.

Dowding, K. (1995) 'Model or metaphor? A critical review of the policy network approach', *Political Studies* 43(1): 136–158.

Dowding, K., Dunleavy, P., King, D. and Margetts, H. (1995) 'Rational choice and community power structures', *Political Studies* 43(2): 265–277.

Ecotech Research and Consulting Ltd with Transportation Planning Associates (1993) *Reducing Transport Emissions through Planning*, London: HMSO.

Engwicht, D. (1992) *Towards an Eco-city: Calming the Traffic*, Sydney: Envirobook.

Fischer, F. and Forester, J. (eds) (1993) *The Argumentative Turn in Policy Analysis and Planning*, London: UCL Press.

Greig, A. D. (1993) 'Urban sustainability: an annotated bibliography', Department of Geography research paper, London School of Economics.

Hajer, M. (1989) *City Politics: Hegemonic Projects and Discourse*, Aldershot: Avebury.

Halcrow Fox (1990) *Joint Activities Transport and Environment Study*, Edinburgh: Sir William Halcrow & Partners and Gower Associates Ltd.

Healey, P., Davoudi, S., O'Toole, M., Tavsanoglu, S. and Usher, D. (eds) (1992) *Rebuilding the City: Property-led Urban Regeneration*, London: E. & F. N. Spon.

Hillier, J. (1993) 'To boldly go where no planners have ever . . . ', *Society and Space* 11: 89–113.

Hood, C. and Jackson, M. (1991) *Administrative Argument*, Aldershot: Dartmouth.

Lindblom, C. (1990) *Inquiry and Change*, Newhaven, CT: Yale University Press.

Majone, G. (1989) *Evidence, Argument and Persuasion in the Policy Process*, New Haven, CT: Yale University Press.

Mazza, L. and Rydin, Y. (eds) (1997) 'Urban sustainability: discourses, networks and policy tools', *Progress in Planning* 74(1): 1–74.

Owens, S. and Cope, D. (1992) *Land Use Planning Policy and Climate Change*, London: HMSO.

Rhodes, R. and Marsh, D. (1992) 'New directions in the study of policy networks', *European Journal of Political Research* 21: 181–205.

Sherlock, H. (1990) *Cities Are Good for Us*, London: Transport 2000.

Stone, D. (1989) 'Causal stories and the formation of policy agendas', *Political Science Quarterly* 104(2): 281–300.

Throgmorton, J. A. (1991) 'The rhetorics of policy analysis', *Policy Sciences* 24: 153–179.

8   Dimensions of sustainable development and scales of policy-making

Tim Marshall

Environmental policy is made at a number of levels in western Europe. This variety of levels is officially encouraged in the EU, by the Fifth Environmental Action Programme, and globally by Agenda 21. But there is considerable diversity in the force of these policy-making efforts at each level, and in the ways in which the levels interrelate. This Chapter explores some aspects of this diversity, by examining the recent experience of two cities, within their regions: Barcelona/ Catalonia and Birmingham/West Midlands. In looking at these places, there are three aims: first, to establish the extent of similarity and difference in environmental policy-making; second, to relate these differences to three facets of the cities/regions – their characters in economic, ecological and political terms; and, third, to comment on the levels of intervention and the powers necessary to make progress in environmental policy.

Two caveats are necessary. First, emphasis is placed on the urban and regional planning dimension of environmental policy, though not to the exclusion of related areas. This is important in considering the relationships with central-state and EU policy-making as these relationships are different in the field of urban and regional planning from those in other fields – fields such as environmental taxation, or direct regulation, of water and air pollution. Second, the discussion focuses primarily on policy-making, not on implementation or on policy impacts. This is inevitable, given that little research exists on the effects of recent policies, if only because of their recentness. In any case, policies and the actions following on from them are not easily separated, and normally policy-makers do pay attention to ensuring that policies are at least potentially implementable.

DIMENSIONS OF SUSTAINABLE DEVELOPMENT

The analysis will make use of a division of environmental policy fields into two zones. One zone may be seen as including softer options, the other harder ones. Table 8.1 shows a number of detailed policy fields placed in either column A or column B. Such a device clearly has all sorts of temporal or spatial limitations, but it is useful for present purposes. The division is not related directly to any previous divisions or categorizations of this type, such as those developed by, or referred to by, O'Riordan (1983), Dobson (1990), Turner *et al.* (1994) or Young (1993). Those divisions refer either to types of environmentalism or environmental politics (technocentric/ ecocentric, light green/dark green and so on), or to kinds of sustainable development to be aimed at (weak or strong, for example). Normally these divisions relate to mainstream economics. The two zones presented here, on the other hand, include rather more concrete lists of objectives to be achieved by environmental policies. They could be more precisely presented as part of an ascending ladder of clusters of environmental achievement. Here, division into two zones makes discussion much simpler. While, coincidentally, some might fit into 'weak' or 'strong' categories of sustainable development, the basis of categorization has nothing to do with concepts of 'natural capital' or 'man-made capital'. All the characteristics listed in Table 8.1 are concerned with biophysical dimensions of sustainable development (considered as 'sustainability' per se), not with the social or political dimensions of equity, liberty or justice, which, it is considered, should be maintained as separate objectives of political activity.The criteria for choice and allocation of the objectives are essentially intuitive, based on an understanding of the amount of 'give' in western European countries at present – in economic, ecological and political terms. A theoretical basis for such intuition could be elaborated, drawing on the ideas of critical realism in the environmental field (Dickens 1996; Bhaskar 1994). This would argue that all western European countries have, in varying degrees, certain critical mechanisms within their economies and polities which facilitate or impede policy development: primarily, at present, the power of capital and the weakness of government, at all levels, and of social movements or forces opposed to capital. These mechanisms intersect with critical ecological processes, as over the different fragility of ecosystems, for example.

Looking, then, at the two city/region cases, the following observations emerge. First, they are *similar*, in that both are making some progress on the A dimensions. Second, they are *different*, in that in

Table 8.1 Examples of 'soft' (A) and 'hard' (B) dimensions of sustainability policies

A – 'soft' dimensions	B – 'hard' dimensions
Reducing slightly domestic and industrial waste streams, and switching between landfill and incineration treatments	Reducing drastically domestic and industrial waste streams
	Reducing car use, with large shift to public transport
Investing in some fields of public transport, especially if technologically smart or fashionable (trams)	Reducing overall water use
	Cutting rate of land urbanization (or de-ruralization) to 0 per cent or close
Reducing some air pollution, via shift of some industries abroad and some technical improvements	Protecting connected ecosystems and especially fragile ones (especially water-based)
Reducing most obvious of water pollution problems, to certain standard	Shifting from road freight to rail and water (or even reducing rate of shift from rail to road)
Reducing slightly rate of land consumption, via urban and regional planning	Reducing mining and quarrying (especially aggregates), except by increased imports
Reducing worst effects on key wildlife ecosystems, especially in famous scenic zones	Reducing air travel (passenger or freight)
	Transforming dramatically processes of chemical industries

Birmingham/West Midlands there has been far more *thinking* about how easy or hard it might be to progress on the B dimensions, within public sector exercises, than in Barcelona/Catalonia. Third, in terms of *formulated policies* the lack of progress on the B dimensions is fairly *similar* in both areas.

It is suggested, therefore, that certain policy fields have been entered, within a quite weak environmentalist discourse; also, that in Britain a more fundamental set of concerns has been raised and debated recently. But the argument here is that this has not been sufficient to progress the more difficult policy areas. The apparently peculiar result is that despite different terms of debate, policies are not greatly different in these two contexts. This is not to say that there is *no* difference. As will become clear, somewhat greater progress has been made in the English than in the Spanish case, especially at city level. The three points above are very general, but the basic point is that strong policies are not being made in either country; the next step is to ask why this is so. If the analysis has some weight it can lead to the formulation of hypotheses on the structuring forces and mechanisms which are affecting environmental policy-making progress, 'underneath' or 'beyond' the variations generated by the different case contexts. This is not a simple statement about the current relative powers of state, capital and social forces – though it is partly that; it points to more complex interrelations between the dominant power mechanisms and the changes in ecological systems, at many levels.

VARIATIONS IN THE POLICY CONTEXTS

The detailed differences between the two cases will emerge below. But there are four key variations. First, there is more overall regional autonomy in Catalonia, with tighter central government control in Britain. Nevertheless, considerable taxation and regulatory power remains with the central Spanish state, through control of infrastructure investment, framework legislation and EU funds. Second, there is rather more of a municipal and regional planning tradition in Birmingham and the West Midlands, although within a fairly centrally constrained planning system. In England there are two strong levels of spatial planning (municipal and central) and one weaker level (regional planning guidance). In Spain there is one strong level only (the municipal), with a weaker regional planning level and virtually no purely planning policy-making by the central state, beyond the basic legislation. Regional planning in Catalonia is carried out directly by the regional government, while in the UK it is a mixed process involving both a forum of the region's local authorities and the regional offices of central government. Third, there is more consciousness of the potential role of urban and regional planning in sustainable development in Britain, with policy development occurring on this at local, regional and central levels. The planning system in Britain is probably more suited to such a role, given its recurrent tendency to go beyond purely physical and land-use issues. Spanish planning's architectural and engineering base makes consideration of ecological issues less immediately easy and attractive, though by no means impossible. Finally, the city–regional balances of population and activity in the two cases are not dramatically different. Birmingham city contains about one-fifth of the region's population, even though the whole conurbation has a proportion nearer to the concentration of the

Barcelona metropolitan region in relation to Catalonia – 50 per cent versus about 60 per cent. But, like Barcelona municipality (which has 27 per cent of Catalonia's population), Birmingham's activity has a disproportionately large effect on the functioning of the region.

Environmental policy-making and planning in Birmingham and the West Midlands

Conclusions in England are based on an examination of Birmingham's Unitary Development Plan (Birmingham City Council 1994b), on environmental strategies prepared by the same authority (Birmingham City Council 1993a, 1993b), and on the documents on advice for regional planning guidance and on regional economic strategy prepared by the West Midlands Regional Forum of Local Authorities (1993a, 1993b).[1] Figure 8.1 shows a map of the region. The regional reports contain numerous references to sustainable development, and the processes behind their preparation involved extensive attempts to build environmental concerns into planning and economic strategies. Statements of a general form ('reducing the need to travel', for example) are often quite strongly environmentalist. However, when fundamental issues affecting economic growth are involved, the needs of the economy and the current lifestyles of residents are given priority. This is most obviously the case in the economic strategy, which formed the basis of bidding for EU Structural Funds. But it also underlies the Regional Forum's submission to central government on future regional planning guidance. In that document this is furthered by a confusing terminology, which presents the two key Chapters under the headings 'sustainable development' and 'sustainable environment'. The first consists simply of the 'normal' proposals for development of a traditional strategy, with only occasional reference to any environmental issues. The 'sustainable environment' section, on the other hand, contains the more immediately 'environmental issues', energy, minerals, waste and 'environmental assets' – anything from air, water and open land to townscape, nature conservation and recreation. This uncomfortable phrasing and division tends to perpetuate the confusions around economy–environment relations, and around planning's role in this nexus, rather than truly integrating sustainable development issues into change (or non-change) of all kinds.

The Birmingham Unitary Development Plan (Birmingham City Council 1994b) was produced in draft form in 1990–1991 (although it was not adopted until July 1993) and therefore predates the main entry of sustainable development into British planning. There is no mention of sustainable development, and 'environment' is used in the traditional planning sense. The 'Environment' Chapter has the following subheadings: built environment, nature conservation, green belt, open

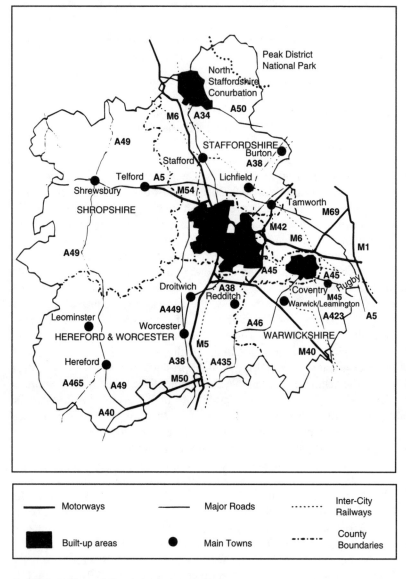

Figure 8.1 West Midlands – spatial structure
Source: West Midlands Regional Forum (1993b, vol. 1)

space, playing fields, children's play, allotments, and sports facilities. The other sections have little or no references to environmental considerations. In the 'Economy' Chapter it is simply stated that environmental quality is a complement of economic success. Both transport and retailing Chapters, with their emphasis on public transport and on protecting existing centres, support key green objectives, but with very little reference to environmental justifications. At the same time, transport policies also contain major support for road-building programmes, and the opposition to out-of-centre retailing is mild. Several of these features no doubt reflect a desire not to go against the government guidance already in place in 1990. At any rate the result is an only very slightly green development plan.

Perhaps more surprisingly (given its later preparation date), the Planning and Architecture Department's *Environmental Strategy: Departmental Action Programme* (Birmingham City Council 1994a) contains a quite traditional approach to greening in most respects – landscaping, environmental improvements, seeking 'economy, efficiency and amenity in the use of land' and referring to the 'nearly 5000 environmental changes' approved each year under planning legislation (Birmingham City Council 1994a: 1). Only in the transportation field is there some sign of a move to look at B dimensions, with strong promotion (or at least argument for) public transport. On the other hand the *Green Action Plan* documents (Birmingham City Council 1993a, 1993b) have a much more ambitious agenda, with a strong statement of environmentalist principles in the general document and some significant starts to initiatives in the programme. These actions include the establishment in 1992 of an Environmental Forum of councillors and a wide range of local organizations, publication of annual State of the Environment reports from 1993, with all the reorientation of data collection required for this, as well as continuing greening of the Council's own operations and interventions. Here the discourse of sustainability is clear and has evidently been thought through corporately. However, even here an enormous gap remains between the taking on of a challenging green agenda and the very modest progress being made – confined primarily to 'soft' dimensions. As in British Local Agenda 21 initiatives generally, there appears to be a great will to advance, at least expressed rhetorically, (mis)matched by an absence of stronger B policy measures. Some Birmingham council officials are clearly aware of this disjunction – the awareness is perhaps a useful first step, but one likely also to generate enormous frustration.

In all these exercises there was wide involvement of non-government actors, especially of business organizations, even though elected councillors had the final say. The exercises can be seen as forms of strategic planning (in the broader-than-urban-planning sense), involving many of the relevant stakeholders at urban and regional level. They therefore constitute a fair representation of those with economic and political power in the city and region, filtered by a particular (mainly Labour Party) ideological viewpoint, between 1991 and 1993.

Environmental policy-making and planning in Barcelona and Catalonia

In Spain environmental issues have come on to political agendas more slowly and unevenly. Barcelona and Catalonia are shown on Figure 8.2. Barcelona City Council was harried by local green activists into producing its first environmental programme in 1994 (Barcelona City Council 1994). This consisted of an introductory explanation of the seven general directions and of twenty action subprogrammes. It is striking that the council argued that their large-scale urban transformations of recent years, including the Olympics, all ran along green lines – a claim most environmentalists would strongly dispute, with the exception probably of the open-spaces programme. The seven general lines also stressed a certain traditional blending of social and environmental objectives, with an emphasis on green space, 'human comfort' and citizen consciousness, as well as on the more familiar (northern European) aspects of energy, pollution and waste.

The twenty subprogrammes in general reflect a relatively early stage of work on green issues, with stress on building up capacity to monitor, to make the initial easier interventions over matters nearer to the control of the council (transport fleets, parks and gardens, building use and so on) and to encourage environmental education and consciousness. An attempt was being made to work with local greens (and with Greenpeace on an energy assessment of the city), but the major coalition of green groups criticized the programme heavily as being long on aspirations and very short on real proposals (Barcelona Estalvia Energia 1994). Certainly the programme has a strong flavour of the date of its preparation, when council spending was being heavily pared back. The subprogramme on planning argued that the present direction of planning strategy had environmental potential, by developing a new polycentric, more mixed-use urban structure, by keeping quite high densities (like in the Olympic village), by improving accessibility (with the ring roads) and extending parking within residential areas (with underground car parks). Again, many environmentalists would dispute some of these claims, though they would support some

Figure 8.2 Catalonia, the Barcelona metropolitan region and the Barcelona urban core
Source: Corporación Metropolitana de Barcelona (CMB) (1983)

of the proposals for more environmentally sensitive planning-control guidelines.

The programme rarely went far beyond existing policies, pursued since environmental efforts began in the early 1980s, and it reveals an inability to move beyond just some of the 'soft' dimensions of sustainability. Environmentally useful policies which already existed included support for public transport, for urban planning, and for some degree of domestic waste recycling, all well-established policy fields. Meanwhile the Olympics strategy had bequeathed, above all, a not very green urban motorway system, and the Barcelona 2000 Strategic Plans begun in 1988 and 1992 contained relatively limited environmental elements. The second strategic plan makes even less reference to environmental issues than the first, having changed its prime objective from that given in an earlier section, which had referred to 'sustainable development' and 'ecology' (Marshall 1990, 1996).

Higher levels of government have not improved the situation much so far. At the Barcelona metropolitan region level, work on a plan since 1989 (the *Pla Territorial Metropolitá* (PTM)) looks likely to result in relatively strong policies for the protection of rural land, but within a broadly developmentalist framework, above all of road-building (Marshall 1993). The Delta Plan, for a key set of infrastructures near to Barcelona city on the Llobregat delta, is equally oriented to economic development, despite commitments to protect remaining wetlands and make some long-overdue environmental investments, such as a water purification plant for the Llobregat river (Marshall 1994).

In Catalonia as a whole, the regional plan (*Pla Territorial General* (PTG)), approved in March 1995 by the parliament of the regional government (Generalitat de Catalunya 1993), is again primarily oriented to unblocking possible impediments to future economic growth – especially from bottlenecks in water supply, energy supply and road systems. In response to green pressures, references were added to sustainable development, but this has not changed the general direction of the plan (Marshall 1995).

In Catalonia, therefore, there is the uncomfortable sensation that some of the sustainability discourse has been heard, and occasionally added on to plans, but that this has never informed processes of preparation or public debates on strategies in any fundamental way. A major piece of 'future studies' work (Institut Català d'Estudis Mediterrànis 1993) confirms this impression, with environmental issues primarily confined to the clean-up and damage-limitation aspects of the 'soft' dimensions. In the West Midlands, at least extensive reflection and debate on the implications of sustainability had taken place, on the very rapid learning curve of the 1990s in the British planning and public policy fields. But the results were only beginning to emerge, to a limited extent, mainly at the city level. One hope for the future is contained at the end of the last volume (vol. 9) of the economic strategy (West Midlands Regional Forum 1993b), where, in addition to presenting an environmental goal and set of objectives, a proposal was made for an environmental assessment of the strategy (see Figure 8.3). This is only a proposal, linked to aspirations in EU and other circles for strategic environmental assessment.

The picture, then, is of a much more sustained effort in the English cases, than can be discerned in the Spanish cases, to *try* to think what sustainable development might mean, and with somewhat more progress on at least the 'soft' dimensions at city level. But the absence of any really strong environmental policies in either region is striking.

Environmental Goal and Objectives of the Regional Strategy

GOAL: To secure an environment which is capable of sustaining a quality of life which renders the region an attractive place in which to live and work and which is capable of providing a valuable economic resource.

OBJECTIVES:

To Protect Assets	To Address Problems	To Ensure Future Patterns of Sustainable Development
– Landscapes	– Dereliction	✓ Recycling industrial land
– Wildlife/semi-natural habitats	– Loss and deterioration of wildlife habitats	– Resources for SMEs to improve environmental performance
– High-quality farmland	– Contamination of water by industry and agriculture	– Education and information and training
– Cultural heritage		– Research and development into clean technology
– Coal and mineral reserves	✓ Deterioration of built fabric	– Introduction of new technology
– Air	✓– Waste disposal	– Support for environmentally friendlier sectors
– Water supplies	– Air pollution	✓ Waste minimization and recycling
– Land for future economic activity	– Congestion	– Reducing emissions
– Open space for recreation		✓ Increasing energy and materials efficiency
– Forestry		✓ Renewable sources of energy
		– Balanced package of transport infrastructure
		– Diversification and deintensification of agriculture
		– Management of visitor attractions

Proposal for an Environmental Assessment Process

State Goals and Objectives

▼

Identify Appropriate Indicators to Measure Quality
(to be refined in association with Regional Planning Guidance monitoring)

▼

Measure Quality Using Identified Indicators
(partially undertaken in Environmental Profile)

▼

Identify Agreed Targets and Timescales
(to be derived from UN Agenda 21, EC Fifth Environmental Action Programme,
UK 'This Common Inheritance', regional and local programmes)

▼

Collect Data Relating to Identified Indicators
(carried out by individual authorities and to be co-ordinated)

▼

Assess Progress Made Towards Achieving Agreed Targets

Figure 8.3 Environmental goal and objectives, and proposal for an environmental assessment process
Source: West Midlands Regional Forum (1993b, vol. 9)

Table 8.2 Some social and economic indicators for Catalonia and the West Midlands

Indicator	Catalonia	West Midlands
Gross value added in manufacturing (% 1989)	40.8	40.3
Gross value added in services (% 1989)	57.1	58.3
Population (1992, 1991)	6,082,534	5,200,000
Population in largest municipality/district (1992, 1993)	1,630,635	988,000
GDP at market prices, % of EU total (1989)	1.5	1.4
GDP per head, % of EU average (1989)	83.5	84.6
Average earnings per head per month (1992)	£950	£1,139
Car ownership (1992, 1993)	2,290,000	2,153,000
Numbers in employment (1992)	2,102,000	1,900,000
Numbers unemployed (1992, 1993)	390,000	294,000
Population density per sq. km (1992, 1991)	190	401

Source: Various, including *Regional Trends 1994*, London: HMSO, 1994; *Catalonia Facts and Figures*, Barcelona: Cambra Oficial de Comerç, Indústria i Navegació de Barcelona, 1993; *Regions: Statistical Yearbook 1993*, Brussels: Eurostat, 1993; *Basic Statistics of the Community*, Brussels: Eurostat, 1993

The following section examines the mechanisms and forces behind these policy-making outcomes. As a means of determining the factors which make for progress, three broad headings are used: economy, ecology and politics. Tables 8.2 and 8.3 summarize some key economic, social and political aspects of the regions.

FORCES BEHIND THE POLICY-MAKING OUTCOMES

Economy

The economic structures and histories of the West Midlands and Catalonia show significant similarities. Both are long-established industrial powerhouses which have undergone major crises in the last twenty years but have emerged with still important industrial sectors, many of these with 'dirty' technologies of various kinds. Barcelona and Birmingham both retain industrial bases, but both are being tertiarized, functioning as higher-order service centres for their regions. The lifeblood of both regions now flows along their motorway

Table 8.3 Government structure and planning powers in each region

Level	Catalonia Number of units Planning powers	West Midlands Number of units Planning powers
Central state	(Via ministerial delegations and funding of provinces and other levels)	(Via central Department of the Environment, with regional offices)
	Makes most laws, and influences policy via funding by Ministry of Public Works, Transport and Environment	Makes laws, issues general and regional guidance, guides via infrastructure investment, vets and manages system of public inquiries of district and structure plans and manages system of appeal against local control decisions
Regional government/ autonomous community	Generalitat – Ministry of Territorial Policy and Public Works	None
	Makes further laws within above, guides via regional planning and infrastructure investment, and supervises local planning legality and performance	Regional planning is carried out by central government (via a regional office), taking advice from a forum of the county and district authorities
County/ comarca	41	5
	Limited powers, still mainly advisory at most since law of 1987	Strategic planning via structure plans and some other powers (e.g. transport)
District/ municipality	943	40
	Prime plan-making and control functions	Make district plans and carry out nearly all control functions

structures, with economies partially dispersed and regionalized, in accordance with fragmented production processes.

This is not to say that the economies are the same. The industrial equipment of Catalonia almost certainly has an older age profile than that of the West Midlands, hence incorporating older environmental technologies. In any case, much multinational investment in Catalonia in the 1960s and 1970s is said to have incorporated plants with lower environmental standards than those in the parent (Dutch, German, Swiss) companies – in petrochemicals, plastics, textiles, food processing and so on. This issue of the layering of rounds of capital investment is significant for comparing regions in economic and environmental terms, as is assessment of the rate of turnover of capital (in both Marxian and standard economic senses). More work on these issues could help to bring out differences between different types of old industrial cities and regions.

Furthermore, Catalonia is much more dependent on tourism and on its international connections, with Barcelona airport acting as a key infrastructure articulator, along with the adjoining port and the port of Tarragona. One of the biggest investments in 1990s Catalonia is the competitor to Euro Disney at Salou, controlled by a consortium including Madame Tussauds (Pearson) and the largest Catalan bank, the Caixa. This is next to a vast petrochemical complex, on the driest stretch of the Catalan coast, in an area already dependent on water brought from far to the south. The West Midlands does not share this ecologically demanding dependence on remote places (it 'exports' the recuperation of its workforce, via package holidays, in large part to Spain). Nor does the English region have to sell its natural resources or landscapes to the same intensive degree.

An examination of those infrastructural sectors most closely implicated in environmental decisions (water, energy, waste treatment, roads, rail, land development) reveals few grounds for differentiating the two regions. Most of these sectors now belong to private companies, some being monopolies in their region, others subject to competition. In Catalonia there is rather more regionalized economic power, in some key areas such as gas and water, with significant control by the Caixa. But this only gives a potential concern for the local and regional environment; so far this has hardly been awoken, given the low political profile of radical approaches to sustainable development in Catalonia.

Both the *existence* of these economic facts (and hence their analysis by planners) and their political *articulation* (partly via electoral systems and partly by business lobbying) have no doubt contributed to the limited leverage of radical sustainable development proposals in both regions. Only detailed research would bring support to this hypothesis, but it appears reasonable. The probably greater dependence of Catalonia on more ecologically threatening economic sectors (and on productive technologies within these) may also be tending to retard the emergence of a serious environmental dimension in the politics of the Generalitat or of Barcelona City Council, even more than in the West Midlands. It is noticeable that the most (apparently) green of the parties in Catalonia is the Left Republican – Esquerra Republicana de Catalunya (ERC). Its manifesto argued for an economic base slanted more towards small but technologically advanced businesses (ERC 1993). Neither the Catalan centre-right nationalists (Convergència i Unió; CiU) nor the Socialists dare to take up such green positions, given their links with, or understanding of, the importance of traditional (1960s–1970s) medium or larger companies.

A similar shared understanding no doubt affects West Midlands politics, with both traditional and modern economic sectors evidently dependent on systems of motorway distribution and relatively cheap energy, water and land supplies. No convincing challenge to the form of the current economic structure, and the international competitiveness discourse which articulates it, has apparently been made in the course of recent debates. This leaves sustainable development economically exposed when 'real world' strategies come to be written.

Ecology

Geographically and historically, the ecologies of Catalonia and the West Midlands are very different. Mainly, this has operated to the advantage of the English region, which is blessed with more reliable rainfall, more tolerant soils, the absence of a too-easily abused waste sink like the Mediterranean, but with an easily used water system around the Severn and Trent. Barcelona's conurbation wins over Birmingham on some counts – its very high density (facilitating public transport), its openness to the sea (removing otherwise probably critical air pollution), and its rich farmland nearby in the Llobregat delta and valley (until much was consumed for port, airport, towns and roads). The subsoil of the West Midlands contained more valuable resources (coal and iron) only partially matched by the hydraulic resources harnessed by the Catalan industrial revolution. But both energy economies now depend above all on remote ecosystemic connections – nuclear, oil and gas in Catalonia, oil and gas in the West Midlands. The two major remaining differences in ecological relations are no doubt the soils – potentially almost certainly more dependable in England – and the sun, which gives Catalonia its competitive advantage in tourism, over 10 per cent of its income. Otherwise, the mountainous character of Catalonia both makes development more expensive and protects many more inaccessible ecosystems.

Clearly these ecological relations have been partly generated by and are still mediated by economic and social processes, continually shifting the effects of geographical/historical inheritances. In principle, one might expect that the problems of Catalonia's ecosystems will place a significant burden on its future development, demanding costly adaptations which will be resisted. The greater ecological vulnerability of the southern region perhaps encourages a more desperate search for forms of future livelihood, rather than an awareness of the dangers of overloading natural capacities. Bringing water from the River Ebro (to the south) is broadly supported by the regional plan and by Barcelona city's strategic plans. This will be one touchstone of the approach to be adopted – whether trying to live within some of the few remaining regional scale limits (those on food, energy, minerals, loan finance having long ago been bypassed) or pushing onwards to wider ecological dependencies.

It is hard to trace the impact of these types of ecological relations on the making of responses to the sustainability agenda. In reality nature and economy do not separate in any tidy way, and the responses of actors incorporate into politics a deeply layered and complexly considered set of understandings on which limits are the ones to take notice of.

Politics

Politics has evidently permeated the discussions on economy and ecology. Here attention will be drawn to just two relatively simple elements. One is the different development of green politics. The significant leverage gained by environmental pressure groups, and then by green ideas in Britain since the mid-1980s is well understood. This may have affected a more traditional and industrial city/region like Birmingham/West Midlands less than some other parts of Britain; but the movement and its impact have been in part country-wide, and the professions, especially planning, and other actors such as business, have been influenced there as elsewhere. This has also been incorporated into the language of the central government, especially within the planning guidance emerging from 1992 onwards. This legitimized pressures from the environmental movements and virtually obliged professionals to make attempts to come to grips with sustainability issues.

In Catalonia, and perhaps even more so in the rest of Spain, green politics is marginal, both electorally and in social movements (Aguilar Fernández 1994). Since the 1970s there has been a significant growth in the number of environmental groups, but most of these focused primarily on wildlife issues until the early 1990s. Broader questions raised by sustainable development have only begun to be tackled by a number of smaller ecological groups and, to a degree, by the ex-Communists and some left-nationalists. Thus, in Catalonia pressure to make green plans and programmes has been restricted to left groups like Iniciativa per Catalunya (the ex-Communists) and a relatively small federation of nature protection groups, DEPANA. The main professionals and academics involved, primarily within the architectural and economics fields, have not been greatly affected by green ideas.

A second important political factor is the overall arrangement of political powers and how these intersects with the green pressures (or their absence) just described. Powers are spread among the three levels in Spain, but this diversity has so far given only limited results in terms of creative environmental policy-making at one level or another. In the UK the power concentrated at the centre has tended to hold back innovation lower down, although some local authorities have pushed to get round these limits. In both cases the EU has proved a relevant but relatively weak supporter of any sustainable development initiatives pursued locally or regionally.

Most Spanish central and regional government programmes and plans have been able to treat green issues on, at most, a rhetorical level, incorporating minimal adherence to EU norms and procedures (such as environmental impact assessment). There has been no equivalent of the vaguely green guidance produced by British central government for planners, from either Madrid or the Generalitat. There is some institutional difference between the central Spanish case, where both environmental and infrastructure responsibilities are in one superministry, and those of Catalonia and England, where environmental tasks are in a different ministry from transport. The main central Spanish 'planning' document, the *Plan Director de Infraestructuras* (Ministerio de Obras Públicas y Transportes 1993), refers to ecological concerns often and promotes inter-urban rail and intra-urban public transport but remains essentially a roads and water-supply expansion plan. Catalonia was the first autonomous community to create an Environment Department, in 1991, and under the guidance of an increasingly environmentalist minister (an engineer) this body has pushed as much as it can for progress on cleaning up, recycling and clean technologies in general. But this has not affected the main developmentalist drive of the Generalitat.

The same applies in most municipalities; again, the most active have been the few controlled by ex-Communists, especially that of El Prat in the Llobregat delta (as described in Marshall 1994). In any case, many of the instruments required for any radical advance are not held by the relatively poor city council or, at most, are effectively shared with the remaining metropolitan agencies, the Generalitat or the State. This is so across several key fields – energy, waste, water, transport, housing, urban planning. In some of these areas the main powers are with strong private enterprises, like Gas Natural, Aguas de Barcelona, region- or state-wide electricity companies and large industrial firms. While Birmingham shares many of these weaknesses, it retains a stronger tax base, a larger professional staff and certainly a longer tradition of confident and independent programmed intervention. In both cases, even in the largest local authorities and despite significant efforts at moving forwards, there is a real problem of scale and power. This must affect implementation, which thus conditions policy-making. Implementation has not been analysed here. However, local green activists are already focusing on this issue, through a project developed by the Barcelona Civic Forum. This seeks to develop environmental indicators (along Seattle lines) and subsequently bring municipal and regional governments to account. This may be helped at the level of Barcelona municipality by the presence of the ex-Communists/Greens in the ruling coalition after the 1995 elections. A member of Els Verds became responsible for 'the sustainable city', though in a relatively junior position inside the predominantly Socialist team.

One aspect of this second factor deserves special attention: the presence of a regional tier in Spain – and its absence in England. This has had several partly contradictory effects. In one respect it has reduced the potential advantage that the higher profile of green ideas in England should give to any city and regional authorities wishing to promote green policies. A regional government in England might be expected to be pushing environmental issues more strongly than does central government – partly in direct party-political opposition to that government – and it would no doubt be able to act more effectively than a municipality like Birmingham (large and powerful though that authority is). This is because so many environmental issues transcend municipal boundaries, requiring greater force and legitimacy to deal with bodies such as environmental infrastructure companies (in water, gas, electricity, waste and so on) and with the remaining central government agencies (in road-building and agriculture, for example).

In principle, the presence of a regional government in Catalonia gives it greater possibilities of future ecological-economic planning. In practice this has not materialized to a significant extent, opposed essentially by the first element described above – the weak green consciousness and movements. But Catalonia's structure of government also interacts with the battle lines of its political struggles. The fact that CiU control the Generalitat while Socialists run Barcelona city has in some respects reduced the capacity for effective forward planning, whether on environmental or any other issues. Urban and metropolitan planning still operate primarily within the predemocratic metropolitan plan, and enormous energies were spent in the 1980s on the battle over the shape of metropolitan government – culminating in the 1987 abolition of the metropolitan corporation. These conflicts have undermined the planning processes at the levels of Catalonia (PTG) and Barcelona region (PTM). Perhaps the absence of strong green pressures makes these conflicts less significant for directly environmental issues, but they have affected forward planning on many relevant questions – metropolitan public transport, retailing and open-space protection, for example.

We can see, therefore, that the interplay of political forces and political structures has tended to impede environmental policy-making in Catalonia, despite their potential regional advantage. In the West Midlands, despite little help from political structures, some attempt at progress has been made at both local and regional level. But such progress *might* have been significantly greater if an English regional-government tier existed.

Caution is certainly in order here, because if one tries to synthesize the effect of all the three facets examined above it is not at all easy to assess how the respective weights of economy, ecology and politics would have played out with a change in one facet. It is possible that forces of economic and ecological reality would have created an outcome in Birmingham and the West Midlands that was not very different: perhaps a greener and more intensely discussed rhetoric, but policies remaining on most points solidly in favour of economic growth and further development. On balance, though, a regional government would probably have begun to try to tackle some of the 'hard' dimensions of sustainability – perhaps on public transport, some aspects of energy, water supply and rural land consumption.

CONCLUSIONS

The main difference between Catalonia and the West Midlands has been observed to be that in the latter at least some *discussion* of B ('hard') sustainability dimensions has taken place. Nevertheless, this has not led to the formulation of policies on these difficult areas. Both regions and both cities have, on the other hand, made some progress on the easier (A) dimensions. It was suggested that the somewhat similar economic characteristics of the cities and regions may have provided a basis for the elements of similar response. This was seen as being reinforced by the political factors, which in part weakened the English response (through the absence of a regional-government tier). Whether the ecological factors have been in play directly is very hard to say; but it seems possible that Barcelona/Catalonia's harsher, potentially more limiting situation may actually reduce the scope for greener politics, even though it may impose its own 'solutions' in the longer run. In any case, the fact that *both* regions can (and do) put off decisions on the hard B dimensions by exporting unsustainability (living off remote natural resources of various kinds) gives *both* a basis for 'business as usual'. In that sense their ecological-economic characteristics are really not so different.

Why are the B dimensions hard? In one sense the answer is simple: they appear to require radical changes in either production forms/social behaviour or overall levels of material throughput, or both. It is difficult to say what sort of societies might wish to make such changes (whether those with western European class/status/power forms, or other types). On a more immediate level, there appear to be issues of both scale and public/private powers involved. Tackling effectively most of these issues would have to include action at scales above the local – that is, generally regionally, nationally or beyond – and involve considerable exercise of public or state power. The presence of strongly neo-liberal policies in British central government (which has constrained local and regional action) and the dominance of centrist or neo-liberal policies at regional level in Catalonia, within a primarily private economy, have served to limit the possibilities of radical environmental policy-making in both countries. A major reforging of public, mainly state, powers would be needed in both countries if such radical change were desired. At present there is little evidence, in fact, that change of the magnitude involved in some B dimensions is widely sought – certainly this is so in Catalonia, but no doubt it is also the case in the West Midlands.

The EU has provided some moral and discursive support via funding (Structural Funds) and advocacy (Environmental Action Programme) channels. These have partly been filtered via national governments, in both states, and partly arrived directly, particularly through partly EU-funded networks like the Eurocities club. But the

EU's leverage remains limited, with most of its funding going to developmental projects of questionable value for ecological protection. In any case, Barcelona, Catalonia and much of the non-metropolitan West Midlands receive relatively small amounts of EU funding compared to many other regions.

The central governments remain key actors, most strongly so in the unitary UK but still to a major extent in semi-federal Spain. Certainly the Catalan regional government has much more scope to promote environmental policies, if it wishes to do so, than the local authorities grouped in the West Midlands Forum; but it remains constrained by central government's control of most infrastructure spending, as well as by the municipalities' hold on most direct planning decisions.

Future prospects depend on the playing out of the factors analysed above. The evidence of the efforts of Birmingham's environmental strategists (more than those of their urban planners) and at least some of the analysis and reflection undertaken for the West Midlands strategies suggest that both the local and regional scales of governmental action have potential in progressing some of the harder B fields of environmental policy. This would only be possible with support from higher levels; the example of the Delta Plan, with major central-state funding, is instructive in this respect, as is the weakness of the East Thames Corridor initiative for the London region, *without* such funding. But the localized and regionalized understandings of the interaction of place and environment and the really variable scales of ecosystemic processes provide persuasive arguments for spreading public environmental powers among the local, regional and national tiers. These would have to include powers of the appropriate form, at adequate scales, to deal with both the economic structural factors identified above and the fields of play of ecological relations (defined partly naturally, partly politically). Urban and regional planning must have a major role in such a foundation for sustainability policies, because of the core spatial dimension of such policies – as with particular rivers, sites or transport networks, for example. But these forms of planning also need the powers involved in industrial and fiscal policies, whether articulated regionally or state/EU-wide. Until some of these lessons are learnt, both national environmental strategies and Local Agenda 21s will remain in part paper exercises in the weakly regulated world of floating privatized powers which increasingly characterize Catalan and, even more so, English society.

NOTE

1 It should be emphasized that the DoE's regional planning guidance for the West Midlands, issued in September 1995, is not considered here as it appeared at too late a stage.

REFERENCES

Aguilar Fernández, S. (1994) 'The Greens in the 1993 Spanish general election: a chronicle of a defeat foretold', *Environmental Politics* 3(1): 153–158.

Barcelona City Council (1994) *Programes d'actuació per una política mediambiental a Barcelona*, Barcelona: Ambit de Manteniment Urba i Serveis.

Barcelona Estalvia Energia (1994) 'El ayuntamiento de Barcelona presenta su primer programa medioambiental en un pleno deslucido', *Mientras tanto* 58.

Bhaskar, R. (1994) *Plato etc.*, London: Verso.

Birmingham City Council (1993a) *The Green Action Plan: Birmingham's Strategy for the Environment*, Birmingham: Birmingham City Council.

—— (1993b) *The Green Action Plan: The Corporate Action Programme*, Birmingham: Birmingham City Council.

—— (1994a) *Environmental Strategy: Departmental Action Programme*, Birmingham: Department of Planning and Architecture, Birmingham City Council.

—— (1994b) *Birmingham Unitary Development Plan*, Birmingham: Birmingham City Council.

Corporación Metropolitana de Barcelona (1983) *4 años de acción*, CMB: Barcelona.

Dickens, P. (1996) *Reconstructing Nature: Alienation, Emancipation and the Division of Labour*, London: Routledge.

Dobson, A. (1990) *Green Political Thought*, London: Unwin Hyman.

ERC (1993) *Pels Catalans, per Catalunya* (Election Programme), Barcelona: ERC.

Generalitat de Catalunya (1993) *Pla Territorial General de Catalunya*, Barcelona: Departament de Política Territorial i Obres Publiques.

Institut Català d'Estudis Mediterrànis (1993) *Catalunya a l'any 2010*, Barcelona: ICEM.

Marshall, T. (1990) 'Letter from Barcelona', *Planning Practice and Research* 5(3): 25–28.

—— (1993) 'Environmental planning for the Barcelona region', *Land Use Policy* 10(3): 227–240.

—— (1994) 'Barcelona and the delta', *Journal of Environmental Planning and Management* 37(4): 395–414.

—— (1995) 'Regional planning in Catalonia', *European Planning Studies* 3(1): 25–45.

—— (1996) 'Barcelona – fast forward? City entrepreneurialism in the 1980s and 1990s', *European Planning Studies* 4(2): 147–65.

Ministerio de Obras Públicas y Transportes (1993) *Plan Director de Infraestructuras 1993–2007*, Madrid: MOPT.

O'Riordan, T. (1983) *Environmentalism*, London: Pion.

Turner, R. K., Pearce, D. and Bateman, I. (1994) *Environmental Economics: An Elementary Introduction*, Hemel Hempstead: Harvester Wheatsheaf.

West Midlands Regional Forum of Local Authorities (1993a) *Advice on Regional Planning Guidance for the West Midlands: 1991–2011*, Stafford: West Midlands Forum of Local Authorities.

—— (1993b) *The West Midlands Region: European Development Strategy*, vols 1–9, Stafford: West Midlands Regional Forum of Local Authorities.

Young, S. C. (1993) *The Politics of the Environment*, Manchester: Baseline Books.

9 Implementing European water quality directives

Lessons for sustainable development

Neil Ward, Philip Lowe and Henry Buller

Meeting the challenge of sustainable development will ultimately require government interventions in social and economic life – in short, regulation. If sustainable development is to be successfully applied beyond the level of rhetoric in the European Union, then attention will need to be paid to the precise means by which EU policies are implemented across Europe. Much can be learnt from experiences with existing policies in different regional contexts. This Chapter examines the local implementation of EU environmental policies, drawing upon evidence from a study of water directives in rural regions of France, Germany, Greece, Spain and the UK.[1] The focus of official attention has been on the formal transposition of European laws into national laws rather than implementation on the ground. Differences in national and local, administrative and regulatory contexts and cultures can hamper the construction of an integrated European environmental policy, however, and they serve to highlight the new challenges to be faced in devising a European strategy for sustainable development. There is a need for greater mutual understanding of how perceptions of environmental problems and priorities differ across Europe, as well as a need for greater consideration of practical implementation issues in the drawing up and drafting of European legislation.

Europe's rural areas are not, of course, homogeneous, and types of development and environmental pressures vary from place to place. In much of northern Europe, intensive agriculture has led to increasing environmental pollution and landscape and habitat destruction, while in rural areas of parts of Southern Europe, such as southern France, central and southern Spain, Greece and Portugal, the intensification of agriculture and land abandonment have led to landscape degradation and increased the risk of scrubland and forest fires. The challenge for European sustainable development is to reconcile the different tendencies in such diverse development trajectories while bringing economic and regional development strategies firmly within environmental limits. Combining environmental concerns with economic and regional development objectives will inevitably complicate the delivery of policy at both regional and local level. This emphasizes the need not only for greater monitoring and regulation, but also for fostering administrative modernization in Europe's rural areas, many of which have seen development objectives drawn up and funded through overly narrow sectoral policies, not least the Common Agricultural Policy.

Recent studies of environmental policy in the European 'periphery' have highlighted the potential for greater conflict between economic development and environmental protection (Yearley *et al.* 1994). The term 'periphery' has different meanings: it can be used to refer to Europe's outlying regions (i.e. those lying furthest from the 'core' of greatest economic growth), including the southern parts of the Mediterranean member-states, as well as Portugal and Ireland, or to Europe's rural areas beyond urban and industrial centres. The core–periphery dichotomy sometimes implies a common identity between peripheral areas which may be far from the case, as well as a form of geographical determinism (i.e. the assumption that an area's rurality or remoteness establishes its socio-economic character). Our research has examined the implementation of European environmental policies in different regions, and it happens that all the regions we studied could be called rural. Rurality, however, like 'peripherality', is a concept that can conceal as many differences as those between urban or core areas and the 'rural peripheries'. Thus we consider that our work has been conducted in 'diverse rural regions' rather than in 'the periphery'.

In what follows, we examine the question of differential implementation of European environmental policies across the EU. First, the way that a perceived implementation problem has emerged is briefly outlined, then we go on to assess recent claims about a 'north–south divide' in the implementation of environmental directives. Finally, through a more detailed examination of the 1980 Drinking Water Directive, a central plank in Europe's high-profile and often controversial set of policies to protect water quality, we highlight the particular problems that have resulted from the (uneven) implementation of a Europe-wide environmental protection policy and draw out the lessons of this for European policies for sustainable development.

THE IMPLEMENTATION PROBLEM

Until the mid-1990s, most interest in the implementation of EU environmental policy has focused on inadequacies in the formal transposition of directives into national law. Debates have been dominated by environmental lawyers and have focused on the differences in the national legal and administrative structures of different EU member-states. As the development of directives has evolved from the drawing up of laws and norms, through the transposition into national law, and then into adjustments in administrative practice, so a gulf has become apparent between the stated aims of EU directives and what actually happens on the ground. As a result, there has been increasing concern about uneven implementation between member-states (see, for example, Collins and Earnshaw 1992; House of Lords 1992a, 1992b). Problems arise in a number of respects: different understandings of the broad objectives of directives; different methods for designating zones for special protection; different relationships between EU directives and national or local priorities for environmental management; and different responses in the monitoring and enforcement of directives by member-states.

Some fear that the project of European integration and the role of environmental policy within it have led to over-rapid harmonization, with a real risk of squandering public legitimacy. What is needed, therefore, is a much greater effort to generate common understanding of why national and regional differences arise in perceptions of the nature of environmental problems and priorities, before legislating to harmonize the policies to solve them. The European experience with water quality directives offers several relevant lessons. In particular, there is supporting evidence that much of Europe's environmental policy, and particularly the earlier anti-pollution directives, was drafted without consideration for how ground-level implementation might be organized. Anecdotal evidence from within the Commission suggests that it is the drafting of new legislation that is seen by Commission officials as most interesting and most prestigious – the 'cutting edge', so to speak, of environmental reform. Monitoring of compliance and dealing with technical and administrative problems arising from the implementation of directives once they have been agreed are viewed as a more routine and mundane set of tasks, and the primary responsibility of national governments.

In assessing differences in the implementation of EU environmental policies across member-states, it is worth assessing the data available from the Commission. Table 9.1 shows the differential progress in transposing EU law into national law and Table 9.2 shows the number of suspected infringements of environmental laws brought to the attention of the Commission. Three important problems need to be recognized when dealing with such data, particularly that contained in Table 9.2. First, monitoring the compliance and enforcement of environmental policies is an enormous task. There are over twenty major water quality directives, several of which require large-scale and regular water monitoring and the reporting of results to the Commission, so generating huge volumes of data. The second problem is in part a consequence of the first. The Commission is ill placed to evaluate and judge all this data and it is not in the interests of member-states to draw the Commission's attention to any shortcomings. The Commission is thus highly dependent upon 'whistle-blowers'. Because such a large proportion of suspected infringements of EU environmental directives are brought to the Commission's attention through the complaints procedure (77.7 per cent of the total), it follows that those member-states with active and well-resourced citizens' groups will tend to generate more complaints than others; and so will those countries where the opportunities for formal challenge of the executive (offered elsewhere through federal systems, administrative courts, incorporation of citizens' groups into parliamentary structures and so on) are limited at the national level. Third, the resources within the Commission given over to monitoring compliance and enforcement are miniscule. Within DG XI there are only a handful of lawyers with responsibility for monitoring all EU environmental laws across all member-states. As a result, only a very small percentage of the complaints received by the Commission end up with the issuing of Article 169 letters – the Commission's means of issuing formal warnings to member-states about failure to apply EU law – let alone action in the European Court of Justice. In other words, the data in Table 9.2 shows only a tiny fragment of the whole picture.

Despite these problems with the ways data are generated and compiled at the European level, the use of such data, particularly those contained in Table 9.1, by politicians, commentators and the press has tended to highlight what might be crudely characterized as a 'north–south divide' in the implementation of EU environmental policy. A similar distinction is emerging in the social science literature on comparative implementation of EU environmental policy (see, for example, Aguilar 1994a, 1994b; La Spina and Sciortino 1993). We now turn to a brief review of the arguments surrounding the so-called 'north–south divide' before going on to examine the implementation of the Drinking Water Directive in more detail.

Table 9.1 Formal implementation of EU environmental directives

Member-state	Directives applicable on 31 December 1993	Directives for which measures have been notified	Percentage
Denmark	117	115	98
France	117	111	95
Netherlands	117	108	92
Luxembourg	117	108	92
Germany	119	108	91
Belgium	117	107	91
UK	117	106	90
Portugal	117	106	90
Spain	117	106	90
Ireland	117	103	88
Greece	117	100	84
Italy	117	95	81

Source: CEC (1994: 83)

Table 9.2 Suspected infringements of EU environmental law, 1989–1993

Member-state	Number of suspected infringements
UK	581
Spain	555
Greece	273
Germany	250
France	236
Italy	207
Ireland	169
Portugal	110
Belgium	95
Netherlands	54
Denmark	42
Luxembourg	19

Note: Suspected infringements consist of complaints received by the Commission, parliamentary questions inferring infringements, petitions placed with the Commission and cases of infringement detected by the Commission itself. In 1993 these sources accounted for 77.7 per cent, 2.2 per cent, 1.7 per cent and 18.4 per cent, respectively, of all suspected infringements.
Source: CEC (1994)

THE NORTH–SOUTH DIVIDE IN EUROPEAN ENVIRONMENTAL POLICY

A comparative social science literature on the implementation of European environmental policy is only in its infancy (Buller *et al.* 1993), but in the few published articles that do exist a model is emerging which distinguishes between 'Northern' (or north-centre) member-states (especially Denmark, Germany and Netherlands), and those of the 'south' (Greece, Italy, Portugal and Spain), with Northern member-states reputedly defending strict pollution control policies and Southern states being characterized as 'backward' or 'laggards' in these respects (see Aguilar 1993, 1994b; Kousis 1994). While such simplified models can lead to caricatures of the respective regulatory arrangements in the 'north' and 'south', they can help sensitize those (mainly Northern-based) policy-makers and academic commentators who tend to equate the environmental agenda and priorities of the EU with those of the most active environmental policy-making states of the north. The notion that Southern member-states have particular and distinctive problems in meeting the requirements of European environmental policies has also prompted a fruitful set of studies of environmental policy and European integration in Mediterranean states (see, for example, La Spina and Sciortino 1993; Pridham 1994). Pridham has suggested that 'the idea of there being a "north/south divide" between member-states over the environment can be overrated' (Pridham 1994: 99), not least because of important differences within the so-called 'south'. However, Southern member-states do appear to share a common (though far from unique) set of characteristics. These include: fragmented environmental policy structures which lead to difficulties in administrative procedures and competence; incrementalist rather than rationalist policy styles; weak policy infrastructure; and a strongly local focus to environmental management. In addition, two Italian social scientists, La Spina and Sciortino, in a provocative exposition on the southern European states' experiences with environmental policy, point to what they call a 'Mediterranean Syndrome' as a generic problem underlying the 'ambivalent' responses of Greece, Italy, Spain and Portugal to European environmental law.[2] The Mediterranean Syndrome involves 'a kind of "civic culture" which sanctions non-co-operative and non-compliant behaviour; administrative structures and traditions which make the enforcement of regulative as well as distributive policies difficult and often random; and viscous, fragmented, reactive, and party-dominated legislative processes' (La Spina and Sciortino 1993: 219). Such an analysis, if correct, would suggest that some of the problems of operationalizing EU environmental policies in Southern states arise from fundamental incompatibilities in political culture.

However, counter to the idea that the political and regulatory 'culture' in Southern member-states is hampering effective implementation of EU environmental policy is the suggestion that an inappropriate environmental agenda is being 'imposed' upon them by Northern member-states. This claim has been made by Aguilar (1994a), with particular reference to the Spanish experience, when she argues that in Southern countries the most pressing environmental problems attracting public and political concern involve soil erosion, desertification and the risk of forest fires, yet the EU agenda has been primarily concerned with setting strict limits on air and water pollution. The agenda, she argues, is Northern-driven: 'North European states have played an essential role, to the detriment of Southern states. The more powerful countries, with advanced policies and environmentally sensitized societies, have often managed to impose their costly pollution abatement measures upon countries with different problems' (Aguilar 1994a: 114). Again, there is a danger here of overplaying the divide, and it is also worth noting that Greece, Portugal and Spain all joined the EU after many of the most important air and water pollution directives had been negotiated and agreed. By joining the EU at a later stage and then 'signing up' to all environmental directives en masse, it is inevitable that Spain would have to cope with an environmental agenda originally devised mainly in the north. The 'imposition' of this agenda might, therefore, be seen as an outcome of circumstance rather than of strategy.

The idea of a north–south divide in the drawing up and impact of European environmental policy contains two quite distinctive sets of arguments. The first of these we might term the *modernization thesis*, following Inglehart (1977), which suggests that different European regions or states lie at different stages on a single development trajectory. Once the stage of high mass consumption is achieved and people's basic material needs are met, post-materialist concerns such as environmental protection become increasingly important. Following this argument, it could be suggested that the environmental agenda of Europe's Northern member-states would eventually be adopted in the south once a certain level of socio-economic development is reached there. European integration is merely forcing the pace.

A second set of arguments, which we might term the *diverse development trajectories thesis*, suggests that there is no single, linear development trajectory along which all countries and regions 'progress', but instead a range of different development trajectories and needs. Following this argument, it is not at all certain that the concerns about air and water pollution in the north will necessarily come to be issues of great public and political concern in the south. While parts of the south, and particularly those regions around large urban centres of growth, might see rapid urbanization and industrialization accompanied by a convergence with the environmental agenda of the North, other Southern regions, and particularly more rural regions, are experiencing quite different trajectories of disinvestment, depopulation and desertification which European integration may actually be accentuating.

One consequence of Southern states having to implement advanced air and water pollution controls is that great demands are placed on local administrative resources. Effective environmental protection requires a sophisticated technical capacity, co-ordination between different state and quasi-state agencies, and the involvement of a complex network of public, commercial and civil actors. Part of the modernization thesis outlined above would suggest that administrative modernization in the field of environmental monitoring and regulation ought to be concomitant with economic development. However, often in the south there is a mismatch between the monitoring requirements of the major water quality directives and what is practically feasible.

The so-called north–south divide in the implementation of European environmental policy therefore highlights several issues. The first is that the political and institutional 'culture' of Southern states has not, on the whole, taken on board environmental prerogatives and is having difficulty adapting to the need to do so under the pressures of European integration. There are several reasons for this: the Southern states tend to be urbanizing nations with weakly developed rural administrative capacities, despite having relatively high rural and agricultural populations; there is little social demand for environmental intervention; and higher priorities tend to be given to economic development. Institutional and management structures in some states in the south have traditionally linked environmental concerns with regional planning (as, until recently, had France). Regional planning structures are ill suited to act as regulators and are characterized by 'facultative styles'. That is to say, environmental quality is used in a flexible and non-normative way as a means of promoting regional or local advantages.

A second issue relates to management and institutional resources. Northern European countries have, for the most part, only had to adapt existing environmental management structures to take on board

the requirements of European directives. Often in the south such structures did not exist, and so implementation of directives is triggering or
forcing institution-building.

A third issue raised by the north–south divide is the problem of
collective responsibility and the notion of 'public health'. In southern
Europe – and particularly in rural areas where there has not been a natu-
ralist tradition of viewing the countryside – the notions of public health
and environmental quality as public goods are largely irrelevant to local
experiences. These are northern European notions borne out of long-
urbanized states with relatively high population densities, for whom
these issues are essential to any notion of sustainable development.

In the next section, we turn to a more detailed examination of the
implementation of the Drinking Water Directive in the diverse rural
regions of Europe we have been studying. Our argument is that, rather
than a 'Northern' European environmental agenda simply being
imposed upon the Southern countries, an 'urban' model of water
quality management has been applied across the European territory,
posing particular problems for Europe's more remote rural regions.
Moreover, the differential impacts of major environmental directives
like the Drinking Water Directive on environmental administration
within different member-states can best be understood in terms of the
institutional adaptations and institution-building that directives set in
train.

THE DRINKING WATER DIRECTIVE IN EUROPE'S RURAL REGIONS

The Drinking Water Directive (80/778) was agreed in July 1980. The
various provisions for regulating the quality of drinking water in
member-states, it was thought, could create differences in the conditions of competition, because of the possible significance of pollution
emission standards for industries' costs, and thus frustrate the achievement of the common market. The directive was therefore intended to
standardize drinking water quality norms across the member-states of
the then Community. It sets down sixty-two standards for the quality
of drinking water in order to protect human health, along with the
frequencies for water quality monitoring, and requires member-states
to ensure compliance of drinking water quality within five years (by
mid-1985).

The approach to drinking water quality assessment and control
contained in the directive differs fundamentally from longstanding
practice in several member-states. Its concern with the quality of

potable water as delivered to the consumer means that its impact on the natural environment is secondary – although, given the wide range of often stringent standards laid down in the directive, water sources used for the abstraction of drinking water need to be sufficiently free from contamination to allow inexpensive water treatment. The implications of the directive have been extremely variable across Europe, depending not only upon the physical characteristics of the water sources used for drinking water abstraction and the local hydrogeology but also upon the quality of existing water-supply networks, the relative importance of other environmental obligations and the economic and demographic structure of regions.

However, the standards laid down in the directive and the amount of sampling required reflect the fact that it was drawn up with an urban model of the structure of drinking water provision in mind. The directive is relatively straightforward to implement when populations are connected to the mains (or public) water supply, as they are across much of northern Europe. Problems arise, however, when it comes to applying the directive in the more remote rural areas of northern Europe and across much of the rural south, where households often depend upon private water supplies from wells and boreholes. Private water supplies raise important difficulties not only in the monitoring of drinking water quality, but also in meeting the strict standards laid down in the directive.

The Commission had felt it necessary to stress that the Drinking Water Directive should be applied to all drinking water supplies. In June 1987, for example, it forwarded an Article 169 letter to the UK because of its failure to satisfy the Commission that the directive had been implemented vis-à-vis private water supplies. There had been no legislation or administrative guidance to implement the directive in the UK as far as private water supplies were concerned but, following the Commission's warning, in 1991 regulations were issued to apply the directive's standards to private water supplies.[3]

At the local level, variations in the implementation of the Drinking Water Directive across Europe often stem from variations in the technical, managerial and institutional capacity of member-states effectively to undertake both the sampling, monitoring and enforcement procedures associated with assessing compliance, on the one hand, and, on the other, the necessary investments in water treatment and supply infrastructure required to meet the quality standards laid down in the directive. Although it is initially tempting to see these variations in terms of a traditional north–south divide in Europe, an important urban/rural distinction also emerges.

Certain factors account for the variability in implementation: the nature and the flexibility of the water-supply system, the balance of private supplies to mains supplies, the existence of dedicated water quality sampling and monitoring organizations and the nature and management of water abstraction sites. On each of these factors, rural areas display common implementation problems across the north–south divide.

The nature and flexibility of the water-supply system

A large-scale water-supply system, drawing upon a number of sources and reservoirs and able to treat raw water before supply, will have a set of alternative provision capabilities in the event of the contamination of one or more sources. Thus, a common response to nitrate contamination of abstraction sites has been to mix contaminated water with cleaner water drawn from sites further away. The larger the water-main system, the greater the capacity to overcome contamination and ensure conformity to standards. The urban regions of the member-states have such systems, which are long established, and necessarily draw on alternative sources to maintain supply. For such regions, infrastructure put in place to meet the traditional concern for maintaining the quantity of water supply is, in principle at least, a means of addressing quality. Beyond urban regions, water-supply systems become much more variable.

In France it is the individual communes that are chiefly responsible for supplying drinking water to their inhabitants. Although intercommunal groupings and contracting out to private concessionaires are becoming increasingly common for all environmental services, including water supply and treatment and waste disposal, drinking water supply in many rural areas is still characterized by numerous, small, closed systems. Such systems may draw water from a number of different sources, which are, nevertheless, often contiguous. In France, as in Germany, a key aspect of long-term compliance with the Drinking Water Directive is, therefore, the interlinking of water-supply systems and the creation of pooled reservoirs. In the Breton department of the Côtes d'Amor, for example, where water supply is provided by eighty-one individual communes and forty-nine intercommunal groupings, a Departmental Water Plan, revised in 1991, foresees the development of a set of mains linking the different supply systems to three departmental supply reservoirs. The central role of local authorities in drinking water provision is also a characteristic of the Greek situation, where the rural–urban distinction is all the more marked. The multiplicity of independent sources and supply systems in the remoter parts of rural Greece, coupled with the shortage of appropriate staff and laboratory facilities, make effective water quality control and monitoring extremely difficult.

Private and public supplies

We have suggested that implementation of the Drinking Water Directive is facilitated by the existence of public water mains. By way of contrast, it is rendered virtually impossible in those areas where there is a high frequency of private water supplies. This is quite clearly a rural issue. In the more rural departments of France, as in much of rural Greece, Spain and Germany, individual supplies (i.e. a single-dwelling unit or hamlet being supplied entirely by a private source) are common. Technically, the problem here is a double one of monitoring ability and effective quality control. Socially or politically, it is a question of public versus private responsibilities, or of the incorporation of rural communities into civic society.

Management organizations

Compliance with the Drinking Water Directive requires considerable staff resources and technical investment in water sampling and quality monitoring. Those states or regions that have been able to build upon existing institutions have been less constrained in this than those that have had to set up specific bodies. Once again, an apparent north–south distinction soon gives way, on closer analysis, to an urban–rural one. Greece is, amongst the nations under study here, perhaps the most constrained by the relative absence of technical infrastructure. The lack of effective public monitoring agencies at the local level is undoubtedly a major stumbling block to implementation, particularly in the rural heartland and on the islands. While larger cities such as Athens, Salonika and Patras have well-established laboratories, monitoring in rural areas is frequently contracted out to different bodies, each responsible for separate parameters. EU aid has been sought for the construction of peripheral monitoring facilities to overcome these unsatisfactory arrangements.

The management of water sources

Significant variations exist in the attention given to the quality of water at abstraction sites. For nations and regions where wide-scale water-mains exist, the treatment or mixing of source water or the eventual shutting down of a source is a relatively straightforward option. Where the relationship between the source and the consumer is more direct, nations and/or regions have been forced to focus their actions on keeping sources relatively clean in order to minimize the often costly options of investing in treatment technology or importing water from other regions. In countries with a surfeit of alternative supplies this is not necessary. In Britain, for example, despite the existence of legal powers since 1974 to create protection zones around water sources, these have not been used. Similarly, in Germany public policy has been moving towards the almost exclusive use of groundwater sources and the connection of all users to water mains. In France, Spain and Greece, however, source protection is at the forefront of national and local policy responses to implementing the Drinking Water Directive. In part, this reflects a shortage of investment resources, as much as the limited availability of alternative water sources. In rural France, establishing rigorous source-protection perimeters is a cheaper alternative to investing in water treatment facilities. In rural Greece, the relatively good quality of surface waters permits a low level of investment in water quality improvement.

THE DRINKING WATER DIRECTIVE IN SPAIN'S GALICIA AND IN ENGLAND'S SOUTH WEST

Spanish research was conducted around the Ria Pontevedra in Galicia (i.e. 'wet Spain'), where the water-supply system is shaped by a dispersed settlement pattern. Around 20 per cent of the population in the study area is scattered through open countryside, but the proportion in some rural municipalities can be as high as 60 per cent. In such areas, drinking water comes from private wells, which has meant that traditionally water has been perceived as abundant, of good quality and free. The public supply of water only reaches larger population centres but is being gradually extended. Water quality and supply are becoming more of a public issue, as sewage seeping from septic tanks contaminates drinking water wells, and since the Spanish drought of the late 1980s.

Local authorities (municipalities) are responsible for the management of water and springs but can delegate some responsibility to water companies. With drinking water, water companies (both public and private) have been given statutory responsibility for monitoring the quality of supplies. Local authorities delegate some responsibility to water companies. Unfortunately, local authorities' environmental and public health responsibilities usually far outstrip their resources. As a result, they often require help from higher-level institutions, normally the Xunta (regional government). In smaller local councils, water quality monitoring is carried out not by the water supply company but by inspectors from the Xunta's Department of Health. A consortium involving five municipalities around Pontevedra has also been created to manage water supplies, but only covers the larger settlements with around two-thirds of the population and has no control over the remaining one-third living in smaller settlements. The significant proportion of drinking water taken from private wells – perhaps in around one-third of households – is not controlled according to the directive.

Water supply companies have responsibility for monitoring the quality of drinking water supplies in accordance with the directive. This self-monitoring role is, in principle, subject to checks by the Xunta's Health Department, who are required to be 'vigilant' and control the monitoring. In practice, however, authorities tend to 'trust' water companies. The Department does not consider it necessary to check sampling procedures and will only test water itself if there is a suspicion that monitoring has not been carried out properly.

In Pontevedra the local authority does not consider it necessary to inform the public about water quality – they are contacted only if the supply is to be cut. It is generally felt amongst local authorities that nobody is interested in drinking water quality information, and this is generally the case. Drinking water quality is not an issue of public concern and is not understood to be a public problem. In any case, the public tend to trust the authorities to supply clean drinking water and rarely suspect that tap water is contaminated.

The British study area for our project is the south west of England, where the bulk of drinking water supplies are provided by South West Water (SWW), one of the privatized regional water authorities. SWW is responsible for abstracting water, supplying water to its 1.5 million consumers, sampling and monitoring drinking water quality, from the abstraction zone to the consumer's tap, and ensuring that this water complies with statutory requirements.

SWW's fifty-seven water treatment works ensure that the quality of drinking water supplied to customers in the region is high. The 1993 report on drinking water quality (South West Water 1994) outlines how over 280,000 measurements of drinking water quality achieved a rate of 99.7 per cent compliance with the statutory standards. The vast majority of breaches of the statutory drinking water standards are a function of old pipe linings within the water distribution system, rather than stemming from the pollution of raw-water sources. Any problems associated with the abstraction of water from rivers are, on the whole, well dealt with by water treatment.

Water sampling and testing are overseen by central government, through the Department of Environment's Drinking Water Inspectorate (DWI). Each year, SWW's practices are inspected by the DWI, which assesses sampling procedures, analytical capabilities, reporting procedures, emergency procedures, operation of treatment works, operation of the distribution system, choice of materials used in the treatment and supply of drinking water, compliance with the standards and progress with improvement programmes. Water companies also have to report drinking water quality monitoring data regularly to their local authorities and to make summary reports on drinking water quality for each year publicly available free of charge.

While SWW is responsible for the public water supply, it is the District Councils' Environmental Health Departments that are charged with ensuring the quality of private water supplies (mainly wells). The Private Water Supplies Regulations 1991 set out the monitoring procedures a local authority must follow (Drinking Water Inspectorate 1994: 231–239). It is first required that local authorities compile a register of all the private water supplies in their area and that each supply be categorized. Sampling of water supplies depends on the classification. Generally, the more people who use a private supply, the more frequent and detailed the tests have to be. Private water supplies are more often bacterially rather than chemically contaminated, with farm effluents or septic tanks usually being the source of pollution. As a result, the Drinking Water Directive's standard of zero coliforms is generally not being met (Barraclough *et al.* 1988).

Drinking water quality issues have not proved to be particularly controversial in the south west. This is not the case with the implementation of the directive across the UK, however. Monitoring of public supplies has brought to light a series of water quality problems including pollution by nitrates and pesticides, and has provided quantitative yardsticks against which the scale of these problems can, for the first time, be effectively measured (Ward *et al.* 1995). The European regulatory approach of standard-setting has, since the late 1980s, had a much greater influence on regulatory policy and practice relating to drinking water quality, has opened up the issue to greater scrutiny by environmental pressure groups, and the adversarial style of political debate they bring, and has meant that the traditional British approach to environmental management, characterized by flexibility, pragmatism and closed policy communities, has been undermined.

CONCLUSION

In considering the implications of our study for the development of European environmental policies, we would suggest that the model of harmonization embodied in the EU's water quality directives (in their current shape and form) will not be an effective means of implementing pan-European policies for sustainable development. First, a massive increase in resources given over to monitoring and enforcement at the EU level (i.e. the Commission) would be required to ensure common compliance and common local practices and procedures. This demand has been made by some commentators (see Collins and Earnshaw 1992), but it could be argued that it runs against some interpretations of the subsidiarity principle (CEC 1993). In turn, those common practices and procedures would involve considerable investment in technical and regulatory facilities and services across the member-states, and particularly in their rural areas and regions.

The design of the Drinking Water Directive – like that of many other water quality directives – is rooted in the notion of control rather than management solutions to water supply problems. It is a directive with a strong end-of-pipe regulatory philosophy that is most applicable to the large-scale, urbanized and sophisticated water supply and distribution systems characteristic of much of northern Europe. This model has been misapplied to rural areas, and particularly those of southern Europe, with resultant implementation problems. Sustainable development might be better served by management solutions set within a broader policy framework which emphasized not only prevention rather than treatment but also equivalent practices and understanding of environmental problems rather than standardized and uniform solutions.

Despite its shortcomings, the Drinking Water Directive has been very successful in bringing to public and political attention the spread and levels of different types of drinking water contamination across Europe. In particular, the problems of nitrate and pesticide pollution from Europe's agricultural regions might not have surfaced had the directive not required that water supplies be monitored for these contaminants. However, with its concern about the quality of water coming from consumers' taps, the directive has as yet not brought about an overhaul in, for example, agricultural production practices or policies. This is the challenge that sustainable development policies will need to address. The Drinking Water Directive has not helped tackle the underlying causes of the contamination of drinking water supplies. A combined approach which not only sets drinking water quality standards but introduces locally sensitive management solutions addressing the use of agricultural pollutants might be the way forward.

Perhaps the most profound conclusion from our study relates to the way that a demanding regulatory directive has been devised with little consideration for the practicalities of implementation. In the new phase of European environmental policy characterized by sustainable development priorities, policy-makers would do well to make sure that such considerations are brought much more fully into play at all stages of the drawing up of legislation, and that the goal becomes equivalence of practices and procedures rather than uniform solutions. An important prerequisite for that goal must be a concerted effort to improve mutual understanding of the variety of environmental problems and priorities facing contemporary Europe.

NOTES

1 The Programme, entitled Conditions for the Integration of European Community Environmental Policy at the Local Level: A Social, Cultural and Political Analysis, was funded by the European Commission's Directorate-General DG XII (responsible for Science, Research and Development) under its SEER (Socio-Economic Environmental Research) Programme. Local work was conducted in Devon in the south west of England, the Ribnitz-Damgarten region on the Baltic Coast of Mecklenburg-Vorpommern in (former East) Germany, the Ria Pontevedra in Galicia in northwestern Spain, the Bay of Salonika in Greece and the basin of St Brieuc Bay in Brittany's Côtes d'Amor in northwestern France. In addition to the authors, the study involved Maryvonne Bodiguel (Project Co-ordinator) and Philip Guttinger at the Centre National de la Recherche Scientifique, Université de Paris X, France; Karl Breckmeier and Bernhard Glaeser at the Science Centre (Wissenschaftszentrum Berlin, WZB), Berlin, Germany; Calliope Spanou at the Department of Political Science and Public Administration, University of Athens, Greece; and Fernando Rodriguez Gomez, Josechu Mazariegos and Simon Pedro Izcara at the Department of Ecology in the Faculty of Political Science and Sociology, University of Madrid, Spain. We would like to acknowledge the contribution of these colleagues to the research which informs this Chapter, and to thank the participants at the International Conference on the Politics of Sustainable Development at the University of Crete, Rethimno, in October 1994 for their constructive comments on an earlier draft of the Chapter.

2 The Syndrome is, however, qualified as an ideal-type or 'structural

tendency' rather than a uniform category where common dynamics can be assumed *ex ante*.

3 In a case against Belgium at the European Court of Justice in July 1990 it was ruled that the Drinking Water Directive need not apply to those private water supplies serving only a single dwelling.

REFERENCES

Aguilar, S. (1993) 'Corporatist and statist designs in environmental policy: the contrasting roles of Germany and Spain in the European Community scenario', *Environmental Politics* 2(2): 223–248.

—— (1994a) 'Spanish pollution control policy and the challenge of the European Union', in S. Baker, K. Milton and S. Yearley (eds) *Protecting the Periphery: Environmental Policy in Peripheral Regions of the European Union*, Ilford: Frank Cass.

—— (1994b) 'The geography of European Environmental policy', *Proceedings of the European Science and Technology Forum's Conference on Scientific Expertise in European Public Policy Debate*, London School of Economics, September 1994.

Barraclough, J., Collinge, R. and Horan, N. (1988) 'The quality of private water supplies in Calderdale – the implications of the EC directive on drinking water quality', *Journal of the Institution of Water and Environmental Management* 2: 487–492.

Buller, H., Flynn, A. and Lowe, P. (1993) 'National responses to the Europeanisation of environmental policy: a selective review of comparative research', in J. Liefferink, P. Lowe and A. Mol (eds) *European Integration and Environmental Policy*, London: Belhaven.

CEC (1993) *Commission Report to the European Council on the Adaptation of Community Legislation to the Subsidiarity Principle*, COM (93) 545 final, 24.11.1993, Brussels: CEC.

—— (1994) *Eleventh Annual Report on Monitoring the Application of Community Law*, COM (94) final, 29.03.1994, Brussels: CEC.

Collins, K. and Earnshaw, D. (1992) 'The implementation and enforcement of European Community environment legislation', *Environmental Politics* 1(4): 213–249.

Drinking Water Inspectorate (1994) *Drinking Water, 1993*, London: HMSO.

House of Lords Select Committee on the European Communities (1992a) *Implementation and Enforcement of Environmental Legislation, vol. I: Report*, HL Papers 53-I, London: HMSO.

—— (1992b) *Implementation and Enforcement of Environmental Legislation, vol. II: Evidence*, HL Paper 53-II, London: HMSO.

Inglehart, R. (1977) *The Silent Revolution: Changing Values and Political Styles Among Western Publics*, Princeton, NJ: Princeton University Press.

Kousis, M. (1994) 'Environment and the state in the EU periphery', in S. Baker, K. Milton and S. Yearley (eds) *Protecting the Periphery: Environmental Policy in Peripheral Regions of the European Union*, Ilford: Frank Cass.

La Spina, A. and Sciortino, G. (1993) 'Common agenda, Southern rules: European integration and environmental change in the Mediterranean states', in J. Liefferink, P. Lowe and A. Mol (eds) *European Integration and Environmental Policy*, London: Belhaven.

Pridham, G. (1994) 'National environmental policy-making in the European framework: Spain, Greece and Italy in comparison', in S. Baker, K. Milton and S. Yearley (eds) *Protecting the Periphery: Environmental Policy in Peripheral Regions of the European Union*, Ilford: Frank Cass.

South West Water (1994) *The Quality of Drinking Water in the South West, 1993*, Exeter: South West Water.

Ward, N., Buller, H. and Lowe, P. (1995) *Implementing European Environmental Policy at the Local Level: The British Experience with Water Quality Directives*, Newcastle upon Tyne: University of Newcastle upon Tyne, Centre for Rural Economy.

Yearley, S., Baker, S. and Milton, K. (1994) 'Environmental policy and peripheral regions of the European Union: an introduction', in S. Baker, K. Milton and S. Yearley (eds) *Protecting the Periphery: Environmental Policy in Peripheral Regions of the European Union*, Ilford: Frank Cass.

10 Community-based partnerships and sustainable development

A third force in the social economy

Stephen Young

The main focus of the Chapters in this book is on the roles of the EU and of national and sub-national governments in promoting sustainable development. This Chapter steps outside the state at the local level to analyse the roles of organizations in civil society in promoting sustainable development.[1] These organizations take many forms, but, essentially, they are partnership bodies, drawing resources from EU programmes, from the public and private sectors, and from charities, trusts and a variety of other organizations. Such organizations are not new. Their origins go back into the nineteenth century. But their numbers seem to be growing in late-twentieth-century Europe (Channan 1993).

Although these partnership organizations vary enormously in their form, they have three defining features. First, they operate on a non-profit or not-for-profit basis. Strictly speaking, it is on a not-for-private-profit (NFPP) basis. Although these organizations often rely on grants, many try to promote income-generating activities. But the key point here is that the profits – or surpluses – are used for reinvestment and community benefit, and not for distribution in the way that dividends are in the mainstream private sector. Second, these organizations focus on the level of the local community. This is usually meant in the geographical sense of a village, an estate or an urban neighbourhood. However, local community also refers to communities of need, interest and experience across a wider area (Haughton and Hunter 1994: 113) – as with people from ethnic groups living in different parts of a city, for example. The contrast with firms is important. Capital is free to move if, for example, more skilled or cheaper labour is available elsewhere. However, community-based partnerships are closely linked to place. Their *raison d'être* is improving local conditions – whether they relate to environment, social deprivation or other issues of local significance. Third, these partnerships emphasize participation and community involvement as key principles. They vary in their success, but almost all try to promote the involvement of local people in defining their needs, developing programmes, and influencing or controlling the development of the organization.

THE SOCIAL ECONOMY AND THIRD-FORCE ORGANIZATIONS

One of the problems with writing about these myriad different organizations is that there is no commonly understood term to describe them. Different types of the NFPP organizations discussed here are referred to by such phrases as community enterprise, community action, third-sector organizations, community-regeneration organizations, voluntary-sector bodies, community-based organizations (CBOs) and local non-governmental organizations (NGOs). In practice, however, they are most easily understood as organizations operating as part of the social economy that has emerged between the private, market, sector on the one hand, and the public sector on the other. Cattell (1994) has brought this concept of 'the social economy' into English from southern European languages. In France and other parts of Latin Europe the concept is well established and clearly understood. It is quite separate from the market economy and the public sector, and is set out in Table 10.1. In both the market sector and the public sector, legal structures have been specifically created, respectively, for companies and for the range of public-sector bodies and government institutions. Another reason for adopting the idea of the social economy is that the European Commision set up a Social Economy Unit in 1989 to focus precisely on this range of organizations.

On mainland Europe the social economy is made up of three types, or families, of organizations, each one of which has its own legal basis. To begin with there are the co-ops. These are democratically-based organizations run by and for their members, with a commitment to the principles of democracy, participation and equal opportunities, as well as economic aims. Next there are the 'mutuals' – organizations created to meet their members' mutual needs, like building societies and mutual insurance companies. These organizations are now more common in the rest of the EU than in Britain. Finally, there are the associations and foundations where people run charities and similar organizations for the benefit of others. These roughly correspond to what is labelled 'the voluntary sector' in Britain.

Within the social economy Cattell uses two criteria to place organizations within each of the three families – the organization's

Table 10.1 The scope of the social economy at the local level

	Market economy		Social economy		Public sector
Legal structures	Specific legal structures for companies			Associations and foundations	Legislation leads to a variety of legal structures
		Co-ops	Mutuals		
Types of organization	Firms of all kinds and sizes from transnationals down to small firms; profit-oriented public/private partnership companies, as in urban renewal	Worker co-ops Food co-ops Community businesses	Credit unions LETS Permaculture schemes Danish community wind farms Training and managed workspace projects Neighbourhood development trusts Community-based forest projects Community co-ops	Self-help organizations with restricted membership Housing co-ops User groups Alternative health projects Recycling schemes Environmental improvement projects	Self-help organizations with open membership Heritage trusts Wildlife bodies Community arts projects Traditional voluntary-sector organizations Small housing associations	Departments, corporations and government agencies at the national level; municipalities, regional and city councils, and other sub-national and local governments

Source: Developed from Cattell (1994: Appendix I)

relationship with its members and the outside world – that is the market and society; and the motive for establishing and maintaining the organization. Cattell applies the concept of the social economy to the UK, drawing in all sorts of organizations outside the public and private sectors. These include consumer co-ops, building societies, political parties, trade associations, pressure groups, charities, fee-paying schools and others.

Here, however, the concept of the social economy and its three families is applied to NFPP organizations at the local level and developed as a way of presenting the range of the community-based NFPP partnership organizations that operate at the sub-national level across the EU. There is no space to get into the complex ways in which some organizations cross the notional boundaries between two of the three families. They are presented in Table 10.1 in columns for simplicity. In reality though, some co-ops, for example, would move away from the market sector towards the centre (Pearce 1993). There is no overall treatment of these NFPP organizations, although some case-study material is available (Warburton and Wilcox 1988; Channan 1993; Department of the Environment 1994; Thake 1995).

Under the co-operative family heading come such organizations as worker co-ops and food co-ops. They are close to the market economy in Table 10.1, as their main activity is trading there. Also, membership of such co-ops is restricted and members gain financially. Community businesses that create jobs for local people also come into this category (Pearce 1993). They frequently relate to the service sector – shops, building, decorating, security, landscaping, cleaning and home helps, for example. The motive here for creating and running the organization is self-help and self-interest, aiming at profits for the benefits of members.

At the other end of the spectrum covered by the social economy are the associations and foundations, a range of organizations where the central motive is philanthropic. People who get involved do so mainly to contribute to the well-being of others. Concerns about sustainable development and the future of the planet fit in well here. With the associations, membership is open, not restricted, and profit is not an aim. Self-help bodies with open memberships which run schemes such as community transport and youth projects are examples here. Heritage trusts restoring canals and old buildings and running tourist projects also fit in. Next, there are the wildlife organizations, community arts projects and traditional voluntary organizations delivering a variety of services. Finally, there are the small church-based housing associations and similar bodies for minorities like ethnic groups and ex-prisoners.

In between the co-op and associational families there are the mutuals. Here membership is restricted and the underlying motive is a mix of self-interest and altruism. Although in reality there are degrees of gradation, the examples are set out in two columns in Table 10.1. The cases of self-interest have some scope for bartering, monetary or other personal gain. They are put next to the co-ops as they are then nearer to the market sector. Those where the motive is more altruistic are put next to the associations. It must be acknowledged, however, that this is complex and can become arbitrary. Although most recycling projects relate to the right-hand mutuals column, for example, not all do. In the column that relates more to self-interest, credit unions, local exchange trading systems (LETS) (Lang 1994), permaculture projects and Danish community wind farms are all clear examples. Also here are the managed workspaces and training projects that specifically target local people in areas of high unemployment.

Some community-based partnerships move on from a focus on a single issue to tackle a range of housing, training, childcare, recreational and other local needs in a holistic way, evolving into what are, in effect, community or neighbourhood development trusts. The same kind of approach has developed in parts of Europe, where local communities manage forests in sustainable ways while generating income from timber products and tourists. The community co-op model is also based on this idea of managing rural resources in sustainable ways to produce income from tourists, fish farms and other sources. The co-op can then run facilities for local people – shops, transport, a village hall, a swimming pool and so on.

The first examples under the mutuals heading that veer towards the associations are the self-help groups with restricted membership. These focus on mutual aid schemes like creches. Next, there are the tenants management and new-build housing co-ops; the welfare projects run by users' organizations; alternative health projects; and most recycling schemes. Finally, there is the whole range of environmental improvement projects. These involve tree-planting, improving open spaces, making ponds, laying hedges, cleaning out rivers, and other amenity and wildlife schemes. Once set up, these are often managed by community-based partnerships.

As can be seen, these community-based NFPP partnerships take many forms and do not fit readily into conventional patterns of analysis. They are not companies in the market. They operate outside government: some have a fierce independence, while others are more subject to government influences. Finally, they are not conventional pressure groups as they are moving on from influencing policy to getting involved in implementation. Accordingly, the term 'third-force organization' (TFO) is used here to refer to those local-level organizations in civil society that are actively involved in running projects on a NFPP basis. Other organizations in civil society at the local level – churches, sports clubs and the like – are excluded. TFO helps to convey the way these NFPP community-based partnerships supplement the mainstream government and market sectors. It also helps to focus the analysis on a particular set of local community and neighbourhood-based organizations for which there is no commonly agreed term. Although the focus here is on sustainable development, the term also covers TFOs dealing with other issues.

TFOS AND THE PROMOTION OF SUSTAINABLE DEVELOPMENT

This section analyses the ways in which TFOs can relate to the promotion of sustainable development. The Introduction discussed how sustainable development is open to different interpretations. The approach taken here is to break the concept down by drawing from the different dimensions identified by different writers (Blowers 1993; Bosworth 1993; Breheny 1992 and 1994; Carley and Christie 1992; Elkins 1992; Goodin 1992; Jacobs 1990, 1991 and 1993; Levett 1994; Pearce *et al.* 1989; Soussan 1992; Stoker and Young 1993: ch. 4; WCED 1987). The contribution of TFOs is then analysed in terms of these different dimensions of sustainable development.

Intra-generational equity

The Brundtland Report stressed the importance of intra-generational equity in the global context of the north–south divide. It argued that equity between existing generations was largely about meeting the basic needs of work, shelter, food and clean water. However, the same principle of redistribution and positive discrimination in favour of disadvantaged groups relates to the deprived urban communities of Northern cities. In these areas, TFOs have emerged to address such issues as housing, fuel poverty, health projects, environmental improvements, and training and support mechanisms for small firms. Councils have also used the flexible model of the TFO to channel resources to special needs groups, including ethnic groups, women, youth and other minorities; and to provide expert technical assistance to groups trying to set up their own schemes. In addition, part of intra-generational equity concerns improving environmental conditions so that the quality of people's daily living experience is improved. TFOs attach a lot of importance to quality-of-life issues and to the environmental context in which their projects are developed. In deprived urban communities TFOs provide a significant mechanism for promoting discriminatory policies that tackle issues of intra-generational inequality. This aspect of sustainable development is thus one where TFOs can make a useful contribution (Stoker and Young 1993: ch. 6; Thake 1995).

Participation

Promoting participation and producing consensus-based approaches is a core part of achieving sustainable development at the sub-national level. Chapter 28 of Agenda 21 stresses the need to draw minorities in, so their needs are defined in the terms in which they perceive them. In developed industrial societies, as in Europe, this means going beyond a situation in which the nature and location of economic development are determined by business and other articulate groups. It means involving minorities, as in inner-city areas, in constructive dialogues with government agencies so that their needs can be met more effectively than they have been.

TFOs can help promote participation by linking into the preparation of Local Agenda 21s, acting as if they were conventional pressure groups. They are well placed to feed in minority views and different cultural perceptions. Their role here is potentially significant because they have unique hands-on experience of the issues they are talking about as a result of the projects they are involved with. They also promote participation by involving people in running the projects that have been established.

In addition, participation relates to broader government strategies to promote sustainable development. A key role for governments is to educate their publics about the seriousness of the environmental challenge. In wartime such consciousness-raising is comparatively simple as governments can exploit the mass media. However, in peacetime, when people cannot see ozone depletion or global warming, it is much more complicated. TFOs can help with the whole education or consciousness-raising process. They attract interest and publicity; they help promote lifestyle changes; and they run demonstration projects – some of which get copied. Some, like the recycling ones, involve members of the public directly, even though they are not actually members of the scheme.

Inter-generational equity

The heart of this much-discussed aspect of sustainable development is the idea that future generations should have access to the same resource base as existing generations, and that our options are made available to them, and not closed. From this two points follow. First, the resource base has to be well managed. TFOs make a small contribution here. By adapting existing buildings and sites they help reduce the pressures for development on the finite amounts of greenfield land. In addition, wildlife TFOs play a useful role in protecting and managing sites of local and regional significance. Indeed, many conservationists argue that the record shows governments cannot be trusted to protect the nationally important sites, whatever their official designation. They see the surest way of protecting such sites as getting them into the ownership of TFOs in perpetuity, thus handing them on to future generations (Young 1995).

The second point to follow on from future generations having access to the same resource base as we do concerns the resources we create. Here the argument is that as we will be using up finite resources and passing on a depleted stock, we have to bequeath other assets to future generations instead. Pearce has argued that this means passing on constant and improving capital stock (Pearce *et al.* 1989). This includes physical and slow-maturing assets, like community forests. It also covers a much wider range of things, including knowledge, skills, financial capital, and institutions that protect the environment and promote sustainable development. In this context the TFO model could be significant. The central point here is that TFOs have been developing in range and scope in spheres that have been neglected by the state and the market. They have expanded at a time when the local state's role as a direct provider has been contracting (Stoker 1994), and have been growing in places neglected by the market. The flexibility of the TFO model and its capacity to mobilize resources suggest that it does have a role to play in helping to fill gaps left by the public and market sectors. An understanding of the dynamics, limits and potential of the TFO model could be one part of the whole jigsaw of constant and improving capital stock that can be passed on.

The need to consider environmental costs in decision-making processes

Throughout history decisions about investment and development have focused on economic costs (Ponting 1991). Brundtland and Agenda 21 recognized that the way in which environmental costs were being taken for granted could not continue. The implication of this analysis seems clear in principle – when decisions on economic development are made environmental dimensions have to be fully considered. This dimension of sustainable development applies mainly to decision-making processes within government and the private sector. In the wider EU context TFOs cannot have much impact here – except by lobbying and by setting a good example with regard to their own decisions.

Built development that is compatible with local ecosystems

Clearly, economic pressures threaten many sites of wildlife and wider environmental value. There is always a delicate balance in nature that human intervention can destroy – whether it is development on an ordinary greenfield site or on a specially protected one. It is necessary here to distinguish between two types of site. First, there are the Special Areas of Conservation – like ancient woodlands and lowland peat bog. Once they are lost they cannot be recreated. They are irreplaceable natural assets – the stuff of critical natural capital (Owens 1993).

On the other hand, it is possible to create habitats of value to local wildlife and to replace many that are destroyed by development. For example, where new industrial or housing developments are undertaken, imaginative planting schemes can link them to wildlife corridors. Such schemes can replace the hedges, copses, ponds and open spaces that are lost to the bulldozer. What matters is the planting of indigenous species ranging from grasses to trees. These will then attract a range of insects for different birds to feed on, give cover to small mammals and provide the variety of host plants that butterflies need to lay their eggs on. With careful planning the landscaping can even create a greater range of wildlife habitats than had previously been there. While it is impossible to eliminate damage to local ecosystems, it is still possible to promote development that is ecologically sustainable. The same principles can promote biodiversity on land surrounding existing buildings, or affected by agribusiness practices.

Environmental and wildlife TFOs can make a significant contribution in this sphere. They have a track record of local knowledge and expertise that public and private sector organizations can take advantage of (Young 1995). This can be focused on the protection of regionally rare or threatened species and on adapting sites to encourage healthy numbers of more common ones. They can own and manage sites, design projects for schools and companies, supplement a council's limited resources and expertise, and take over management and maintenance tasks.

Environmental capacities

This aspect of sustainable development relates to the capacity of the planet to cope with human demands on it. The environment – air, water, land – can absorb human wastes, but only so long as the rates at which they are deposited do not exceed certain thresholds. If these are breached, delicate ecosystems can be endangered. Acid rain, for example, threatens the planet's capacity to provide resources of timber and fish, to operate the carbon cycle and to maintain the natural world. Thus thresholds need to be established to ensure that environmental capacities are not breached. However, the TFO contribution to this aspect of sustainable development is very marginal in the wider context of government policies to tackle all the different kinds of waste and pollution.

A different kind of economic growth

At its heart, sustainable development is about changing the whole nature of economic growth and conventional approaches to investment to make them compatible with environmental needs. The Brundtland Report stresses the importance of thinking about the quality of growth rather than the quantity of growth (WCED 1987: 52–54). This is necessary partly because of the concept of futurity. This is about limiting the long-term cumulative impacts on the biosphere from economic growth and development. Thus economic growth cannot be environmentally sustainable if it 'depletes the future viability of the resource base' (Soussan 1992: 25); nor 'if it increases vulnerability to crises' (WCED 1987: 53), as through rising sea-levels.

Clearly, TFOs are marginal to attempts to amend conventional government, EU and private-sector approaches to running economies in the context of globalization processes. But the development of the idea of the social economy as a whole falls within their sphere of influence. The argument here is that, collectively, TFOs can help develop local economic self-sufficiency and the notion of the steady-state economy (Daly and Cobb 1989). Thus, neighbourhood development trusts, small housing associations, credit unions, a city farm, a multipurpose community centre, environmental groups and others can trade, barter and interact with each other. Enthusiasts for this argument point to the way in which LETS schemes have been spreading ideas about an economy based on needs not wants.

LETS schemes also accept and institutionalize an important point argued about the nature of economic growth by greens and feminists –

that society needs to recognize the value of what is at present unpaid work, as in the home and through supporting the housebound. The conventional approach in the post-Rio era is to view people not employed in the mainstream economy as being out of work and contributing nothing of value to society (Ekins 1992: 62–71; Dobson 1995; Young 1993: 98–99). TFOs can relate very positively to this issue. While they do create some full- and part-time jobs, part of their contribution comes from valuing the unpaid involvement and commitment of local people in running TFOs.

RELATING TFOS TO SUSTAINABLE DEVELOPMENT

Although the numbers of TFOs grew during the 1970s and 1980s, this was largely unconnected to sustainable development. There were some exceptions. Some TFOs were promoted by farsighted environmentalists who understood the green analysis. They were developing small-scale local solutions without using the language of sustainable development. Those involved saw what they were trying to do as being common sense and relevant to their needs. Similarly, some government agencies were developing enabling approaches during this period, as with the Danish community wind farms and, more widely, in the cases of wildlife and community development in the inner cities. But their approaches were narrowly conceived and not integrated into broader, more holistic programmes to promote sustainable development. Pre-Brundtland, the process of linking TFOs to sustainable development was thus very haphazard. However, the post-Brundtland debates began to focus attention more sharply on the breadth of sustainable development and the need for broad-based holistic approaches. Both before Rio and afterwards, in various UN fora like the Commission on Sustainable Development, NGOs in particular pushed the argument about developing the roles and capacity of TFOs.

In the early 1990s this new understanding of the potential TFO contribution to sustainable development expressed itself in two important ways. The EU's Fifth Environmental Action Programme highlighted the role of the social partners in promoting sustainable development (CEC 1992). In addition, Agenda 21 and the debates both at Rio (Grubb 1993) and after Rio (Department of the Environment 1994, 1995) emphasized what were often referred to as 'partnerships for change'. This refers to the need to involve local communities in running projects to promote sustainable development. These documents and debates also showed a growing appreciation of the important contribution that city councils, municipalities and other sub-national governments could make, both by themselves and through involvement in partnerships for change, to the promotion of sustainable development.

As a result of these debates in the early 1990s, policy-makers at all levels from the EU downwards were becoming more aware of the ways in which community-based partnerships could contribute to partnerships for change at the local level. This led to a shift away from a few isolated bottom-up approaches and some scattered initiatives from pioneering municipalities. A new, more focused approach started to emerge from policy-makers – but still only in a limited number of places.

TFOs and sustainable developments at the local level

Up until the mid-1990s most sub-national government involvement in the promotion of sustainable development via TFOs of the kinds discussed above related to sectoral approaches – as in recycling, energy, wildlife and so on. The challenge for the second half of the 1990s is to link TFOs more explicitly to sustainable development across a broader front. Local Agenda 21 (LA21) is a significant opportunity here, for although much of the implementation of LA21 will be done via public- and private-sector organizations, the TFO model provides a useful supplement. One of its advantages is its flexibility. It can relate to an area as big as a municipality, but also to smaller areas – right down to the level of the urban neighbourhood or village. Apart from relating to geographical communities, it can channel resources to communities of interest or need across a wider area – to ethnic groups or the disabled, for instance. It also can be used in areas neglected by the market. In addition, there is a link between the analysis of bottom-up approaches in the Introduction and the discussion of participation above. TFOs can inject into the policy-making process the indigenous community's own understanding of how people relate to their natural environment and surroundings. These bottom-up perceptions are often different from those of policy-makers. TFOs can thus provide a positive and creative link between the process of local people being involved in designing projects that address local needs at the policy-making stage, and the implementation phase.

The role of sub-national government here is complex. Most successful TFOs have grown in spite of the local state, often because people have given up on it, and decided to meet their own needs. Their independence is one of their greatest assets. The result is a paradox. Municipalities and councils have to act in a top-down way to promote bottom-up spontaneity. It becomes a bit like trying to organize anarchy. It tests the sensitivity of a council to its limits. In this situation municipalities can respond in three ways; first, they can ignore potential TFOs and leave them to make their own way; second, they can develop supportive frameworks by running training courses to develop relevant skills in the community and by establishing grant funds to support initiatives that relate to LA21 aims; and, finally, they can – as in parts of Denmark and in some Dutch cities like Rotterdam – take a stronger line and take over initiatives that emerge, and manipulate them in a neo-corporatist way. If the second and third courses are to be followed, then it is important that potential TFO projects are identified during the LA21 participation process.

However, taking a positive approach is not straightforward (Stoker and Young 1993: ch. 6; Young 1996). The experience of the 1980s and early 1990s shows that sub-national governments face four main problems in these circumstances. The first problem is that policy-makers have a limited understanding of the dynamics of TFOs. Appreciating the barriers to their operation and to participation in this sphere is complex. This reflects the fact that TFOs are creatures of their local conditions, rooted in a variety of local political cultures. These vary enormously, not just from country to country across the EU, but from the rural periphery to the inner city.

Trying to develop relevant policies is made more difficult by the second problem. This is the lack of a cross-departmental, holistic approach towards TFOs from within local government. Too often policy-makers approach them from a narrow housing, recreation, energy or other perspective, without appreciating the need to take the broader approach that sustainable development requires.

Third, promoting TFOs tends to be resource-intensive. They can be demanding in terms of staff time. It is not just the launch phase that is important here. There is also the need for aftercare support. Here again, the dynamics of what is happening are not fully understood and the principles on which policy should be based are not always clear. Surprisingly, TFOs are not always funded through grants from the municipality. They can draw from organizations that councils do not have access to, bringing in public-sector funds from the EU downwards and approaching firms for sponsorship, discarded equipment and seconded staff, and charities and others for grants. Often there are financial implications for the municipality, but they are not as great or as frequent as is often assumed.

Finally, there is the difficulty of measuring the benefits that TFOs can bring. TFOs need resources, but resources have to be allocated according to prevailing criteria. TFOs do not readily relate to these. During the 1980s and early 1990s the conventional approach within government towards assessing which projects to support revolved around assessing outputs and outcomes in terms mainly of economy, efficiency and effectiveness. In some respects, measuring the tangible benefits (hard outputs and outcomes) that TFOs can bring against these criteria – as, for example with recycled buildings, houses renovated, trees planted, numbers of people gaining skills, and so on – is straightforward. However, much of what TFOs can contribute relates to the more intangible aspects of what they can deliver – soft outputs and outcomes. Examples here include quality-of-life issues like improved local environments, distracting young people from drugs and crime, and alleviating some of the social costs of unemployment. TFOs can provide a structure for people's lives – a place to go, a reason to get up in the morning. Part-time involvement in schemes can help give people a sense of worth and help them cope with some of the social effects of unemployment – heavier smoking, money, depressive illness, suicide and so on.

The problem here is that if TFOs are to expand they need more resources. But decision-makers find it difficult to relate conventional criteria to the soft, intangible benefits that TFOs can bring. However, approaches do vary across Europe, and by the mid-1990s there was evidence to suggest that criteria were becoming more flexible. For example, in terms of hard outcomes it is difficult to measure some environmental education schemes, demonstration projects and the benefits that promoting participation and community development can bring. But such schemes are more readily supported. However, by the mid-1990s objections were still frequently raised about promoting projects solely on the basis of new ideas about valuing unpaid work and promoting the social economy.

TFOs and sustainable development at the EU level

In the late 1980s the European Commission had very few links to the level at which TFOs operate, and a limited understanding of their contribution. But by the mid-1990s its approach was changing. It became more aware of the role of TFOs as a result of setting up the Social Economy Unit in 1989, and because of the wider process of the EU reaching down to the sub-national level, to the regions (Baker *et al.* 1994). Mazey and Richardson (1993) argue that the Commission presents itself as pluralist and open, and encourages the development of new links to it. The various Directorate-Generals (DGs) are open and easily accessible to trade associations and bodies representing industrial interests, national NGOs, unions and other major groups. At the sub-national level they relate to existing bodies, like the regional councils in Spain. Where organizations do not exist at the regional level, local councils, business groups and other organizations come together to create a regional grouping which the various DGs can relate to. In the north west of England, for example, there was no organization that the Commission could relate to – and it had to be created (Stoker and Young 1993: ch. 7)

The Commission's approach is thus based on having substantial organizations with which it can easily build links at the sub-national level. The mutuals and the co-ops are fairly well organized and have representative bodies. But TFOs at the local level cannot relate easily to this approach. They are small and scattered, and they lack representative bodies to put their case. They thus lack easy access. In addition, city councils and other sub-national governments often misunderstand the nature and needs of TFOs and take a top-down, instrumental approach towards them. Sub-national government can become a barrier between the Commission and TFOs.

The Social Economy Unit was set up in DG XXIII. DG XXIII was chosen because of its responsibility for small and medium-sized businesses. During the early 1990s the Unit focused mainly on the bigger co-ops and mutuals (CEC 1995). The co-ops dominate the social economy in the EU in terms of jobs and turnover. However, after the Rio Summit it began to move on to do surveys of the smaller co-ops and mutuals, and in particular the associations and foundations. It began to appreciate more the benefits they offered and the potential they had for providing jobs. In the areas of the small co-ops, the urban environment and wildlife, for example, their contribution was becoming clearer. In Italy over 1,500 co-ops were established to provide services and jobs for disadvantaged people, for example.

The surveys led on to support programmes (CEC 1995). In 1994 a budget of 2.5 million ECU supported fifty-one projects. Apart from survey work, this covered such things as research into non-commercial criteria, training needs and programmes, and information networks. The aim is to use the information gathered to develop enabling policies aimed in particular at the associations. This all reflects the way that the Fifth Environmental Action Plan (CEC 1992) had echoed the Brundtland Commission's (WCED 1987) talk of empowerment. As a result, the EU now seems to be trying to develop stronger links down to the level of TFOs, or at least to the levels of the NGOs developing advisory programmes that empower them, and to the municipalities supporting them and working with them. In time it is likely to develop more detailed policies. Nevertheless the response from the whole range of organizations in the social economy is likely to be very varied. Some will welcome projects channelling resources to them; but others undoubtedly will maintain their independence and not be interested in trying to develop links up to the EU.

THE SIGNIFICANCE OF TFOS

In the context of what governments and firms are doing to promote sustainable development across the EU as a whole, the contribution of TFOs is limited and marginal. They do not yet amount to a significant third force, but they have become an identifiable one.

In the short term, TFOs appear to be contributing most in terms of intra-generational equity; participation; and the biodiversity aspects of inter-generational equity, and making development compatible with ecosystems. In particular, discussion of Table 10.1 described the importance of the multi-sectoral neighbourhood development trusts. In a few urban areas and remote villages, these organizations do have a strong local presence.

Some aspects of the TFO contribution are likely to become more significant in the longer term. The passing on of knowledge about the TFO model in the context of inter-generational equity is one example here. In addition, it is not yet possible to assess the significance of their contribution to creating a different kind of economy – based on quality not quantity. Jacobs (1993) argues that the important point is about changing direction via small changes. Here the initial moves to create small collections of interacting TFOs within the emergent social economy could be of significance.

The other way to assess the significance of TFOs is to relate them to the Ladder of Sustainable Development (Table 0.1) in the Introduction. The examples vary, but the material in this Chapter shows that they are certainly capable of making small but positive contributions in terms of the columns dealing with nature, holistic integrative approaches and appropriate technology. They can make a limited but more substantial contribution in terms of promoting bottom-up community structures in the civil society column, tackling equity issues in the redistribution column and promoting decentralized social institutions in the institutions column.

In the policy instruments column they have, in sustainable develop-ment terms, an advanced approach to accounting and are one of the tools that governments can deploy. The significant point here is that TFOs can be used to tackle problems in locations that are unattractive to firms. This links with the geographical focus column, and with moves towards local self-sufficiency. The social economy as a whole reflects new ideas about the role of the economy and the nature of growth.

The other point that arises here is that TFOs have a potentially significant role to play during the transition to sustainable development. In the section on bottom-up approaches in the Introduction it was argued that sustainable development will only come about if it is strongly participatory. Then it will grow from below as people come to realize that it is in their interests; about a broad mix of social, economic and environmental issues; and about much more than simple environmental management. Ultimately it is about control over local resources, participation and empowerment.

The most significant aspect of TFOs in the context of sustainable development may well turn out to be not so much the limited direct contribution that they make, but rather how they relate to the whole process of persuading people that there is a need for change. Ultimately, sustainable development will only come about if it is widely accepted and politically acceptable. TFOs involve people in projects and draw them into thinking about environmental issues. This is especially significant in two contexts. First, there are the cases where they manage an environmental resource – like an urban allotment or a forest.[2] Second, there are cases where sustainable development is approached via gates on social issues – as with health, creches and safe play areas for children of all ages, and other aspects of involving people via local community development approaches.

There is an important link here to an earlier point. There is a continuing mismatch between TFOs addressing these social dimensions and promoting participation and environmental education, on the one hand, and policy-makers finding it hard to relate their project assessment criteria to the intangible benefits TFOs offer, on the other. This constrains the growth of the social economy.

CONCLUSION

In the late 1990s TFOs relate to the changing nature of local democracy. The empowerment of people through their involvement with TFOs that address some of their needs is part of the wider process of reforging the links between the local state and civil society. TFOs do not replace the local state, but become part of the process of democratizing it. Their expansion seems to represent a strengthening of the organizations in civil society against the local state. The balance between them varies partly according to the extent of the local TFO presence. This suggests that the new social movements' rejection of the state and the old politics is giving way to a new engagement with the state at the local level.

Finally, TFOs need to be placed in the context of debates about participation. Traditionally, political scientists have interpreted participation in political systems broadly to include such activities as voting, lobbying councillors and MPs, contacting officials and demonstrating and taking part in direct action (Parry *et al.* 1992). The involvement of people in organizing and running TFOs seems to represent a growing area of activity, and an addition to the usual list of participatory involvements in the politics of industrialized democracies like those within the EU.

NOTES

1   The author is grateful for the financial support for this research from Phase Two of the UK Economic and Social Research Council's Local Governance Research Initiative – grant ref. L311253061.
2   I am indebted to Tim O'Riordan for this point.

REFERENCES

Baker, S., Milton, K. and Yearly, S. (eds) (1994) *Protecting the Periphery: Environmental Policy in the Peripheral Regions of the European Union*, London: Frank Cass.
Blowers, A. (1993) *Planning for a Sustainable Environment*, London: Earthscan.
Bosworth, T. (1993) 'Local authorities and sustainable development', *European Environment* 3(1) (February): 13–17.
Breheny, M. (1992) 'Towards sustainable urban development', in A. M. Mannion and S. R. Bowlby (eds) *Environmental Issues in the 1990s*, Chichester: Wiley.
—— (1994) 'Defining sustainable local development', paper presented at the Global Forum June 1994 Academic Conference, Manchester, mimeo.
Carley, M. and Christie, I. (1992) *Managing Sustainable Development*, London: Earthscan.
Cattell, C. (1994) *A Guide to Co-operative and Community Business Legal Structures*, Leeds: Industrial Common Ownership Movement.
Channan, G. (ed.) (1993) *Out of the Shadows*, Dublin: European Foundation for the Improvement of Living and Working Conditions.
CEC (1992) *Towards Sustainability: A European Community Programme of Policy and Action in Relation to the Environment and Development*, Brussels: COM(92) 23 final.

—— (1995) *The Social Economy Unit of the European Commission*, Brussels: European Commission.

Daly, H. E. and Cobb, J. B. (1989) *For the Common Good: Redirecting the Economy Toward Community, the Environment, and a Sustainable Future*, Boston, MA: Beacon Press.

Department of the Environment (1994) *Partnerships in Practice*, London: HMSO.

—— (1995) *First Steps: Local Agenda 21 in Practice – Municipal Strategies for Sustainability as Presented to Global Forum Manchester 1994*, London: HMSO.

Dobson, A. (1995) *Green Political Thought*, London: Routledge.

Ekins, P. (1992) *Wealth Beyond Measure: An Atlas of New Economics*, London: Gaia Books.

Elkin, T. and McLaren, D. (1991) *Reviving the City: Towards Sustainable Development*, London: Friends of the Earth.

Goodin, R. (1992) *Green Political Theory*, Cambridge: Polity.

Grubb, M. (1993) *The Earth Summit Agreements*, London: Royal Institute for International Affairs.

Haughton, G. and Hunter, C. (1994) *Sustainable Cities*, London: Jessica Kingsley.

Jacobs, M. (1990) *Sustainable Development: Greening the Economy*, London: Fabian Society.

—— (1991) *The Green Economy*, London: Pluto.

—— (1993) *Sense and Sustainability: Land-Use Planning and Environmentally Sustainable Development*, London: Campaign for the Protection of Rural England.

Lang, P. (1994) *LETS Work – Rebuilding the Local Economy*, Bristol: Grover Books.

Levett, R. (1994) 'Options from a menu', *Town and Country Planning* 63(7/8): 206–207.

Mazey, S. and Richardson, J. (eds) (1993) *Lobbying in the European Community*, Oxford: Oxford University Press.

Owens, S. (1993) 'Planning and nature conservation', *Ecos* 14(3/4): 15–22.

Parry, G., Moyser, G. and Day, N. (1992) *Political Participation and Democracy in Britain*, Cambridge: Cambridge University Press.

Pearce, D., Markandya, A. and Barbier, E. B. (1989) *Blueprint for a Green Economy*, London: Earthscan.

Pearce, J. (1993) *At the Heart of the Community Economy: Community Enterprise in a Changing World*, London: Gulbenkian Foundation.

Ponting, C. (1991) *A Green History of the World*, London: Penguin.

Soussan, J. G. (1992) 'Sustainable development', in A. M. Mannion and S. R. Bowlby (eds) *Environmental Issues in the 1990s*, Chichester: Wiley.

Stoker, G. (ed.) (1994) *Local Government in Europe*, Basingstoke: Macmillan.

Stoker, G. and Young, S. C. (1993) *Cities in the 1990s: Local Choice for a Balanced Strategy*, Harlow: Longman.

Thake, S. (1995) *Staying the Course: The Role and Structures of Community Regeneration Organisations*, York: Joseph Rowntree Foundation.

Warburton, D. and Wilcox, D. (1988) *Creating Development Trusts: Case-Studies of Good Practice in Urban Regeneration*, London: HMSO.

WCED (1987) *Our Common Future*, Oxford: Oxford University Press.

Young, S. C. (1993) *The Politics of the Environment*, Manchester: Baseline Books.

—— (1995) 'Wildlife conservation policies 1988–94: running up the down escalator', in T. Gray (ed.) *British Environmental Policy in the 1990s*, Basingstoke: Macmillan.

—— (1996) *Promoting Participation and Community-Based Partnerships in the Context of Local Agenda 21: A Report for Practitioners*, Manchester: Government Department, Manchester University, European Policy Research Unit Paper.

11 Grassroots environmental movements in rural Greece

Effectiveness, success and the quest for sustainable development[1]

Maria Kousis

Critics of sustainable development insist that if it is to achieve its true goal, development should grow from within and rely on sustainable forms of resource use. Simultaneously, it should foster local control over resources, participation in decision-making and empowerment for local people, more especially the underprivileged and marginalized (Thrupp 1989, 1990; de la Court 1990; Gow 1992).

Sustainable development policies should be more collaborative, making use of people's knowledge and experience of their environments (Redclift 1987). Recent research carried out at the United Nations Institute for Social Development reiterates the idea that external agents and local inhabitants should engage in genuine collaboration (Ghai and Vivian 1992). Policy analysts such as Liberatore (1993) take their turn to point out that effective sustainable policies would involve the establishment of new institutions and acknowledgement of the need to widen the scope of participation for practical (i.e. compliance of businesses) and ethical (e.g. public involvement) reasons. The significant rise in the number and activities of non-governmental organizations concerned with environmental issues that occurred during the 1980s indicates a willingness and readiness on the part of the public to collaborate with decision-makers (Brechin and West 1990).

Unfortunately, however, as many works observe, decision-makers do not show similar intentions, and non-sustainable development policies and projects have given rise to fierce public opposition at the grassroots level. This has been the case especially as regards nuclear power plants, toxic waste and chemicals (Walsh 1988; Stevis and Mummee 1992; Szasz 1994).

Grassroots environmental movements spring from the conflict which is produced when state and capitalist interests enter local communities in order to use and control local natural resource systems essential to local subsistence. Local resistance is not centred just on pure environmental protection issues but also on economic, socio-political and ethical ones as well. According to Redclift (1992), research examining in detail the way in which different groups establish power relations through their control over resources and the evolution of these relations over time is overdue. Inevitably, following Redclift's proposition, questions arise: do grassroots environmental movements achieve their goals? And, if they do, what does this mean for sustainable development?

International social movement research (Klandermans 1989) has proposed that a critical question to deal with is what makes social movement organizations 'effective'. This question invites the study of their internal (organizational) characteristics as challenging groups. The resource mobilization theory, as coined by Gamson (1990), closely links effectiveness and success but fails to deal with the ideological motivations of the struggle (Ingalsbee 1994), and leaves the role of the challenging group's main opponent, the state, outside its analysis. The state is often involved directly or indirectly as the movement's main antagonist. Therefore, this Chapter aims to answer the question at hand by combining three different theoretical poles: resource mobilization, new social movements and state theories. Many works by social and other scientists which address environmental disputes using case studies implicitly refer to issues embedded in these theoretical poles (e.g. Regan and Legerton 1990; Bullard 1990; Ekins 1992; Ghai and Vivian 1992).

This Chapter presents, first, a summary review of the literature on resource modilization (RM) and the state. Second, it looks at the effectiveness and success of three grassroots environmental movements in Greece. Third, by bringing into the analysis the role of the movements' main opponent, the state, the Chapter proposes a synthesis of the theoretical poles. Fourth, it presents a very brief comparative analysis of grassroots environmental movements in Greece and in countries of the European 'core'. Fifth, it addresses the ideological motivations of grassroots environmental movements which the resource mobilization model downplays. Finally, the Chapter raises some key questions concerning grassroots movements and sustainable development.

LITERATURE REVIEW

The effectiveness of challenging groups

Community- or locally based grassroots social movements constitute a 'temporary, specialized and relatively rich mobilization by members of a connected community against a specific threat' (Tilly 1994: 18). In the context of the present Chapter the threat is environmental. Such movements pose 'a sustained challenge to powerholders in the name of a population living under the jurisdiction of those power-holders by means of repeated public displays of that population's numbers, commitment, unity, and worthiness' (Tilly 1994: 7). For Gamson (1990), a challenging group operates effectively when two functional problems are solved, those of 'pattern maintenance' and 'internal conflict'. First, for 'pattern maintenance, the group must be able to maintain a series of commitments from members that can be activated when necessary. Second, internal conflict influences a group's ability to act effectively. These two problems are dealt with by 'bureaucratic organization' and 'power centralization', respectively. That is, the first problem is solved by creating a structure of roles with defined expectations so that necessary tasks will be routinely performed, while the solution to the second problem is achieved by avoiding undesired factional splits. Bureaucracy in this context means 'formalization and role differentiation'. In defining bureaucratic challenging groups, Gamson (1990) uses three minimum characteristics: a written document (a constitution or charter); a formal list of members; and three or more levels of internal division. Both bureaucratic organization and power centralization contribute to the effectiveness of a group. The importance of recruitment networks and interpersonal ties to activate and maintain commitment is only later considered by Gamson (1990).

Although within the RM model, Morris (1984) strongly emphasizes the role played by the movement's local participants (or indigenous activists) and not that of external resources. Morris's view is supported by works on grassroots environmental movements. Freudenberg and Steinsapir (1991), for example, describe in detail the dramatic increase in local environmental activism which is characterized by volunteerism and a broad cross-section of gender, class, regional and occupational groups. This view is emphasized and labelled differently by Ingalsbee (1994). The action mobilization theory he proposes is contrasted with the resource mobilization one, as a new social movement theory which rests upon the assumption that only actors' mobilizing actions can bring life to such things as organizations, resources and (cumulatively) movements (Ingalsbee 1994: 141).

Regarding ideological motivations for struggle, grassroots environmentalists share certain perspectives, two of which are relevant to the theme of this Chapter. According to Freudenberg and Steinsapir (1991), they implicitly challenge the belief that economic growth is good per se and ultimately benefits everyone, by asking who bears the costs and who gets the benefits of growth. At the same time, they question the rights of producers to make decisions lacking the community's input, believing that citizens have every right to participate in making decisions on environment and development. This view is reinforced by local experience with the government and its experts. The mistrust that developed led them to view participation as mandatory for the representation of their interests in this process. New social movement theories stress these issues, which clearly reflect the desire for more autonomy, self-organization and/or self-determination (Ingalsbee 1994).

Other researchers emphasize the role of external resources in local environmental mobilization. Gould and Weinberg (1991) argue that local citizens are able to mobilize if they can gather key social resources. Thus, they argue that the impact of national and regional environmental social movement organizations (ESMOs) on local environmental political mobilization decreases with the remoteness of contaminated communities from the metropolitan social resource centres in which the larger organizations are located. External resources are usually available there in the form of scientific or technical information and strategic planning, consciousness raising, and conferment of legitimacy on the problem and the local coalition. It appears, therefore, that research on grassroots environmental movements will be enriched using both resource mobilization theories and new social movement ones. The success of challenging groups has a multidimensional character, since characteristics of the environment – such as the political opportunity structure – are interacting with characteristics of the movement itself – organizational structure, membership commitment, strategy and tactics (Klandermans 1989). In this Chapter characteristics of the environment will be studied by examining the role of the state.

The RM model, as developed by Gamson (1990), closely links group effectiveness and success. Both bureaucratic organization and power centralization contribute to the success of a challenging group, as does feistiness. Feistiness means the willingness to break rules and use non-institutionalized means, such as economic boycotts, building occupations, demonstrations and other non-violent disruptive tactics – not simply verbal feistiness – to disrupt the antagonists. Furthermore, non-violence and unruliness interact with media coverage to limit the effectiveness of overt repression as a means of social control. Success itself is seen by Gamson (1990) as a set of outcomes surrounding the acceptance of a challenging group by the antagonist, with new advantages gained during the challenge and its aftermath. These outcomes are measured at the end of the mobilization when the challenging group ceases to exist as a formal entity, when mobilization activities stop, or when the group is accepted by the antagonist as part of the constituency. Indicators of acceptance are acts which involve a change from hostility or indifference to a more positive relationship. These are consultation, negotiations, formal recognition and inclusion. No assumption is made that those mobilized necessarily caused the benefits. Instead, Gamson aims to show whether desired results did occur after the period of the challenge by coding four perceptions of goal achievement – those of historians, the challengers, the antagonists and the challenging group's level of satisfaction at the end. A more general but similar measure of success, according to Zimmerman (1990), is the change in the response set pattern of the state being in the position of the antagonist, i.e. whether a reaction lower in the hierarchy is moved up by the challenge of a social movement. He points out, however, some problems with this measure, since some responses may be independent of the challenge, administrative rules may not allow for hierarchical response changes and, finally, some states may choose not to respond at all or may react only to the means they elect to use (e.g. oppression).

The state as the movement's antagonist

In the modern capitalist world, especially the periphery, the central state appears to be the major antagonist of grassroots environmental movements, either directly or indirectly. Since it requires growth to avoid political instability, modern capitalism neglects the future and provides no mechanisms for dealing with the common property and public goods problems which markets generate (Dryzek 1992). The administrative state is highly constrained in its responses to these problems given severe difficulties in policy implementation, the inability to deal with complex problems due to the non-neutrality of expertise, and its obstruction of the free transmission of information. Structural theories emphasize the economic role of the state as an institution having a special interest in enhancing the conditions of capital accumulation and growth (FitzSimmons *et al.* 1991; Poulantzas 1973).

Supporting structural theories, Humphrey and Buttel (1982), Schnaiberg (1994), Gould (1992) and Kousis (1994) maintain that in a dynamic capitalist society the state performs two main functions: *accumulation*, by ensuring the conditions for profitable capital accumulation and economic growth; and *legitimation*, by maintaining social harmony. Under the first role, the state is committed to looking at environmental resources for their exchange-values. Thus, producers are permitted to externalize the environmentally damaging costs of production and limit corporate liability (Cable and Benson 1992). The state's managed scarcity intervention is limited by the following four different types of producer strategies: reducing initial problem consciousness, constraining implementation of environmental protection policies, restricting enforcement actions or evading controls, and increasing public and political resistance (Schnaiberg 1994). These strategies have been labelled by some as 'corporate environmental crimes', since they point to the failure of the state's environmental regulatory process due to the inherent contradictions of the liberal democratic state (Cable and Benson 1992).

The state's legitimation function concerning environmental demands is to preserve the ecosystems' capacities so that they can produce the use-values of various political constituencies of state actions. The failure of the state to provide adequate levels of legitimation, and thereby social harmony, often generates public opposition (Cable and Benson 1992; Modavi 1993; Kousis 1994). In conflicts over the implementation of state policies, state agencies and actors benefit from solutions mollifying these movements without imposing high exchange-value costs on local capitalist producers (Schnaiberg 1994). Simultaneously, however, legitimation concerns of the polity can act as political opportunity structures for grassroots movements to pressure the state and gain concessions (Modavi 1993).

The study of grassroots environmental movements reveals important characteristics for producers, consumers and the state. The producers' characteristics, whether capitalist or socialist, appear to be:

- largely organized around environmental resources;
- highly conscious of their material interests in access to such natural resources;
- ready to mobilize all forms of control capacity (social, political and economic assets) in order to capture the exchange-value in markets, as well as the influence of the state (Schnaiberg 1994).

Local environmental movement groups, workers and residents have both exchange-value interests (as workers in production organizations) and use-value interests, as citizens living in ecosystems disrupted by such organizations (Schnaiberg 1994). They usually organize around grassroots issues focusing on health impacts on family members, economic impact on the family, and community property and environmental impact. The central state's role is significant yet paradoxical, with a conflict of interests between the functions of accumulation and legitimation.

A recent study (Flam 1994) focusing specifically on anti-nuclear movements and state interactions provides cross-national analyses illustrating how these interactions contribute to the mobilization and demobilization of specific movements, and how they make for successive shifts in movements' dominant goals and strategies. Flam also traces the impact of interactions on shifts in policy goals and conflict-managing styles of decision-makers across eight state apparatuses.

GRASSROOTS ENVIRONMENTAL MOVEMENTS IN RURAL GREECE

Grassroots environmental movements in rural Greece have mushroomed in numbers and diversity, covering a wide range of ecosystem issues (Kousis 1994). Three such movements which have received extensive publicity will be the subject of this section from the resource-mobilization-state theoretical perspective in the context of sustainable development.

The selection of the three case studies is based on criteria referring to the grassroots character of the mobilization, the sustainable development attributes of the projects and the features of the antagonists challenged. Specifically, all three grassroots environmental mobilizations fit the definition of ad-hoc social movements as described by Tilly (1994) and Gamson's (1990) definition of a challenging group. In addition, they challenged three very different forms of sustainable development projects: a municipal sewage treatment plant, a toxics storage–treatment corporate facility and a geothermal powerplant which uses renewable energy, widely accepted as sustainable. The challenged antagonists cover the wider spectrum of producers usually involved in environmental conflicts: a private foreign company, a government-controlled company and a local authority. In all these cases the state becomes directly or indirectly involved and plays a most significant role with its responses to the specific mobilizations.

The data for this section are drawn from a variety of sources.

Relevant agencies supplied publications and reports, while two of the three action committees (hereinafter called Struggle Committees) permitted access to their archives, which included minutes of meetings, incoming and outgoing correspondence, protest activity information, local and national press cuttings and other relevant documents. Informal and telephone interviews with leaders of the movements and state employees provided information not appearing elsewhere. Local and national newspapers, as well as the major ecology magazines, have proved to be a very important data source. The data set covers issues which have raised important questions for students of environmental movements, especially in rural developing areas. There follows a brief account of each dispute.

In northwestern Greece locals from 102 villages and three towns in the Thesprotia region and the island of Corfu strongly resisted the construction of a sewage treatment plant which would handle domestic and other wastes from the urban centre of Ioannina and dispose the treated effluents into River Kalamas (Kousis 1991). Their major antagonist was not the Ioannina municipal authority but the central government, which had provided construction grants and technical support. The locals' aim was to protect the river ecosystem which they depend upon for their livelihood. The area covers 45,000 stremmata of irrigated fields, scenic resorts for recreationists, and potential sites for fish farming and the further development of tourism. State authorities and the municipality of Ioannina were attempting to 'solve' a problem which modern urbanization creates. From May 1987 to November 1990 and continuing through May 1992, the locals from Thesprotia and Corfu mobilized effectively. All plant construction activities were halted until further studies were carried out to investigate alternative sewage treatment and disposal solutions.

On the island of Milos the 4,500 locals from its five villages mobilized intensely against the operation of a 2MW geothermal power pilot station on Zefyria, the island's most fertile valley (Kousis 1993). The station was built by the government-controlled Public Power Corporation (PPC), with financial assistance from the government and the European Community. The locals produced evidence that geothermal energy development exerted negative impacts on public health, the local economy, and the terrestrial and marine ecosystems of the island, while technical studies carried out on behalf of the PPC revealed no such negative impacts. The intense mobilization activities of the Milians against the pilot station took place from September 1988 to July 1989. This mobilization eventually led to the suspension by the state of all geothermal-energy-related activities on the island.

In west-central Greece the 2,000 inhabitants of the small coastal town of Astakos learnt from a national newspaper article that a north European company had applied to the government for a license to install a toxic waste storage and treatment facility in their area. An immediate and strong mobilization effort followed (Kousis 1991). The locals realized that such an installation would generate adverse and irreversible consequences on their quality of life and the physical environment. Although the state did not identify with the company's position, it did not side readily with the locals either. In promoting its interests, the company persistently argued publicly that the facility would offer only positive benefits to the local and national economy, without any threats to the environment. The intense mobilization activities in Astakos between May 1989 and February 1990 eventually resulted in the company's failure to obtain a government license to install the facility in the area.

Bureaucratic organization and power centralization

As outlined earlier, bureaucratic organization basically refers to formalization and role differentiation, and when examining for its presence at least three characteristics ought to be found: a written document, a formal list of members and the presence of three levels of constituency (Gamson 1990). However, for the three cases considered here, although there are written documents and at least three levels of members, a 'formal list of members' does not exist. This is because Gamson studied challenge groups in a developed urban environment rather than a rural setting and, given the developing character of the Greek regions, the non-existence of a formal list of members is not viewed as crucial. What *is* crucial is that the indigenous movement organizers did present documents stating their cause as well as provisions for effective operation. In addition, they distinguished between three levels of members. In Kalamas and Astakos there are executive committees, subcommittees with various tasks and rank-and-file levels of members. In Milos a 37-member committee was established with a seven-member executive and a planning and co-ordinating subcommittee.

The committees and subcommittees serve several functions. They inform local, regional, state and international bodies about the problem, as well as local concerns and aims. They call public meetings and organize mobilizations after public referenda, which lead to strikes, blocking of regional transportation routes and occupation of public buildings. In addition, in the case of Milos, which had already experienced negative impacts and needed to document them, an additional important function was the collection of funds. An account in the name of the Struggle Committee was opened with a local bank. The amount, which accumulated in that account very quickly through local contributions alone, was enough to hire an Athens-based environmental research centre to conduct a study on the impact of geothermal energy in Milos.

Based on the above, the bureaucratic organization in these grass-roots movements appears to be as strong as that described by Gamson. The absence of the formal list of members did not hinder the smooth organization of activities which led to the success of these mobilizations. In these rural developing areas such a list was not required, since all locals were involved in the events that took place. Communication was not pursued through the mail, but orally through social contacts and via publicly posted written announcements. This means of communication was extremely effective, well suited to the village populations concerned. Formal written communications were limited to local organizations, associations, unions, clubs and societies and were used when needed.

Regarding power centralization, none of the three movements was dominated by one leader. Instead, power rested with top-level committees with central authority. The Kalamas committee was managed by a rotating chair. These committees played a very crucial role in preventing factional splits. They changed very little since the beginning of the mobilization, and kept the movement alive and successful, without any important factional episodes.

Local activism and perspectives

The participants in the Kalamas, Milos and Astakos movements were all volunteers. Furthermore, they came from all the different classes, occupational groups, subregions and both sexes. The movement organizers were locals, usually with more education and/or experience than the rest of the active participants. In the Milos case, the chair of the Struggle Committee was a Milian repatriate from the capital, Athens, while in Kalamas some of the committee's most active members were local engineers. In Astakos the chair of the committee is a local doctor also serving as the mayor of the town.

As far as grassroots perspectives are concerned, the mobilizing locals share very similar, if not identical, views. These views surround the wider issue of economic growth and question who gets the benefits and who bears the costs. In addition, given the locals' experiences, which led them to mistrust the state and its experts, they were led to demand the right to true and meaningful (not just formal) participation in the making of decisions concerning the environment and development in their regions.

The locals mobilizing around Kalamas claim that their region is underdeveloped and in desperate need of assistance from the state to foster true local development and not the degradation of local natural resources. In support of their case, they point to their region having the second highest rate of emigration in Greece. The movement's participants believe that if the disposal of Ioannina's domestic sewage into Kalamas becomes a reality, Ioannina's citizens will benefit but the people in the river basin will dearly pay the costs. Regions which survive on agriculture and tourism will no longer function as they have done up to now. Furthermore, there will be no other development options, such as fisheries or other tourism activities, with a deteriorated river ecosystem. Finally, public health costs and the cost of damage to the natural environment will also be borne by locals in Thesprotia and Corfu.

In Milos, air, land and water resources had been affected by geothermal activities. The local doctor's attempt to make the pilot station's negative health impact known rendered the Milians highly conscious and ready to protect their families, especially their children. Crop production in Zefyria, the only valley of the island, was shrinking. Plant life near the station was drying out and 'dying'. In the summer preceding the massive mobilizations, grain harvest production was only about 25 per cent of the normal annual grain crop, while that autumn and winter the locals had to get rid of all their olive oil produce in the light of laboratory tests which showed that it contained the highly poisonous substance arsenic. Other damages included plant and field destruction from the 'lava stream' which had occurred during the drilling operations and from leaks from the pipes of the disposal system which ran from the valley to the coastal zone.

The small community of Zefyria, adjacent to the geothermal station, was subjected to high levels of pollution and experienced grave difficulties in continuing its normal life. Domesticated animals became sick and many died. As high hydrogen sulphide concentrations in air made normal breathing impossible, many people fled their homes. The newly established tourist businesses were also concerned about losing clients, given the unexpected deterioration of the natural ecosystem. One of the most beautiful beaches, which also happened to be a very important archaeological site, was the disposal point for the geothermal station's untreated liquid effluents, and was deserted. Thus the Milians felt that they were paying very dearly for geothermal energy development. Although this renewable energy project had promised to turn their island into a green paradise, it actually deprived them of their minimum right to clean air. And while they – the Milians – were paying the costs, it was the Public Power Corporation and the state, far away from the damages, who were reaping the benefits.

In Astakos the movement stood against the installation of a toxic waste treatment and storage facility with a capacity to process large volumes of imported toxic waste – Greece itself produces only a small proportion of such toxic substances. In this case, since the head of the Struggle Committee and mayor of the town was a medical doctor the dangers from such a facility were carefully considered immediately. Intrinsically, the preservation of the ecosystem where Astakos is located is extremely important for the continuation of the agricultural and fishing activities which are the main sources of rural income. Furthermore, the balance of this ecosystem is important for the future of small-scale tourism which some locals hope to see. Most important, however, has been concern over the impact of the proposed development on family health, especially the health of children. Locals thus viewed themselves as those who would be paying the social costs of processing and storing foreign toxic waste, and the company (and possibly the state) as those who would reap the monetary benefits.

In all three cases the mobilizing locals developed a mistrust of government and company reports, documentation and 'expert' knowledge. In Astakos the company presented an environmental impact assessment (EIA) study which had been carried out by its own 'experts', concluding that no negative impacts would be produced. In Milos all pollution measurements taken by experts appointed by the state and the PPC were many times lower than those presented by the Panhellenic Centre of Environmental Studies (PAKOE) – a private laboratory which had been hired by the Struggle Committee. In Kalamas the locals distrusted state-sponsored technical reports which insisted that domestic waste disposal into Kalamas would not carry any negative effects on their health and the natural ecosystem of the area.

This mistrust of state-affiliated and company-sponsored technical reports was reflected in the public referenda which the three grassroots movements unanimously approved to demand that the locals truly participate in the decision-making process on the environment and development in their regions. For Kalamas and Astakos this meant that locals were seeking assurances that alternative solutions would be seriously considered and adopted. For Milos the target was the cessation of all geothermal development activities which had been degrading the island's air, land and water resources.

Tactics

The willingness of challengers to break rules and use non-institutionalized means to disrupt antagonists ('feistiness') is usually accomplished via economic boycotts, occupation of buildings, demonstrations and other non-violent tactics. All three cases present vivid examples of the above. The mobilization for the protection of Kalamas was characterized as the first environmental mobilization of its kind. In addition to demonstrations in Athens, strikes and occupation of public buildings, Thesprotians managed successfully to isolate their provincial capital, Igoumenitsa, for forty-one days. For several weeks the city did not function at any level. In public referenda, all unions and associations and individual locals voted to cease all activities – even schools and hospitals were closed – and to block all routes of transportation to the city. The municipal town hall was chained and locked up by members of the Struggle Committee and public buildings were occupied by local citizens. On a number of occasions farm tractors were used in these mobilizations, though the actions were characterized by non-violence. These mobilization tactics were also used in Athens, in front of the Parliament and in front of the major TV stations, by internal migrants from Thesprotia and Corfu. Similar non-violent but non-institutionalized means were used in Milos. Because the locals' requests for systematic and credible measurement and impact assessment were left unanswered, an occupation of all municipal buildings was organized – and in such a way as to avoid arrests. The occupation was followed up by an 80 km march of the entire population of the island to the geothermal pilot station, under unfavourable weather conditions. Participants with cars surrounded the station, blocking its entrances and exits. Non-violence also characterized the mobilization efforts in Astakos. After a public referendum deciding never to let the company into the area, strikes and a public-service-building occupation followed. The climax of these mobilization efforts was the blocking of the motorway to Astakos and the occupation of the site wanted by CBI. The entire Astakos population, along with other locals from nearby areas, was gathered with signs stating their aim. In this instance, rifles appeared in the hands of locals while tractors blocked the road.

External resources

External resources played a role in these grassroots mobilizations. The Kalamas issue attracted the attention of several Athens-based environmental organizations. One of them, RIXI, helped the local movement by organizing informative meetings for locals and inviting any interested Greeks to them. It also organized an excursion to the Kalamas river area in order to disseminate information and raise consciousness. Finally, it requested technical assistance from foreign ecological organizations. In this way RIXI also conferred legitimacy on the local problem and the local mobilization. Other environmental organizations, some of which were political, such as DOKE, played similar roles. In addition, twelve environmental organizations travelled to Thesprotia in support of the mobilizers. Furthermore, following DOKE's communication with the German Green Party, a German TV crew came and filmed the mobilization. It should be noted here that a major Greek ecological magazine (*New Ecology*) tended to support the view that domestic sewage could be safely disposed of in Kalamas if it was subjected beforehand to tertiary (not just secondary) treatment. In Milos the Struggle Committee hired the Athens-based PAKOE to carry out a small-scale study on the effects of geothermal energy development in Milos. PAKOE was selected as an independent, environmentalist-oriented private research centre, and it carried out environmental impact tests in collaboration with a German University since it did not have all the required equipment itself. In December 1988 PAKOE announced the test results on sampled olive oil, sea water, ground water and air and made two proposals. First, it recommended the shutdown of the station as it detected dangerous concentrations of arsenic, positive ions and hydrogen sulphide. Second, it suggested a feasibility study for geothermal activity development in Milos. PAKOE thus not only provided scientific information but simultaneously conferred legitimacy on the Milian mobilization. As a result, local cohesion was enhanced. Any political obligations felt toward state policy were abandoned since everyone's primary concern centred on the health of the family and the protection of the Milian ecosystem. In practice, PAKOE went even further. It took top-ranking PPC officials and ministry executives to court, seeking private litigation for the Milians. These managers, claimed PAKOE, had not carried out an environmental impact assessment study, as was required of every new development project by the National Environmental Policy Act of 1986. Simultaneously, PAKOE asked the courts to order an assessment of the pilot station's effects on the environment.

In Astakos, by way of contrast, there was no external support. The mobilization was carried out by locals, which proved both difficult and painful since the company used various tactics to co-opt some of the mobilizers. Among other methods, it offered a number of local authority figures and press reporters an all-expenses-paid trip to a similar facility in northern Europe. The severity of the issue involved, however, kept the locals united until they finally saw the signs of success.

The role and response of the state

The conflict over Kalamas is rooted in the government's planning and decision-making processes. Before 1975 no action was taken, as legislative provisions for sewage treatment did not exist. However, since 1981 the government had been advised about environmental issues by its scientific collaborators from engineering schools. It organized relevant meetings with all interested parties and exerted influence especially on the municipal authority. Between 1985 and 1987 the government held a dialogue with local-authority representatives about prospective technical studies on the disposal of treated wastes in Kalamas.

In February 1988 the Struggle Committee for the protection of Kalamas announced that, although funds and time had been made available, the appropriate study that should have been carried out had not been. Thus, in September 1988 the frustration over the government's lack of action led the committee and its supporters to initiate an intensive mobilization. The Thesprotians demanded not only that the appropriate studies be carried out but that the state and its scientific collaborators, as well as the political parties, assume responsibility for their actions/inactions. The Ioannina municipality, dependent on the government's economic and technical support, announced that the river and the lake would be destroyed if the sewage treatment facility was not constructed and set in operation.

The forty-five days of strikes, the blockades, rallies and occupation of public buildings eventually led to the involvement of the local police department, which invited the Struggle Committee to take part in a dialogue. Then, at the end of October 1988, the Minister of the Interior visited the area and held talks with the mobilizers, and an agreement was reached that until new studies were carried out both treatment plant construction activities and mobilization efforts would cease. Furthermore, these new studies would not focus on Kalamas as the only viable option; they would also place emphasis on environmental impacts. More importantly, the studies would be evaluated by a panel which would include Struggle Committee members and World Health Organization representatives selected by the local authorities of Thesprotia and Corfu.

In the case of Milos, between 1975 and the summer of 1988 the PPC, in close collaboration with its supervising Ministry of Industry and Energy, escalated activities which would help exploit the geothermal potential on the island. Initially, the PPC claimed that geothermal energy would turn their island into a true paradise. During the autumn of 1988, however, accumulated environmental and health impacts due to the PPC's activities led to the formation of the Struggle Committee for Geothermal Energy. The subsequent mobilization of the Milians aimed to suspend all geothermal activities until precautionary measures were taken which would protect the health of the locals as well as the Milian ecosystem. In response, in January 1989 the ministry requested assistance from other ministries and government agencies, and sent its secretary-general to the island for consultation with the locals. Nevertheless, at the secretary's departure, the government-controlled TV station announced that all PPC activities in Milos were to proceed normally. In response to this news, the locals renamed their committee as one *against* geothermal development and mobilized by striking, marching, demonstrating and giving press releases. As these mobilizing activities were climaxing in March 1989, the Ministry decided to halt all PPC activities until all groups agreed to collaborate. In addition, the government promised to fund a general environmental impact study for the island.

In the case of Astakos, the government took on the apparent role of the middleman between a private company and the locals, but in essence it played a central role since it had the power to decide whether the foreign company in question would be granted permission to use the local resources. During the spring of 1989 the Ministry of the Environment, Physical Planning and Public Works (MEPPPW) requested additional information from the foreign company regarding its application to buy or lease the Astakos site. The specific site had a ship-repairing installation which was the property of a state bank supervised by the Ministry for Industry. In an internal memo, the bank described this type of exchange as too risky and (perhaps as a competitor for the site) would not accept the company's proposals. For its part, the MEPPPW initially responded to the company's application by agreeing that the appropriate studies and controls be carried out. In early autumn 1989, however, by which time the Ministry for Industry had asked the MEPPPW to sign the transfer without consulting the local authority, the latter had requested a feasibility study for the site. In the circumstances the locals' response was an intensive mobilization that took place between November 1989 and January 1990. As a consequence, in January 1990 the Ministry for Industry annulled all relevant written agreements with the company, and in February 1990 the MEPPPW finalized the government's negative position towards the company with a statement in Parliament.

CONCLUSION

The success of grassroots environmental movements in less-developed rural Greece, typically exemplified by those of Thesprotia, Astakos and Milos, is apparent, according to Gamson's (1990) and Zimmerman's (1990) criteria. Although there have been dormant periods for these movements, the organizational structure which they developed may still be effective in furthering their goals. What has made these movements successful thus far? The specific focus of this analysis points to various factors which are related to both their organizational effectiveness and the role of their antagonists. These factors also illuminate some similarities and dissimilarities with the experience of grassroots movements in the developed world.

Looking at bureaucratization, the formal list of members, which is viewed as an essential characteristic of ESMOs in the developed world, is not found to apply to the case studies from a less-developed country. Indeed, it is considered insignificant given that oral communication has proved more effective. Conversely, power centralization is found in the form of a top-level committee that remains more or less unaltered and prevents the creation of any factional disruptions. Thus, as in the developed world, problems of internal conflict management are solved via similar internal structures in all cases. Feistiness is present in its fullest potential, as locals mobilized to safeguard their community against environmental and public health impacts.

As regards non-institutionalized forms of action, however, the evidence shows a tremendous effort on the part of the mobilizing forces to make their problem known and to get it corrected, using all institutionalized means available. It cannot be overstressed that local people resort to non-institutionalized means and mobilize only after the institutionalized routes fail to address the issues of concern. Moreover, this frustration makes their 'struggle' more intense and their efforts stronger and persistent. The non-existence of public participation mechanisms in the selection of development projects in less-developed countries leaves the use of non-institutionalized actions as the sole alternative.

The role which external resources played was important during the mobilization to save Kalamas and Astakos, and vital in the case of Milos. For reasons which remain unclear, the Astakos case did not attract the attention of any of the capital-based national or foreign ESMOs, although there was a mention of the problem in an ecological magazine. More research is needed to qualify these peculiarities. Finally, proximity to Athens – where most, if not all, national ESMOs are based – does not appear to affect the relationship with these grassroots organizations as it does in developed countries. Significantly, Astakos is located closer to Athens than Thesprotia or Milos.

Voluntarism in rural Greece is similar to that experienced in grassroots ESMOs in the more developed world. Men and women, old and young, from all occupational and class groups, volunteer to carry out the goals of their movement. However, in their perspectives on economic growth and participation in the decision-making process, locals in these rural mobilizations appear to be more persistent than their counterparts in the United States. This may be attributed to their persistent desire to see 'sustainable development' truly taking place in their regions, to the absence of public participation procedures or to the fact that they are not totally dependent on one income source. Local perceptions, however, are very indicative of the mistrust of the state and thus strongly support new social movement theories.

Therefore, the evidence from this work on three significant grassroots environmental movements in rural Greece indicates that their effectiveness and success can be explained using the resource mobilization paradigm, as developed by Gamson (1990), Morris (1984), Gould (1991) and Weinberg (1990; see also Gould and Weinberg 1991), as well as parts of the new social movement paradigm, as described by Ingalsbee (1994). At the same time, the evidence points to the importance of the dynamic interaction between the challenging groups and the state. Analysis also demonstrates the potential discrepancy between the state's accumulation and legitimation functions. The participants of the three challenging groups were frustrated when they tried to collaborate with the state initially. Over long periods of time, locals exhausted every legal and formal means of communication with state actors. Given the state's obligations to accumulation issues, their collaboration efforts were ineffective – which led locals to resort to social movement tactics. The interaction of these challenging groups with the state, however, needs to be studied in more detail in future works.

A number of questions arise. Is the state ready to accept individual ESMOs because it fears the political cost of a negative response? Or is it merely performing a legitimation function while waiting for a stronger comeback later on, when economic motives can be used to convince the locals? In the analysis above, three 'sustainable development' projects, according to the more conventional use of the term, gave rise to mobilizations whose constituency aimed to protect local resources from the environmental impacts of these externally generated projects. The inhabitants of the communities involved requested from the state a sustainable development path which is geared to local needs, i.e. to the use of local resources for local purposes. They resisted the state's support of powerful non-local agents who intended to use the local ecosystem for projects that were not just non-locally sustainable but locally *un*sustainable. Locals insisted that they participate in decisions that directly affect their health, economy and ecosystem, and that their development path should be selected *in collaboration with* them and not by the state alone. Whether they have fully succeeded in achieving all of these goals has yet to be seen. What this Chapter is suggesting is that there are two sides to the sustainable development issue, the social and the ecological. The evidence provided shows that distributing the negative externalities of developed regions in less-developed rural areas, or exploiting a rural area's local natural resources for a developed region's needs, cannot be labelled sustainable. Characterizing such activities in this way implies imposition by the more powerful centres upon the less powerful groups. In contrast, not only is the sustainable development sought by the locals characterized by justice, but it also causes less damage to the local ecosystem.

This, perhaps, is the ideal route to sustainable development. Certainly, if the social and political side of the sustainable development issue is the most crucial, the ecological side may become less polemical. Future research needs to address systematically the conditions under which community-based social movements arise around environmental issues, and the relevance of these movements to the different dimensions of the concept of sustainable development.

NOTE

1 This work was supported in part by the University of Crete Research Fund, contract no. ELKE-376, and by the European Commission, DGXII, contract no. EVSV-CT94-0393.

REFERENCES

Barkin, D. (1991) 'State control of the environment: politics and degradation in Mexico', *Capitalism, Nature, Socialism* 2(1): 86–108.

Brechin, S. R. and West, P. (1990) 'Protected areas, resident peoples, and sustainable conservation: the need to link top-down with bottom-up', *Society and Natural Resources* 3: 77–79.

Bullard, R. D. (1990) 'Environmentalism, economic blackmail, and civil rights: competing agendas within the black community', in J. Gaventa, B. E. Smith and A. Willingham (eds) *Communities in Economic Crises: Appalachia and the South*, Philadelphia: Temple University Press.

Buttel, F. H. (1991) 'Environmental quality and the state: some political-sociological observations on environmental regulation', in R. G. Braungart and M. M. Braungart (eds) *The Political Sociology of the State*, Greenwich, CT: JAI Press.

Cable, S. and Benson, M. (1992) 'Acting locally: environmental justice and the emergence of grassroots environmental organization', revised version of paper presented at the 1992 meetings of the American Sociological Association (ASA), Pittsburgh.

de la Court, T. (1990) *Beyond Brundtland: Green Development in the 1990s*, London: Zed Books.

Dryzek, J. S. (1992) 'Ecology and discursive democracy: beyond liberal capitalism and the administrative state', *Capitalism, Nature, Socialism* 3(2): 18–42.

Ekins, P. (1992) *A New World Order: Grassroots Movements for Global Change*, London: Routledge.

Faber, D. (1992) 'The ecological crisis of Latin America: a theoretical introduction', *Latin American Perspectives* 19(1): 3–16.

FitzSimmons, M., Glaser, J., Monte Mor, R., Fincetl, S. and Rajan, C. (1991) 'Environmentalism and the American liberal state', *Capitalism, Nature, Socialism* 2(1): 1–16.

Flam, H. (1994) *States and Anti-nuclear Movements*, Edinburgh: Edinburgh University Press.

Freudenberg, N. and Steinsapir, C. (1991) 'Not in our backyards: the grassroots environmental movement', *Society and Natural Resources* 4(3): 235–45.

Gamson, W. A. (1989) 'Reflections on the strategy of social protest', *Sociological Forum* 4(3): 455–467.

—— (1990) *The Strategy of Social Protest*, Belmont, CA: Wadsworth.

Ghai, D. and Vivian, J. M. (1992) *Grassroots Environmental Action: People's Participation in Sustainable Development*, New York: Routledge.

Gould, K. (1991) 'The sweet smell of money: economic dependency and local environmental political mobilization', *Society and Natural Resources* 4(2): 133–150.

—— (1992) 'Putting the [W]R.A.P.s on participation: remedial action planning and working class power in the Great Lakes', *Sociological Practice Review* 3(3): 133–9.

Gould, K. and Weinberg, A. S. (1991) 'Who mobilizes whom: the role of national and regional social movement organizations in local environmental political mobilization', paper presented at the meetings of the American Sociological Association (ASA), Cincinnati, Ohio, August.

Gow, D. D. (1992) 'Poverty and natural resources: principles for environmental management and sustainable development', *Environmental Impact Assessment Review* 12: 49–65.

Haigh, N. (1989) *EEC Environmental Policy and Britain*, Harlow: Longman.

Humphrey, C. R. and Buttel, F. H. (1982) *Environment, Energy, and Society*, Belmont, CA: Wadsworth.

Ingalsbee,T. (1994) 'Resource and action mobilization theories: the new social psychological research agenda', *Berkeley Journal of Sociology* 38: 139–156.

Klandermans, B. (1989) 'Introduction: social movement organizations and the study of social movements', in B. Klandermans (ed.) *International Social Movements Research* 2: 1–59.

Kousis, M. (1991) 'Development, environment, and social mobilization: a micro level analysis', *Greek Review of Social Research* 80: 96–109 (in Greek).

—— (1993) 'Collective resistance and sustainable development in rural Greece: the case of geothermal energy on the island of Milos', *Sociologia Ruralis* 33(1): 3–24.

—— (1994) 'Environment and the state in the EU periphery: the case of Greece', *Regional Politics and Policy* 4(1): 118–135.

Liberatore, A. (1993) 'Beyond the Earth Summit: the European Community towards sustainability?', Florence: European University Institute working paper EPU no. 93/5.

Modavi, N. (1993) 'The political economy of state intervention in land use conflicts: a case study of community opposition to golf course development in Hawaii', *Case Analysis* (spring–summer).

Morris, A. D. (1984) *The Origins of the Civil Rights Movement: Black Communities Organizing for Change*, New York: Free Press.

Morris, A. D. and McClurg Mueller, C. (1992) *Frontiers in Social Movement Theory*, New Haven, CT: Yale University Press.

O'Connor, J. (1988) 'Capitalism, nature, socialism: a theoretical introduction', *Capitalism, Nature, Socialism* 1: 11–38.

Poulantzas, N. (1973) 'The problem of the capitalist state', in R. Blackburn (ed.) *Ideology in Social Science*, New York: Vintage Books, pp. 238–253.

Redclift, M. (1987) *Sustainable Development: Exploring the Contradictions*, London: Routledge.

—— (1992) 'Sustainable development and popular participation: a framework for analysis', in D. Ghai and J. M. Vivian (eds) *Grassroots Environmental Action: People's Participation in Sustainable Development*, London: Routledge.

Regan, R. and Legerton, M. (1990) 'Economic slavery or hazardous wastes? Robeson County's economic menu', in J. Gaventa, B. E. Smith and A. Willingham (eds) *Communities in Economic Crises: Appalachia and the South*, Philadelphia: Temple University Press.

Schnaiberg, A. (1985) 'Capital flight from environmental regulation: nonmetropolitan industrialization and "folk" resistance', paper presented at the annual meeting of the American Sociological Association (ASA), Washington, DC, 30 August.

—— (1994) 'The political economy of environmental problems and policies: consciousness, conflict and control capacity', *Advances in Human Ecology* 3: 23–64.

Stevis and Mummee (1992) 'Nuclear power, technological autonomy and the state in Mexico', *Latin American Research Review*: 55–82.

Szasz, A. (1994) *Ecopopulism: Toxic Waste and the Movement of Environmental Justice*, Minneapolis: University of Minnesota Press.

Thrupp, L. A. (1989) 'Politics of the sustainable development crusade: from elite protectionism to social justice in third world issues', *Environment, Technology and Society* 58: 1–7.

—— (1990) 'Environmental initiatives in Costa Rica: a political ecology perspective', *Society and Natural Resources* 3: 243–256.

Tilly, C. (1994) 'Social movements as historically specific clusters of political performances', *Berkeley Journal of Sociology* 38: 1–30.

Walsh, E. J. (1988) *Democracy in the Shadows: Citizen Mobilization in the Wake of the Accident at the Three Mile Island*, New York: Greenwood Press.

Weinberg, A. S. (1990) 'Community right to know and local mobilization', *Environment, Technology and Society* 59: 8–9.

Zimmerman, E. (1990) 'Social movement and political outcomes: why both ends fail to meet', paper presented at the XIIth World Congress of Sociology, Madrid, 9–13 July.

12 Postscript

Sustainable development in the twenty-first century: the beginning of history?

Michael Redclift

This book has examined the politics of sustainable development at the end of the twentieth century. Where will it lead us in the twenty-first century? In this Chapter I want to look ahead, to 2020 and beyond, and try to envisage a future which makes new demands on the global environment and on the European Union. Will the European idea survive the next quarter-century? Will it be sustainable? What will our children and grandchildren make of our attempts to operationalize sustainable development? Is European unity the next 'big idea' or is sustainable development just such an idea? Do we need utopian visions to provide a contrast between the way we live now and the way we might live? Did history 'end' in 1989, with the collapse of communism, or is it only beginning? Might sustainable development actually mark the beginning of history rather than its end?

The editors of this volume reviewed the various meanings of sustainable development at some length in the Introduction, and it is unnecessary to repeat their efforts in this postscript. Instead, I want to begin by illustrating some of the ways in which the environment and sustainability assume importance today, drawing on real-world examples. These examples also serve to illustrate another concern of the editors, and several of the contributors to this book: that we need to develop a better understanding of what sustainable development might mean to people in their daily lives.

In October 1995 I visited the University of California at Berkeley. It had been over ten years since I was last there, and the changes showed in a number of ways. I was struck by the forceful arrival of 'identity politics' reflected in student clubs and societies, which seemed to have replaced most of the Left activism of the 1970s. Today Berkeley's students endeavour to enlist their fellows in groups whose main objective is to help provide (or reinforce) personal identity, especially around ethnic membership, gender and, significantly I think, the environment. Advertisements throughout the campus offer job opportunities to 'Hispanics who want to put their environmental credentials to the test . . . by working for green businesses in Central America'. Another advertisement I spotted spoke of 'training in environmental assessment . . . essential for gaining a satisfying career'.

While it is clear that such job openings still remain relatively few and demonstrate more than anything the manipulative possibilities of the market, they are none the less interesting. Environmental commitments, and interests, are now one of the hooks being used to draw young people into corporate America. This may constitute 'weak sustainable development', as the editors suggest, but it clearly represents a strong motivational message.

Several weeks later I joined a train in Strasbourg, bound for Stuttgart. In my experience one of the joys of travelling by rail (apart from it being relatively environmentally benign) is that people actually talk to each other, which they rarely do on aeroplanes. Just as rail termini are fascinating milieux of sound, smells and emotions, airports are, by contrast, relatively dull places, full of shopping malls and men wearing suits. They lack, as spaces, what we recognize as sociability.

On this occasion I was travelling in a compartment with a corridor (an additional aid to sociability, this!). An Indian man entered, and within a matter of minutes we were talking about our jobs, families and the state of the world. He told me he was a film director, making documentary films, usually for television. He had just completed a film about the Hindu pilgrims to Benares, who bathed in the Ganges. 'It is a wonderful place,' he said, 'where, together with several million others, you can buy and sell anything, eat anything and spend anything on a hotel . . . but the environmental problems have to be seen to be believed!' Evidently, in planning for several million pilgrims bathing in an already polluted river, nobody had looked into 'pollution' in the secular, rather than the religious, sense.

My friend asked me what I did for a living, and when I told him that I undertook research on the environment he became very animated. His brother owned factories all over India, and had just been to visit him in Strasbourg. His brother knew that his factories produced appalling environmental effects in the communities where they were situated but he simply discounted these dangers, saying that they were 'the price we pay for progress; we have to get capitalism moving in these villages'.

My companion told me that his brother was aware of environmental problems, and the part he played in them, but his brother believed that recognizing the need to act more sustainably was not enough, you also had to be prepared to do something about it. This his brother was simply unprepared to do. My travelling companion was very concerned that I should succeed in getting the environmental message across to more people, especially in the South. 'You need to think of yourself as John the Baptist', were his last words to me on alighting at Stuttgart railway station.

This struck me then, and subsequently on reflection, as quite a responsibility (and might, anyway, end in my decapitation!), but it also brought home the difference between endorsing the idea of sustainable development and being prepared to do something about it. How do we unravel people's social commitments from their environmental effects, and yet gain assent for structural changes beneficial to the environment but also undermining of our lifestyles? This is the subtext of much of this book.

My third example brings me back to North America again, just over a week later, when I visited British Columbia for the first time. As soon as you consider moving from an urban centre in western Canada you begin to appreciate the immensity of the wilderness areas that engulf you.

In British Columbia the political tensions reflect the way these wilderness resources are developed. For many of the local people the tension is between creating new jobs from the extractive economy and protecting the forests at the cost of local livelihoods. For over a century people who warned about the destruction of the natural environment have been pictured as meddling outsiders. Interestingly, the real 'insiders', native Americans, the First Peoples, have spent the same length of time pursuing their land claims, to no avail.

Some years ago in the Choco, on the Colombian coast, I met men who were paid US$10 per cubic metre to cut and transport valuable hardwoods, and still they waited outside the company's office in Buenaventura for the chance to get their hands on a chainsaw. On Vancouver Island loggers are paid much more than that, indeed they are relatively well paid. British Columbia resembles a resource-exporting economy in some ways, not unlike those of Latin America. However, in the city of Victoria, and elsewhere on the Island, there is also heated opposition to clear-cutting of forests and the trail of devastation that extends right up the west coast of Canada to Alaska. Canadians have a strong cultural attachment to the idea of wilderness, but economic benefits are hard won, and most Canadians also enjoy a high standard of living. The more removed they have become from primary economic activities, such as lumbering and fishing, the more they value conservation as a goal, at least in principle.

Disputes over the environment are no longer resolved between environmental activists and frontiersmen. They are increasingly the province of environmental managers and consultants: professional midwives to sustainable development. This prompts a reflection. In the last few years I have noticed what amounts to almost a hunger for environmental policy expertise, especially in southern Europe, and there is a growing army of consultants who here, as elsewhere in the European Union, act as the interpreters of new environmental policy measures. In Spain there are relatively few environmental activists, especially outside Catalonia and the Basque Country. There are also few local-level initiatives, such as you find in Germany, the Netherlands and Britain. There is little chance of finding a cycle lane or an opportunity to separate your domestic waste in the average urbanization outside Madrid. However, at every meeting and conference I have attended in Spain there are dozens of environmental professionals, whose goal is to find their way inside, or around, the body of regulatory rules and practices that increasingly constrain Spanish businesses and government in the European Union. There seems to be an enormous demand for environmental intelligence, and foresight, in the future environmental agenda in Europe. This is also a process that is occurring rapidly in Central and Eastern Europe, as they take anticipatory measures in preparation for their expected accession to the European Union.

The question I want to explore is whether this growing expertise is sufficient. Will pressing the right buttons stop the bus? Alternatively, how will my travelling companion's brother, apparently not indifferent to environmental problems in India, respond to the 'greening' of production, known as 'ecological modernization' in Europe?

Can a profit-motivated Indian capitalist, wedded to the market and with little incentive to behave differently, meet the environmental standards imposed by the European Union? Or the standards currently being interpreted by new generations of Spanish environmental economists? And who benefits, and loses, from this process – India's poor or Europe's new professionals? Does it contribute to the more sustainable use of natural resources? Why should the unemployed in British Columbia care about the next generation in Europe, or India or, indeed, in British Columbia itself? To begin to answer these questions, we need to step into the next century.

THE ROLE OF THE NORTH IN GLOBAL SUSTAINABLE DEVELOPMENT

To begin to assess the prospects for sustainable development in the European Union, we need to pose the problem at the global level. Even comparatively modest environmental targets are difficult to meet given the expected rise in global population and levels of consumption in the next twenty-five years. By 2025 the population of East Asia will be 1.7 billion, and that of South Asia 2.1 billion.

Many of these people will enjoy a higher standard of living; they will have access to electricity and clean water. In most cases their personal consumption of energy and goods will have risen. By 2020 China is expected to be the largest economy in the world, with a gross domestic product 40 per cent larger than that of the United States in terms of purchasing power. India, Indonesia, South Korea, Thailand, Taiwan and Brazil will be among those countries with larger economies than that of the United Kingdom. In the case of China, this will return it to the position it occupied before the Industrial Revolution in Europe, as the world's largest manufacturer.

Another example which serves to illustrate the point is that of Brazil. There are a number of important constraints on the development of sustainable energy policies for the Amazon. These include population growth. In 1990 Brazil's population was growing at 1.7 per cent a year. In the 1980s it grew at 1.9 per cent a year. In 1992 the population of Brazil stood at 152 million people. By 2020 it is expected to reach 234 million, even with a reduced rate of population increase (down to 1.3 per cent per annum). Among other things, more people mean a greatly increased demand for energy. Higher living standards for the majority of Brazil's people mean much more energy will be consumed.

If Brazil is to meet the energy demands of its growing population it will need to continue to grow economically. The Brazilian economy is currently growing by about 3.5 per cent a year. This means that the installed energy capacity will need to increase by nearly 50 per cent simply to keep pace with population growth. In addition, the increase in energy consumption per capita during this period will itself require a much greater installed capacity – probably almost four times that of 1990. The problem is not that Brazil's rate of economic growth cannot keep pace with the increased demand for electricity, but rather that the scale of economic development and electricity generation seems set to transform the country's natural resource base. By 2020 the Amazon could account for over half the installed capacity of Brazil. There will be more damns, most of them large, less biodiversity and a reduction in tropical forest cover. The Amazon, we might reflect, contains one-fifth of the globe's freshwater resources and half of the globe's tropical forests.

Where do these dramatic shifts in population and economic activity leave our concern with sustainable development? In its Second Assessment, the Intergovernmental Panel on Climate Change (IPCC) concluded that at some stage major reductions in carbon dioxide emissions, of the order of 50 per cent of current emissions, will be required in order eventually to stabilize concentrations (IPCC 1995).

According to IPCC, stabilization of atmospheric concentrations of all greenhouse gases at today's levels requires very low population and economic growth rates, major changes in energy technologies, and intervention to reduce emissions and enhance sinks (IPCC 1995). These proposals are not those of a radical green pressure group, but the considered opinion of some of the world's most distinguished environmental scientists. To what extent can these targets be approached given the scale of global development?

The problem of meeting middle- to long-range environmental targets is not confined, of course, to climate-change scenarios, but includes other environmental factors that are usually more critical to personal livelihoods in the short term, particularly in developing countries. These include: water quality, land degradation, environmental health, local air pollution and even biodiversity losses. The challenge to move towards increased sustainable development is one that needs to find expression in every aspect of economic and social life. It is unlikely that attempts to address 'environmental issues' in isolation from those of development will enable us to reverse the deeply embedded processes of unsustainable development which have contributed to environmental problems. At the moment, policy interventions are either regulatory, and based on legal compliance, or market-based, and dependent on price and fiscal incentives. Both approaches, however, depend critically on public endorsement and voluntary compliance. They are intended to influence existing human behaviour towards better resource conservation and pollution abatement, but we cannot police the planet. We also know very little about the effect of these policy mechanisms on long-term behaviour.

Environmental management has also taken important strides towards endorsing the precautionary principle, but this principle has not been incorporated into everyday economic and social decisions nor, in most cases, into the policies of governments and international actors, such as business corporations. Thus, it is becoming clear that achieving even modest environmental targets requires a third, more profound, process which would involve radical changes in behaviour, lifestyle and mobility, particularly (although not exclusively) in the industrialized North. Such changes would also contribute to the resolution of global problems by helping to give credibility to the industrialized world in future negotiations with the South. At the moment the effect of emulating Northern consumption, often using dirty technology, is proving detrimental to the environment in many of the newly industrialized economies. In most of the Asian 'Tigers', for example, the increase in urban air pollution exceeds even the dramatic increases in economic growth. It is a delusion to view these market success stories as examples of sustainable development.

We need to begin by analysing the connections between existing development in the European Union and the models of development which are advancing elsewhere in the world. This does not mean 'putting the clock back' to import substitution or heavy-handed state intervention, but it does imply a decision to consider what is unsustainable about past experience, as well as a 'revisioning' of the future.

Mapping out a global profile for sustainable development in the next century also has implications for research. Several lines of enquiry are open to the social sciences. We need to integrate what we currently know about the management of the environment from a variety of different disciplines, and assess the extent to which economic and social institutions might be made more responsive to change and made to incorporate a concern with enhanced sustainability. This means subjecting existing institutions and policies to rigorous scrutiny to establish the extent to which they might be the instruments of sustainable development, rather than the obstacle.

In outline, this means breaking the problem down into two parts. First, we need to establish the current social processes, which are constantly changing and which define consumption and human commitments. This requires greater specification of where social processes are located and at what level they operate environmentally: locally, regionally and internationally. Second, we need to establish the feasibility of intervention in these processes. To facilitate this we need to know more about existing experiences of positive environmental action to establish the conditions of their success. Currently, throughout Europe, from Baden-Württemburg to Teesside, local-government authorities are seeking to make such an assessment, often prompted by Agenda 21. Most of these efforts are being undertaken despite, rather than because of, national government policies. These experiences can help us to develop local scenarios of sustainable futures, and help to close the gap between civil society and government which lies at the heart of much of the ambiguity surrounding sustainable development.

It is clear that we bequeath social institutions, as well as an 'environment', to future generations. Most of these institutions were devised within a context of unsustainable growth. The role of the social sciences, in particular, is to provide key understanding and information which will contribute to the refashioning of core economic and social institutions. Hence our research will also need to focus upon the everyday institutional practices through which society reproduces itself. We will need to consider the 'environmental stakeholders' and 'users', for whom research can be expected to play a key role in the future and whose influence on the way it is conducted needs to be considered before new economic and social institutions can be fashioned.

In view of the breadth of the issues, as well as the need to specify much more clearly both the nature of existing social commitments and the feasibility of policy interventions, we need to recast the distinction between 'ecocentric' and 'anthropocentric' referred to at the beginning of this book. The discussion of the Sustainable Development Ladder in the Introduction made a valid distinction between 'strong' and 'weak' definitions of sustainable development. But why should 'ecocentrism' and 'biocentrism' be equated with strong sustainable development, towards the top of the figure? In what sense does the primacy of nature imply 'stronger' sustainable development? Indeed, it is clear that to make sustainable development operable will require structural interventions in the economy and the global political system, without which global trends in population and consumption will prove irreversible.

The anthropocentric perspective under 'strong' sustainable development is based on global equity and concern for future generations, too – which is neither more nor less ecocentric/biocentric. If intra- and inter-generational equity between humans is the foremost objective of sustainable development one must remain sceptical of ecocentric/biocentric positions devoid of political and social objectives. The issue becomes not how we in the North pay our debt to nature but, rather, how many of the countries of the South escape from their own burden of debt to us! We need, if we are to address global inequalities, to transform our trading relations with the developing world. And we need to do this not simply because of its ecological effects, but because 'free trade' cannot be fair between such unequal partners. The failure to do so inevitably increases human inequalities.

MEETING ENVIRONMENTAL TARGETS: SUSTAINABLE DEVELOPMENT AND SOCIAL COMMITMENTS

In a provocative paper about sustainability, Robert Goodland (1994), an economist with the World Bank, makes a challenging assertion. He argues that it is quite possible to raise per capita incomes in poor countries to between US$1,500 and US$2,000. If this were to be done then people living at these levels would benefit from about 80 per cent of the basic welfare currently provided by incomes ten times as high (c. US$15,000–US$20,000). Goodland adds:

> [those] working on Northern overconsumption should address the corollary – can $21,000 per capita countries [OECD] cut their consumption by a factor of ten, and suffer 'only' a 20 percent loss of basic welfare?
>
> (Goodland 1994: 8)

If we lowered our consumption by this amount, what effect would it have on economic development in East and South-East Asia? In the context of continuing economic growth and the expansion of world markets, especially in Asia, we surely need to ask some leading research questions of this kind.

How much welfare does additional material consumption actually buy? Does increased welfare reflect increased security, including environmental security? What would be the environmental and social benefits of reducing our consumption to more modest proportions? Can we design an alternative vision which enables progress to be made in improving quality of life without damaging the environment, and without significant welfare costs for most people in the North? What is the role of Northern consumption in changing habits and lifestyles in the rapidly developing economies of the South? Does the 'identity politics' of the Berkeley campus facilitate more sustainable development in Asia? How can research into existing practices pave the way for effective policies for enhanced sustainable development?

Can we harness our environmental science to the demands of more sustainable policies? In effect, the 'science agenda' inherited from the IPCC needs to be placed alongside the 'civil society' agenda emanating from the work of the Brundtland Commission, through the Earth Summit and Agenda 21. Some strides have been made, in the United Kingdom and other countries such as the Netherlands and Germany, in reviewing the building blocks of a more sustainable society, but they are recent and, on the whole, modest. Current thinking needs to be given a clearer focus and to be better integrated with shifts in the global political economy. Policy instruments have rarely been placed within the social and institutional context in which they are expected to work.

Too often, global environmental management is expected to deliver behaviour which is unsupported by relevant social and economic institutions in the countries concerned. Such institutions can only be built up through international political action. The focus of future research should be to examine the effectiveness of pursuing international policies to enhance sustainable development, and to seek more information about the impact of more sustainable policies at the national and sub-national levels.

Policies for achieving environmental targets need to take cognizance of the social and economic forces which have served to institutionalize unsustainable practices. We need to know, for example, how shifts in energy or food policy in the European Union might affect global resources and global sinks. We also need to know whether cultural practices might be developed which give greater credence to enhanced sustainable development. We need, in fact, to take stock of the corpus of everyday behaviour and institutions before we can formulate effective policies to change them. We also need to get behind the structural barriers to sustainable development represented not only by Indian factories, but also by Indian poverty. We need, in fact, to reintegrate the environment, and a concern with sustainable development, into global political economy and the cultures of global consumption.

REFERENCES

Goodland, R. (1994) 'The concept of environmental sustainability', *Annual Review of Ecological Systems* 26: 1–24.

IPPC Working Group Three (1995) *Second Assessment Report: Summary for Policymakers* (unpublished).

Index